Artemis, Eve, *and the* Image of God

Artemis, Eve, *and the* Image of God

A Case of Mistaken Identity in Paul's Ephesian Marriage Code

JOSEPH A. BRENNAN

Foreword by Kent E. Brower and MiJa Wi

☙PICKWICK *Publications* · Eugene, Oregon

ARTEMIS, EVE, AND THE IMAGE OF GOD
A Case of Mistaken Identity in Paul's Ephesian Marriage Code

Copyright © 2024 Joseph A. Brennan. All rights reserved. Except for brief quotations in critical publications or reviews, no part of this book may be reproduced in any manner without prior written permission from the publisher. Write: Permissions, Wipf and Stock Publishers, 199 W. 8th Ave., Suite 3, Eugene, OR 97401.

Pickwick Publications
An Imprint of Wipf and Stock Publishers
199 W. 8th Ave., Suite 3
Eugene, OR 97401

www.wipfandstock.com

PAPERBACK ISBN: 979-8-3852-1220-0
HARDCOVER ISBN: 979-8-3852-1221-7
EBOOK ISBN: 979-8-3852-1222-4

Cataloguing-in-Publication data:

Names: Brennan, Joseph A [author]. | Brower, K. E. (Kent E.) [foreword writer] | Wi, MiJa [foreword writer]

Title: Artemis, Eve, and the image of God : a case of mistaken identity in Paul's Ephesian marriage code / Joseph A. Brennan.

Description: Eugene, OR: Pickwick Publications, 2024 | Includes bibliographical references and index.

Identifiers: ISBN 979-8-3852-1220-0 (paperback) | ISBN 979-8-3852-1221-7 (hardcover) | ISBN 979-8-3852-1222-4 (ebook)

Subjects: LCSH: Bible.—Ephesians, V, 22–VI, 9. | Artemis (Greek deity)—Cult—Turkey—Ephesus (Extinct city). | Women in the Bible. | Motherhood—Religious aspects—Christianity. | Bible.—Feminist criticism. | Families—Biblical teaching. | Ethics in the Bible.

Classification: BS2695.2 B74 2024 (paperback) | BS2695.2 (ebook)

10/08/24

For Lara, my equal partner in all of life (Gen 2:18)

Contents

	Foreword by Kent E. Brower and MiJa Wi	ix
	Acknowledgments	xiii
	Abbreviations	xv
	Introduction: Why This Book?	xvii
1	The Problem	1
2	Writer Context and the Ephesian Marriage Code	36
3	Reader Context and the Ephesian Marriage Code	54
4	Competing Concepts of the Image of God	77
5	The Image of God, Marriage, and Celibacy	109
6	An Evangelistic Marriage Code	138
7	Conclusion	155
	Bibliography	163
	General Index	183
	Scripture Index	193

Foreword

THE USE OF SCRIPTURE to undergird differing views of human relationships within the people of God is timeless. But the precise way in which it is used differs. In the comparatively recent past, for instance, scripture was used to prop up human trafficking in the iniquitous slave trade. One would be hard-pressed to find anyone who would overtly use scripture to support such a view today. But the question of gender roles within marriage and the community of faith as set out in scripture is still contentious. The so-called complementarian and egalitarian positions are both contested areas of hermeneutical engagement, with the NT *Haustafeln* prominent in the discussion. Despite the much-rehearsed and sometimes heated discussions on gender roles in light of intertextual analysis of Genesis 1–3 and lexicological study over the meaning of *kephalē* (headship), no prospect of consensus has yet emerged.

In this context, Dr Joseph Brennan's excellent book offers a fresh and persuasive perspective that should reshape this discourse. Brennan starts with the notion of the *imago Dei* seen in those in Christ, both male and female, asking a different set of questions from those proposed by previous scholarship in his re-reading of the Ephesian *Haustafel*. For instance, why did Paul, the implied author, devote so much space to these household social relations (in fact, the Ephesian *Haustafel* is the longest one in the NT)? When his audience/readers listened to his letter, what might they have heard about the *imago Dei* in people, most crucially considering the influence of the Artemis cult upon Ephesian thought life?

In what proved to be a critical and very creative move, Brennan proposed re-reading the Ephesian *Haustafel* alongside of the available rich epigraphic and artifactual evidence of the Artemis cult. This material from the first century establishes the ubiquitous and influential presence of the Artemis cult in Asia during the period. This leads to the crucial question:

FOREWORD

How might the cult of this female goddess have shaped the way in which female (and male) devotees understood what bearing the image of Artemis entailed in human relationships? If this was the essential background against which the Ephesian *Haustafel* must be read, to what extent have Paul's readers unconsciously viewed their new freedom in Christ in Artemisian terms? What if Paul intentionally penned the Ephesian *Haustafel* to challenge the adverse influence of the Artemisian model for image-bearers? Paul's new kingdom model, already set out earlier in the epistle as well as in Paul's other letters, was based on love, trust, and mutual respect. It was directly opposite to the Artemisian model that pictured the female image-bearer of Artemis as, as Brennan characterizes it, "an independent honorary male" with "marital independence rather than marital interdependence."

In fact, Brennan argues, Paul had no real interest in "Hellenistic hierarchical realities." Rather, his countering of the Artemisian model was all part of his struggle to, as Brennan puts it, "implement evangelistic new kingdom values in a resistant first-century world." The Artemisian model had "become a troublesome syncretistic influence polluting Paul's evangelistic *Haustafel*." Paul wants the Ephesian readers to replace their previous model as image-bearers of Artemis with a new identity as image-bearers of Christ. Paul writes so extensively because the Ephesian wives were still at risk of being image-bearers of Artemis rather than modelling their *imago Dei* on that of Christ. Thus, on Brennan's reading, the Ephesian *Haustafel* has nothing to do with gender hierarchy and everything to do with the attractive model of Christ-like mutuality and interdependence in which mutual submission, trust, and loving self-sacrifice are of the essence.

This study has the potential for re-setting the discussion about the Ephesian *Haustafel*. It may also have significant implications for re-reading the other NT *Haustafeln* with respect to gender roles. By Brennan's careful re-construction of the *Sitz im Leben* of the Ephesian audience in which Artemis, in his words, "herself is the nearest, albeit incorrect, reference for the gentile believer trying to imagine what God in them looks like," he shows clearly how Paul works to reshape their understanding of how they are to bear the *imago Dei*. Paul's interest is essentially evangelistic. Paul wants his Ephesian readers to see the other as bearers of the image of Christ and so become image-bearers themselves. As Brennan concludes, "Notions of who is in charge, so ever-present in their former lives now have no grounds. Paul's particular attention to the wife's 'submit' and 'respect' as bookends to the husband's 'love' is Paul's assurance to her that this is not a return to an old way of living, but a mutual submission to sacrificial love that she need not fear."

Brennan's exceptional piece of careful scholarship, written in an engaging fashion and emerging out of deep personal passion, should have a profound impact on the discussion. Its particular attention to epigraphic and artifactual evidence on the Artemis cult to set the context for understanding this NT *Haustafel* should enable contemporary readers to understand Paul's language of mutual submission, love, headship, and trust in a way that eliminates the power/authority dynamic in favor of the new kingdom realities.

KENT E. BROWER AND MIJA WI

Acknowledgments

THIS BOOK WOULD NOT have been possible without the support of so many. I am incredibly grateful to have Dr Kent Brower as my main PhD supervisor, twice! Never could I have imagined that after departing academic life in 1999 to pursue business interests would I be permitted to return to doctoral study upon retirement, and to have the privilege of Dr Brower once again as my supervisor. True, I had to start over from the beginning since much has been written in my subject area over the years, but my interest in the Ephesian marriage *Haustafel* never left and how very fortunate I am to complete my research with whom I began those many years ago. I also wish to express my deepest appreciation to Dr MiJa Wi, co-supervisor, for her tireless reading, re-reading, and insightful comments on each line of text, encouraging me to think in directions I had not previously considered. I owe special thanks to Dr Dwight Swanson for probing my reasoning at each stage of the assessment process, which strengthened my argument. And I would be remiss not to mention my internal and external examiners, Dr Svetlana Khobnya and Dr T. J. Lang, who amid teaching, publishing, and supervising PhD students, so graciously took time to evaluate my thesis and ask penetrating Viva questions, truly a labor of love on their part.

I must thank Nazarene Theological College and the University of Manchester for the opportunity to present aspects of my work across multiple research seminars. Presenting one's research in progress among such esteemed scholars can be a frightening experience, but I was met with grace mixed with critical insight that has been formative in the work before you now.

Finally, I wish to thank the women in my life: my daughters Kelsey and Kendall, who were so very young when I initially began this research out of concern for their future; for who they are today and for their husbands, Ryan and Brandon, who see the same strength and beauty in them

ACKNOWLEDGMENTS

that their mother and I do; for my cherished granddaughters Cora and Ada, so young and full of imagination, may you see the world for what it can be and help make it so; and for my wife, Lara, my equal partner in all of life (Gen 2:18) whose unwavering love and belief in who we can be makes all things possible. To you I dedicate this book.

Abbreviations

IN ADDITION TO ABBREVIATIONS given in the SBL Handbook (second edition), please note the following:

bNid	Babylonian Talmud Niddah
bSan	Babylonian Talmud Sanhedrin
IEPH	Die Inschriften von Ephesos
Paed	Paedagogus
PGrenf	Alexandrian Erotic Fragment and Other Greek Papyri Chiefly Ptolemaic
pKid	Jerusalem Talmud Kiddushin
POxy	The Oxyrhynchus Papyri
SRI	Scriptural Research Institute

Introduction: Why This Book?

FOR TWO DECADES AS an executive recruiter no one ever asked what my degree was in. Not once. Looking back, it seems like the craziest thing now. At the time I held both undergraduate and graduate degrees in Bible and theology, in addition to graduate and post graduate work in counselling psychology. I was fortunate to place candidates in promising career opportunities, including multiples of V-Suite candidates, with client companies ranging from start-ups to Fortune 500s. One would assume I held a business or finance or human resources degree that would make me uniquely qualified, but nope, nothing of the sort. I had been an education pastor in a large church, a marriage and family therapist, full-time university lecturer, and director of graduate degree programs. I was fortunate to recruit and place highly competent female and male professionals in great careers, yet no one asked about my education. Ever.

I have my wife, Lara, to thank for this. She paved the way for me. While I taught courses in biblical literature, critical thinking, and effective interpersonal relationships at Colorado Christian University, and travelled to the UK in pursuit of a PhD in theology, she was the top billing, executive recruiter at her firm. When I decided to break from academic life, leaving PhD research behind, she landed me an interview with her firm's president. Given that she was their most productive recruiter, he could hardly say "No."

In her career Lara regularly conversed with senior executives in supply chain management, logistics, distribution, eCommerce—individuals responsible for millions in revenue for their companies, her counsel and negotiation skills helping them make life-changing career and family decisions for the better. Lara was a successful female executive recruiter. And together we raised two daughters of whom we are very proud.

Yet in the large church where I was once one of several pastors, Lara would not have been permitted to teach a mixed group of men and women in Sunday School about scripture, unless I was present in the room while she taught "under my authority" as her husband. Fortunately for us she had no desire to teach! Moreso, according to our understanding of scripture, she was to follow my loving leadership in marriage as the male head of the household, based on her responsibility to "submit to" and "respect" my God-given authority, according to 1 Peter 3, Colossians 2, Titus 2, and Ephesians 5.

This presented a big problem. Despite my being a pastor in such a socially conservative church, our marriage did not function this way at all. If we were honest with ourselves, we'd have to admit that our marriage did not align with the "go to" scriptures often used by so many well-meaning scholars to define "biblical" marriage. If we were honest, we had to admit that we worked best when we shared family leadership together as fully functioning equals based on our individual areas of giftedness. If we could not come to agreement on a decision, one of us trusted the other to make the best choice. I never had "carte blanche" as the final authority in the home. Such choices were shared. And as I observed the marriages of others around me, many were the same.

So, then what might this mean for us in relation to texts such as the Ephesians 5:21–33 marriage code? Were our lives somehow out of alignment with scripture? Had society moved on in such a way that this ancient text was no longer relevant to modern day living? And what might this mean for our young daughters, for their future husbands, should they marry? I was more than just concerned. I needed answers. After reading a sea of unsatisfactory explanations about the text, I still needed them.

In 1996 I picked up my pen as PhD student to write on the Ephesians marital *Haustafel*, under the supervision of Dr Kent Brower of Nazarene Theological College/University of Manchester. And for the following three years I continued research as his student until departing in 1999 to become a recruiter. Our daughters grew up, married, and launched careers of their own. Lara and I retired from professional life. Still, gnawing questions surrounding Ephesian marriage never left, haunting me all those years, until now. First Peter only has seven verses about marriage. Colossians only has two. Titus only has two. What had gone so horribly wrong with believing spouses in Ephesus that Paul felt compelled to write a whopping thirteen? Did Paul wish to carve in stone the structure of gender relationships across all cultures for all of time? Was he trying to ensure the survival of the emerging church amongst harsh Hellenistic realities of hierarchic marriage? Or was Paul contemplating something else, something more important? And

INTRODUCTION: WHY THIS BOOK?

what of the single mother? Was her home leaderless? I still needed answers. The college, university, and my supervisor, Dr Brower, graciously permitted my return to study, adding an additional supervisor, Dr MiJa Wi. I am eminently grateful for both of them. This work, before you now, represents three years of intense research under their tutelage.

This is a book about the Ephesians 5 marriage code, the goddess Artemis, Eve, and the image of God in the believer. Re-reading the marriage code against the background of epigraphical, artifactual, and literary evidence reveals that the influence of the virgin goddess, without need of male protection, made believing spouses value independence over interdependence as they sought to work out their "new creation identity" as God's image bearers. When one compares the revered reception history of the powerful celibate Artemis with the tattered reputation of dependent married Eve it comes as little surprise who qualifies as the more compelling candidate to emulate for the believing, albeit disillusioned wife working out what it means to be like God as a new creation in Christ.

Artemis is getting in the way. Paul is determined to rectify this misguided notion among Ephesian spouses of what it means to be like God (4:24; 5:1–2) and takes thirteen verses to do so (5:21–33), extolling the infinite value of the "holy and blameless" Ephesian wife to the husband that he might love her self-sacrificially as Christ does the church and as Adam loved Eve, leaving behind all for her to become one with her (Eph 5:31, cf. Gen 2:24). Paul goes on to entreat her to "respect" and "submit to" her husband's example of self-sacrificing, Christ-like love, nothing more. Notions of who gets to lead and who gets to follow in terms of "rule" or "authority" have nothing to do with the text. Intent on evangelizing the unbeliever to Christ-like new kingdom relationships that are a slice of heaven, Paul appeals to spouses to love one another in a manner that represents their new identity as God's united image bearers of what restored relationships in Christ can become.

For two decades as an executive recruiter no one ever asked about my degree. Not once. Perhaps the question of who gets to lead and who gets to follow also need not be asked when it comes to gender, leadership, and the home. But if the question about the Ephesians 5 marriage code is not who gets to lead and who gets to follow, then what is the appropriate question, and answer? My hope is that the contents of this book will provide a satisfying reply.

1

The Problem

Mistresses we keep for the sake of pleasure, concubines for the daily care of our persons, but wives to bear us legitimate children and to be faithful guardians of our households.[1]

DEMOSTHENES, *AGAINST NEAERA*

Husbands, love your wives, just as Christ also loved the church and gave himself up for her so that he might make her holy, cleansing her by the washing of water through the word, so he might present her to himself as a glorious church, not having stain or wrinkle or any such thing, but holy and blameless. So, husbands also ought to love their wives as their own bodies. He who loves his wife loves himself.[2]

EPHESIANS 5:25–28

1.1 THE PROBLEM: MARRIAGE HIERARCHY OR NOT?

FOLLOWING HIS PROCLAMATION IN the Ephesian letter that the kingdom of God is newly inaugurated on earth and in the heavenlies (1:10, 18–20), and that believers now have elevated social status befitting new creatures

---

1. Demosthenes, *Neaer.*, 59.122, LCL 351.446–47 (c. 343–340 BCE).

2. Source text from Greek: *Nestle-Aland, Novum Testamentum Graece,* 28th ed. Source text from Hebrew: *Biblia Hebraica Stuttgartensia.* All translations are my own unless otherwise noted.

(3:22–23; 5:1, 8) who are seated with Christ in the heavenlies (2:6), does Paul go on to endorse continued earthly hierarchical relationships in his marital code of 5:21–33?[3] Engagement with this question has resulted in a range of less than satisfying, diverging responses among scholars: 1) Paul's believed earthly gender subordination to be God-ordained; 2) Paul's accepted gender subordination in the Hellenistic world as an unfair necessity to avoid devastating consequences for the emerging church; 3) Paul appeared to endorse gender subordination on the outside while subverting it from the inside. Lack of consensus remains, opening the door for this work to suggest that Paul uses the Ephesian marital code as a tool to achieve a far more significant goal.

Scholarly discussion of the Ephesians marital table of the *Haustafeln*[4] historically has led to a choice between two diverging interpretative roads; complementarian (favoring male leadership) and egalitarian (favoring equal leadership).[5] For much of the late twentieth century,[6]

---

3. See 1.2 regarding Pauline authorship.

4. *Haustafel* (house table), plural *Haustafeln*, is a table of responsibilities members of each household pair are expected to fulfill. A *Haustafel* is included in Martin Luther's *Der Kleine Katechismus* (Small Catechism), published in 1529 for the training of children. Included in Luther's Small Catechism is a review of the Apostles Creed, The Ten Commandments, The Lord's Prayer, Sacrament of Holy Baptism, Sacrament of the Eucharist, and the Office of the Keys and Confession.

5. There is an ocean of scholarship concerning the *Haustafel*, Paul and gender, first-century Greco-Roman culture, and the treatment of women in Hellenized Rome, far more than can be categorized within the parameters of this chapter or this book. While its scope will not permit a detailed review of all *Haustafeln* related scholarship, the highlighted authors in this chapter offer recent work that is inclusive of prior scholarship and reflects the general themes of *Haustafeln* scholarship today. For further investigation, a summary of selected authors follows:

For a sampling of scholarship that is specific to the marriage *Haustafel* see Osiek, "The Bride of Christ (Ephesians 5:22–33)," 29–39; Bilezikian, *Beyond Sex Roles*; Ortland, "Male-Female Equality and Male Headship (Genesis 1–3)," 95–112; Gombis, "A Radically New Humanity," 317–30; Balch, *Let Wives be Submissive*; Blomberg, "Neither Hierarchicalist nor Egalitarian," 283–326; Dawes, *The Body in Question*; Keener, *Paul Women & Wives*; Payne, *Man and Woman, One in Christ*; Padgett, *As Christ Submits to the Church*; Hering, *The Colossian and Ephesian Haustafeln in Theological Context*; Beattie, *Women and Marriage in Paul and his Early Interpreters*; MacDonald, "Beyond Identification of the Topos of Household Management," 65–90; Redding, "Not Again: Another Look at the Household Codes," 456–63.

For a sampling of scholarship that is focused on first-century culture, see Winter, *Roman Wives, Roman Widows*; Cohick, *Women in the World of the Earliest Christians*; Engberg-Pedersen, *Paul in His Hellenistic Context*; Webb, *Slaves, Women and Homosexuals*; Horrell, *Becoming Christian*; Meeks, *The First Urban Christians*.

6. Although late twentieth century is when most of the κεφαλή debate took place, it

scholars sought to resolve the question of who leads and who follows with lexicological studies of the word "head" (κεφαλή) in first-century and classical Greek to ascertain what the writer meant when he said in Ephesians 5:23, "for the husband is the head of the wife as also Christ is the head of the church."[7] Egalitarians accused complementarians of a patriarchal interpretation of κεφαλή that marginalized believing women,[8] while complementarians accused egalitarians of imagining first-century themes of marital mutual submission and gender equality where there were none.[9] Studies that focused mainly on lexical exegesis of κεφαλή in biblical and extrabiblical contexts shed some light on first-century human relationships, but lexical unrest remained.

Marriage *Haustafel* scholarship then moved in new directions with a focus on inaugural eschatology[10] and the restored *imago Dei*,[11] in male and

---

continues to receive limited discussion in the twenty-first century. See Lee-Barnewall, *Neither Complementarian nor Egalitarian*, ch. 8; and Westfall, *Paul and Gender*, ch. 1.

7. "ὅτι ἀνήρ ἐστιν κεφαλὴ τῆς γυναικὸς, ὡς καὶ ὁ Χριστὸς κεφαλὴ τῆς ἐκκλησίας." See Grudem for an example of complementarian scholars who view κεφαλή as "authority": "Does Kephale Mean 'Source' or 'Authority Over' in Greek Literature?," 38–59; "The Meaning of Κεφαλὴ ('head')" in Appendix 1 of Piper and Grudem, *Recovering*, 436–40, and their "The Meaning of *Kephalē* ('Head')" in *JETS* 44.1.

A sample of Egalitarian scholars who argue for alternative meanings of κεφαλή include Fitzmyer, "Another Look at Kephale in 1 Corinthians 11:3," 503–11; Cervin, "Does *Kephale* Mean 'Source' or 'Authority' in Greek Literature? A Rebuttal," 85–112; Mickelsen and Mickelsen, "What Does *Kephale* Mean in the New Testament?," 102–3; Payne, "Response," 118–24.

See sect. 1.7 for detailed definitions, but to briefly sum the two positions: 1) egalitarian scholars maintain that God created men and women fully equal in all respects. The fall of humankind in Genesis 3 has led to gender dominance by the male but, with the inauguration of the kingdom of Christ, marital relationships have been restored to full equality; 2) complementarian scholars maintain that both genders are equal before God as persons, but that God has ordained masculine and feminine hierarchical roles in the created order.

8. For example, Perriman, "The Head of a Woman: The Meaning of Κεφαλή in 1 Cor 11:3," 617–18; and Payne, "Response," 123.

9. For example, Piper and Grudem, *Recovering*, 463.

10. This book accepts the consensus within NT scholarship that NT eschatology, however challenging it is to define the word, has a tension between "the already" and "not yet."

11. For its development in late twentieth and early twenty-first centuries, see Wright, *Jesus and the Victory of God*; Moltmann, *The Coming of God*; Beale, "The Eschatological Conception of New Testament Theology," 11–52; Dunn, *The Theology of Paul the Apostle*; Payne, "Galatians 3:28's Application of Paul's New Creation Teaching to the Status of Women in Christ," 11–16; Beale "The End Starts at the Beginning," 7–21.

female believers, which opened the door to apply new creation language to gender. Scholars further unpacked the social dynamics of first-century Roman life,[12] how harmony in the Roman household was essential to harmony in the Roman city-state,[13] and the literary context of the household codes in light of the eschatological hopes of Second Temple Judaism.[14] Consensus arose that the conversation has moved on from lexicology; that the *Haustafeln* must be viewed through new kingdom realities; and that the context for understanding the household codes is the struggle of the emerging church.

In line with much of contemporary scholarship, I have moved beyond the debate over the meaning of κεφαλή, likewise turning to new kingdom discourse to illumine the nature and function of relationships in the emerging church on earth as representative of heavenly relationships. As the temple of the Holy Spirit, purchased by God through the blood of Christ (1 Cor 6:19–20), first-century believers became the conduit of Christ's new reality breaking into the present reality of the Hellenistic world. Across the Pauline corpus, righteous living, peace, and joy (Rom 14:17; Eph 5:19–20) were new realities for believers who, with the writing of the Holy Spirit on their hearts, were transformed into living letters from God to all of humanity (2 Cor 3:2–3). As his image-bearers of what Christ's reign looks like in the heavenlies, the formation of the church, populated with believers sealed by the Holy Spirit as God's inheritance were also marked as beneficiaries of a future inheritance (Eph 1:18). T. J. Lang defines it as such, "As for the nature of this inheritance, it is elsewhere identified with the kingdom of God

---

12. For example, see Meeks, *The First Urban Christians*; Winter, *Roman Wives, Roman Widows*; Witherington, *Women and the Genesis of Christianity*; Kearsley, "Women in Public Life in the Roman East," 189–211; Balch, "Paul, Families, and Households," *Paul in the Greco-Roman World*, 258–292; Horrell, "Ethnicisation, Marriage, and Early Christian Identity," 439–460; Oakes, *Empire Economics and the New Testament*.

13. First century household management finds its origin in Greek philosophy. The rule of "harmony" in the household stems from Aristotle's *Politics* (c. 350 BCE). Aristotle argued that to maintain harmony in the city-state one must have harmony in its most basic unit, the household. Without this the stability of the city-state was in danger (*Pol.* 1.1253b.1–14). Unfortunately, for slaves and women, the price for such harmony was subjugation. The Greco-Roman context of the Pauline and Petrine *Haustafeln* has implications interpretation of the household codes in light of new creation theology. See Balch, "Household Codes," 25–50, also Osiek and Balch, *Families in the New Testament World*. See also, Hengel, "The Pre-Christian Paul," ch. 2.

14. For example, see Valentine, *For You Were Bought with a Price*; Osiek, MacDonald, and Tulloch, *A Woman's Place*; Smith, *Strangers to Family*, Lee-Barnewall, *Neither Complementarian nor Egalitarian*; Westfall, *Paul and Gender*.

(1 Cor 6:9–10; Gal 5:21), the promises to Abraham (Gal 3–4), recompense (Col 3:24), and that which is imperishable (1 Cor 15:50)."[15] Hence, the use of new creation "kingdom language" for the church as the *imago Dei* is appropriate since believers, in the form of living letters on earth, represent Christ's kingdom while also inheriting it.[16]

Albeit helpful, the influence of women's evolving social status in the vast Roman empire across hundreds of years and diverse economic disparity spoke little to the *Sitz im Leben* of the Ephesian readers.[17] Further, when it comes to describing Christ's kingdom realities and gender, application of new creation language to the marriage *Haustafeln* has led to *more* diverging interpretative roads, not fewer. In the Ephesus NT marital codes some scholars see gender transformation and equality,[18] others see subversion and defiance of Roman authority,[19] others see strategic survival for the emerging church,[20] and still others see marital unity within gender hierarchy.[21] A precise

---

15. Lang, "Sealed for Redemption," 165.

16. See 4.1 for more on Paul and the *imago Dei*.

17. Scholars may not directly instruct one to use these generalized examples as a framework to interpret indigenous household codes, but the volume of attention such background has received over three decades (including, at times, a discussion of various NT *Haustafeln* on the heels of the discussion of the status of women in Greco-Roman culture, Second Temple Judaism, Egypt, and Roman politics) implies their prominence.

Twentieth-century examples of this generalized approach include Witherington, *Women in the Earliest Churches*; and his *Women and the Genesis of Christianity*; Balch, *Let Wives be Submissive*; Keener, *Paul Women and Wives*; Osiek and Balch, *Families in the New Testament World*.

Twenty-first-century examples include Balch, "Paul, Families, and Households," 258–92; Keener, "Marriage," 680–93; Campbell, *Marriage and Family in the Biblical World*.

Examples of the attention given to the status of women in the western Roman Empire which is then applied generally to Ephesus and Asia Minor: Osiek, MacDonald, and Tulloch, *A Woman's Place*, 20–25; Cohick, *Women in the World of the Earliest Christians*, 100–106 (for examples from western Roman empire) and 106–10 (for examples from Egypt); also her *Ephesians: A New Covenant Commentary*; Westfall, *Paul and Gender*, 7–24; Smith, *Strangers to Family*, ch. 3.

Examples of scholarship that focus on the indigenous status of women in Ephesus and Asia Minor include Karaman, *Ephesian Women in Greco-Roman and Early Christian Perspective*; Rogers, "Constructions of Women at Ephesos," 215–23; Boatwright, "Plancia Magna of Perge," 249–72. Gritz, *Paul, Women Teachers, and the Mother Goddess at Ephesus*.

18. Westfall, *Paul and Gender*.

19. Osiek, MacDonald, and Tulloch. *A Woman's Place*.

20. Smith, *Strangers to Family*.

21. Lee-Barnewall, *Neither Complementarian nor Egalitarian*.

grasp of Paul's application of the restored image of God to marriage remains unclear. A precise grasp of the Ephesian reader's notion of themselves as new creatures in the restored image of God is even more ambiguous.

This book proposes that fresh insight into the Ephesians 5:21–33 marital *Haustafel* can be achieved with an examination of 1) the influence of the goddess Artemis upon Ephesian thought life, 2) the rise of two traditions for believers to manifest the *imago Dei* as witnessed in the reception history of Eve as compared to Artemis, 3) and Paul's evangelistic intent for the Ephesians marital code as its primary goal. A detailed examination of local inscriptional evidence with close reading of the marital code will reveal that, due to the continued influence of the virgin goddess upon their thought world, Ephesian believing spouses misunderstood their new creation identity to be one of independence from each other rather than interdependence with each other. Second, when compared to the revered celibate goddess, the reception history of Eve the matron makes her an unlikely candidate for the Ephesian woman to emulate, which Paul seeks to rectify in the text. Third, in the context of equality, trust, and mutual submission, Paul appeals to the husband and wife to be "slaves to one another" as a united new creation in marriage that transcends the Hellenistic social structures of honor and shame.

Building upon the substantial attention scholarship has placed on intertextuality and writer context, this book draws more attention to reader context of the text. Most scholarship has not considered local epigraphical evidence, the influence of Artemis, or the weight of her enormous temple upon the thought world of the Ephesian reader. Typically, the background construction of the Ephesian *Haustafel* has been the text itself, other NT marital codes, or Pauline intertextual references unrelated to marriage.[22] When literary or archaeological evidence has been used it is often based on the diverse history of women's status across hundreds of years and thousands of miles from the first century Ephesian home. Reading the Ephesian marriage code in tandem with local epigraphy that was visible to all social levels in Ephesus brings clarity to the letter in a way that embraces both reader and authorial context. Moreover, most scholarship has not considered the place of this lengthy marital code within Paul's explicit evangelistic intent in the letter.

---

22. The terms "marital *Haustafel*" and "marital code" are used interchangeably in this book.

This book demonstrates that Paul, as an interpreter of scripture who understands his audience, borrowed terms prevalent in the Ephesus inscriptions about the cult of Artemis, applied them to Christ to announce his superiority over the Ephesian goddess, and applied them to the Ephesian believer to announce a new identity that surpasses that of Artemis worshippers and even the goddess herself. This new identity is one of mutual submission in relational unity as Christ's image-bearers, visible across social structures mentioned in the letter: Jews and gentiles, husbands and wives, parents and children, slaves and masters. Constructing a background from inscription, allusion, and allegory, Paul seeks to replace the believing couple's misunderstanding of the *imago Dei* in them as independent, and perhaps even celibate, with an entreaty to live as the unified *imago Dei* in mutually submissive marital togetherness. Paul uses the notion of a newly created marital relationship in the *imago Dei* as an evangelistic, attractive alternative, inviting the outsider in and transforming Hellenistic social structures from the inside out.[23]

Reading the marital code alongside a detailed examination of inscriptional evidence from Ephesus reveals that believing spouses misunderstood who they were as new creatures in Christ due to the continued influence of Artemis upon their thought world. In Paul's mind, they have chosen to manifest independent identity as new creatures to the exclusion of shared identity in a family of new creatures. Given the negative reception history of Eve as the matron of Adam, the notion of strong, celibate, Artemis would hold up as the superior near-reference to the Ephesian female of what it means to be god-like. This mistaken notion enabled her to live without submission to (5:22, 24) or respect for (5:33) her husband; while her husband continued in the first-century Mediterranean tradition of honor and shame, valuing his wife as household manager and bearer of legitimate offspring while not loving her as an equal partner in a new kingdom (5:25–33). Paul reorients them as to who they are as bearers of Christ's image who mutually submit to one another (5:21), with loving actions, based on trust in Christ (5:22), his example of self-sacrifice (5:25–27), and each other in shared identity (5:28–30). Reunited as the *imago Dei* in Christ's body (5:30) they form a new ideal of marital oneness,

---

23. In this book the word "evangelistic" refers to the force of Paul's missional intent to draw entire households (husbands, wives, children, extended family, slaves, and so on) into the newly inaugurated kingdom of Christ on earth.

reflective of the very first marriage (5:31), which attracts the outsider to the new kingdom with new kingdom realities.

1.2 INTRODUCTORY QUESTIONS

Following are introductory questions relevant to the outcome of this book. Who wrote the letter, and does this matter? From the earliest apostolic fathers forward Pauline authorship found acceptance in the early church, however, by the nineteenth century the authenticity of Pauline authorship was contested[24] and continues as such with half of scholarship affirming the letter came from Paul's pen and half denying it.[25] The success of my argument is not dependent on an authentic Paul or pseudonymous Paul. The

---

24. Evanson considered it a forgery and omitted it from his *A New Testament: or the New Covenant According to Luke, Paul, and John*; cf. Gnilka, *Der Epheserbrief*, 13. Schleiermacher suggested it was commissioned by Paul but composed by Tychicus in *Sämmtliche Werke*, 1:165–66. De Wette concluded that Ephesians was an expansion of Colossians and not to be attributed to Paul in *Introduction to the Canonical Books of the New Testament*, 277.

25. Common denials of authorship center around: 1) Ephesians' use of vocabulary so heavily dependent on the undisputed letters; 2) the epistle's "new" theological focus on cosmic Christology, ecclesiology, and inaugural eschatology in response to a delayed *parousia*; 3) the impersonal tone of the letter (1:1, 15; 3:2; 4:21), Ephesians dependence on Colossians; 4) and a different writing style that cannot be Paul's. Common affirmations of Paul's authorship center around: 1) autobiographical material (3:1–13); 2) early attestation to Paul by apostolic fathers such as Clement of Rome, Ignatius, and Polycarp; 3) a theological focus that is not new but merely emphasized to suit the needs of the readers in Ephesus and Asia Minor; 4) and Paul as one capable of multiple writing styles and literary flair. See Baugh, *Ephesians*, 1–25, for a full discussion of authorship debate.

A sampling of advocates for Paul's authorship includes Thielman, *Ephesians*, 1–5; Arnold, *Ephesians*, 58–64; Wood, *Ephesians*, 3–9; Sanders, "The Case for Pauline Authorship," 9–20; Guthrie, "Appendix C: Epistolary Pseudepigraphy," 1011–28; Barth, *Ephesians 1–3*, 36–50. Hoehner, *Ephesians: An Exegetical Commentary*, notes that 50 percent of commentators over the last century and the majority (54%) from 1519 to the present have held to Pauline authorship, 2–60.

A sampling of advocates for deutero-Pauline authorship include Best, *Ephesians*, 6–36; Lincoln, *Ephesians*, xlvii–lxxviii; Kitchen, *Ephesians*, 22–28; Schnackenburg, *Ephesians*, 24–29. Mealand, "The Extent of the Pauline Corpus," 61–92, took samples of a thousand words from the Epistles, analyzing twenty-five stylistic variables to conclude that the distinctiveness of Colossians and Ephesians confirm that these letters are deutero-Pauline. Goodspeed, *The Meaning of Ephesians*, claimed that out of 618 short phrases no fewer than 550 could be matched to Paul's undisputed letters, calling Paul's authorship into question since he would not have needed to depend heavily on his own writings if he were the actual author.

following by Martin Kitchen best reflects my agnostic approach to authorship for the argument of this book:

> Either Paul allowed his style, language, and thought to develop to such an extent in all these respects, or another writer so breathed the atmosphere of Paul's thought, perceived in Paul's writing the essence of the gospel as he understood it, and used his knowledge of Pauline tradition to inspire an "epistle" of his own in conscious continuity with the voice of an apostle, with its own particular language, style, and theological emphases.[26]

Whatever one's view of who authored Ephesians, agreement with the argument of my work is possible. While the precise determination of who wrote Ephesians is not of first importance, the provenance of Pauline thought is. It is regrettable that once a text is declared pseudonymous it can be pushed to the side as perhaps unauthoritative, or not as authoritative. Authorship does not have to be a choice between authentic provenance and spurious pseudonymity. The canonical acceptance of Ephesians by the early church invites a sympathetic reading of the letter as extending the provenance of Paul's apostolic witness to the first-century Ephesian believer, and beyond, whether written by his hand or that of a Paulinist. From this point onwards the book will refer to epistle's author as "Paul," the implied author from the NT canon, while being mindful of the nuances of authorship.[27]

Whether authentic Paul or implied Paul, he was an interpreter of scripture for his readers, at times moving beyond the literal meaning of Hebrew texts according to the needs of his audience.[28] Paul is not a sole practitioner in this methodology. Interpreters in the early rabbinic era (c. 100 BCE–100 CE) had to address situations no longer germane to daily Jewish life. The old kingdom of Judah no longer existed. The temple had been rebuilt with permission of Persia, but this did not mean that the Jews were once again an independent nation. The Greeks replaced the Persians as occupiers and the Romans replaced the Greeks, and by this time the Jews were scattered

---

26. Kitchen, *Ephesians*, 7.

27. For more, see Petroelje's discussion of authorship in *The Pauline Book and the Dilemma of Ephesians*, 21–23; and Campbell, *Framing Paul*, 32–33, where he considers Ephesians to be authentic (as one of ten authentic canonical epistles that bear his name). Whether the letter was written by the authentic Paul who had lived in Ephesus for three years, or a Pauline admirer who was equally well aware of the situation in Ephesus, the essence of Pauline theology is common to both.

28. For more see Hays, *Echoes of Scripture in the Letters of Paul*; and Isbell, *How Jews and Christians Interpret Their Sacred Texts*.

through Babylonia, Egypt, and Asia. Rabbinical scholars were tasked with interpreting Torah in light of new geography, decentralized places of worship, and various socio-political structures. Scripture had to be interpreted in ways applicable to wherever people lived.[29] Paul, putatively a classically trained Pharisee, was also such a practitioner, reinterpreting the Hebrew Bible in light of the coming of Christ, clarifying the OT in light of revelation that would become the New in a way that allowed him to evangelize everyone:[30]

> To the Jews I became as a Jew, in order to gain Jews. To those under the law I became as one under the law (though I myself am not under the law) so that I might gain those under the law. To those outside the law I became as one outside the law (though I am not outside God's law but am within Christ's law) so that I might gain those outside the law. To the weak I became weak, so that I might gain the weak. I have become all things to all people, that I might by all means save some. (1 Cor 9:20–22 NRSV).

What does this mean for the Ephesian letter with its marital *Haustafel*? Chapter 6 argues that Paul's evangelistic passion is of central importance in the Ephesian marriage code whether written by the apostle himself or a Pauline admirer aware of Paul's passion and intent on carrying it forward.

The question of "when was Ephesians written" has importance to this book when related to historical events impacting the 60–90 CE window in Asia Minor. Both those embracing an early composition date (60–62 CE) for Ephesians and those embracing a late date (80–90 CE) can affirm the impact of Caesar's *Lex Julia* laws for marriage and adultery (23 BCE), adultery and promiscuity (17 BCE), and prohibiting celibacy (9 BCE).[31] Unique to a late date for Ephesians is the 66–70 CE Jewish War with the sacking of Jerusalem, destruction of the temple, and Jewish Diaspora.[32] These late-date

---

29. This would become even more pronounced with the loss of the capital city of Jerusalem and destruction of the temple by the Romans in 70 CE.

30. For more see Isbell, *How Jews and Christians Interpret Their Sacred Texts*.

31. See 5.2 for detail on the *Lex Julia* laws.

32. Entwined with authorship, the composition date for the letter remains an ongoing debate (see fns. 26 and 28). An early date (60–62 CE) presumes Pauline authorship since the apostle would have been alive to write the letter. The date of 60–62 is the early date majority position. See Arnold's discussion of early dating (*Ephesians*, 55–57). In support of an early date: 1) the personal reference in 3:1, "I, Paul, the prisoner of Christ Jesus" (ἐγὼ Παῦλος ὁ δέσμιος τοῦ Χριστοῦ Ἰησοῦ) is deemed authentic; 2) making the letter a prison epistle written while Paul was under house arrest in Rome (60–62 CE); 3) following his

events, when paired with the heightened persecution of Christians under Domitian's reign, better explain the abundance of *Haustafeln* for Asia Minor (Eph 5:21–33; Col 3:18–19; 1 Pet 3:1–7) than an early-date composition of the letter. Given a late date strengthens the book with evidence that heightens the tension of prying eyes, eager to find fault with the emerging church. But the focus of the argument on Artemis and the believers' distorted notion of the restored image of God in them remains intact whether early date or late. Chapter 6 will demonstrate that Paul's intent was for the marital code to be used as an evangelistic tool, whether written by him personally in 62 CE from his Roman imprisonment or in 80–90 CE by a Pauline admirer.

Is the Ephesian letter a circular letter for Asia Minor, or specific to the residents of Ephesus? As with authorship, the destination of the letter has been debated. In support of a circular letter the description of the recipients is general. They are designated as saints (1:1, 15, 18; 3:18; 5:3; 6:18); as faithful (1:1,13, 15; 2:18; 3:12); among those loving Jesus Christ with an incorruptible love (6:24); who experience his grace (1:6, 8; 2:5, 8) and his love (2:4; 5:2, 25). The title, "To the Ephesians" (ΠΡΟΣ ΕΦΕΣΙΟΥΣ) was not added until the middle of the second century but appears on all subsequent Greek MSS.

In some early and important manuscripts (𝔓46 ℵ* B* 424c 1739), the words "in Ephesus" (ἐν Ἐφέσῳ) are absent as well as from manuscripts used by Basil, Origin, Marcion, and possibly Tertullian,[33] giving rise to the

---

appeal to Caesar (Acts 22–26); 4) and is harmonious with the procurator transition from Felix to Festus (Acts 24:27) which most scholars date at 58–60 CE. According to Bruce, *New Testament History*, 345, "The date of his [Felix's] recall and replacement by Porcius Festus is disputed, but a change in the provincial coinage of Judaea attested for Nero's fifth year points to A.D. 59."

A late date (80–90 CE) presumes pseudonymous authorship since the apostle would have already died. In support of a late date: 1) A date of 80–90 CE would allow for the letter's post-apostolic theological perspective of a delayed *parousia*; 2) account for the writer's extensive use of Paul's undisputed letters; 3) and provide enough time for Ephesians to become part of a collection of Paul's authentic letters, its canonicity supported by Ignatius' heavy reliance on the Ephesian epistle in his *Letter to Polycarp* (c. 108 CE) as a testimony to its perceived genuineness and placing the epistle's composition during the reign of Domitian 81–96 CE. See where Ignatius' *Pol* (5.1) has a clear allusion to Eph 5:25, and his letter to the Philadelphians (4.3) alludes to Eph 5:22, 24, 28. See also Best, 15; and Hartog's "Polycarp, Ephesians, and Scripture," 255–75. Since dating of the epistle has been discussed and debated at great length among others, a full review is not required here.

33. Tertullian says that Marcion has the wrong title for the letter, calling it "Laodiceans" rather than "Ephesians," but does not seem bothered: "There is no importance

hypothesis that the phrase is missing in the autographs and supporting the notion that the letter had a general target audience to include the churches in Asia Minor. If ΠΡΟΣ ΕΦΕΣΙΟΥΣ and ἐν Ἐφέσῳ were originally absent, this suggests that the letter was encyclical, with copies being sent to multiple churches in Asia Minor, of which Ephesus was most prominent. Hence, the location could be filled in wherever the epistle was read. This suggestion is supported by the influence of Paul's three-year ministry in Ephesus (Acts 20:31) that spreads the gospel to the outlying communities (19:9–20, 23–27) much like when Epaphras heard the gospel in the hall of Tyrannus (9–10) then carried it to Colossae.[34]

In support of the letter being just to Ephesus, examples in scripture of other letters where the writer left a blank in a circular letter for the location to be filled in are absent. To the contrary the cities and provinces are specifically addressed or not addressed at all. In Revelation 1, when more than one church is addressed (1:4), each is specifically addressed (1:11). In Galatians "to the churches of Galatia" is given (1:2). In 1 Peter multiple provinces are given (1:1). In 2 Corinthians Paul identifies both the city of Corinth and the province of Achaia (1:1). The circular letter, James, is "to the twelve tribes in the Diaspora" (1:1). Similarly, Jude writes to "those who in God . . . who have been called" (1:1); and 2 Peter to "those having received a precious faith" (1:1). Hence, it is difficult to support the notion Ephesians had a blank space to be filled in by the reader in whatever city in Asia Minor the epistle landed. It is more likely that "in Ephesus" (ἐν Ἐφέσῳ) was mistakenly omitted in an early copy of Ephesians and copied as such by a few scribes, then ἐν Ἐφέσῳ was reinserted by scribes to correct the

---

in titles, since when the apostle wrote to some, he wrote to all" (*Marc.* 5.17.1). For more see Wright, *The Dividing Wall*, 56; Wood, "Ephesians," 11–14, 121; Best, *Ephesians*, 13–14; Schnackenburg, *Ephesians*, 40; Lincoln, *Ephesians*, 1–4. Metzger, *A Textual Commentary on the Greek New Testament*, writes, "Since the letter has been traditionally known as 'To the Ephesians,' and since all witnesses except those mentioned above include the words ἐν Ἐφέσῳ, the Committee decided to retain them, but enclosed within square brackets," 532.

34. Other suggestions include: 1) the letter was written from Ephesus itself; 2) because of Paul's association with the church at Ephesus and the importance of the Ephesian church in Asia Minor, the address ἐν Ἐφέσῳ was attached; 3) when Paul's letters were being collected there was no letter from Paul to Ephesus and since the letter had no name it was given that of Ephesus; 4) the letter was found in the archives in the church at Ephesus and the name Ephesus was supplied. See also, Campbell, *Framing Paul*, 32–33, where he considers Ephesians to be written to the Laodiceans mentioned in Colossians 4:16.

mistake.[35] Further, early testimony from church fathers Irenaeus, Cyprian, and Origen attest that the letter was directed to Ephesus thus supporting that ἐν Ἐφέσῳ was part of the original autograph.[36]

Whether a targeted letter for Ephesus or a circular letter for Asia Minor, the success of my argument is not inextricably tied to the city, albeit the volume of Ephesus inscriptions related to Artemis in support of the text makes for a stronger argument if tied to the city. Ephesus, the ruins of which lie near the modern village of Selc̆uk in western Turkey, was the most important city in Ionian Asia Minor, well known, constantly visited by pilgrims, famously wealthy, and the seat of Roman government for the province. Artemis, patron goddess of Ephesus, was worshipped there for thousands of years and revered throughout all of Asia. Built outside the city walls, two kilometers from the city center, her enormous temple, the Artemision with its 127 columns, held vast wealth as the bank of Asia.[37] The temple was destroyed by flood in 456 BCE, rebuilt by the Ephesians and stood for another 100 years before being destroyed again, this time by fire in 356 BCE, and rebuilt again by the Ephesians in 323 BCE.[38] This final form of the temple was four times the size of the Parthenon; 137 m (450 ft) long by 69 m (225 ft) wide and 18 m (60 ft) high, and is described in Antipater of Sidon's list of the Seven Wonders of the Ancient World.[39] Adorned with the works of the greatest painters and architects of the age, it contained five statues of the Amazon founders[40] and a painting of Alexander the Great holding a thunderbolt.[41] Following each catastrophe, the Ephesians were united in rebuilding the residence of their goddess, bigger and better each time, the marvel of the temple attracting tourists and worshippers to the Artemision from around the world.

---

35. For more see Baugh, *Ephesians*, 32, and textual notes referencing additional scholarship, 50–54. See also Arnold's detailed discussion, *Ephesians*, 24–31.

36. Irenaeus, *Haer.* 5.2.3, 8.1, 14.3, 24.4; Cyprian, *Test.* 12.7, 8, 11, 13, 41, 70, 72, 117; Origen, *Princ.* 3.4.5.

37. Dio Chrysostom, *Disc.* 31.54, LCL 358.58–59; Strabo, *Geogr.* 14.1.22, LCL 90.400–401; Xenophon, *Anab.* 5.3.4–6, LCL 223.224–27.

38. Strabo, *Geogr.* 14.1.22, LCL 223.224–27, reports that Herostratus set the fire to ensure that his name live on in history. Alexander offered to pay to rebuild the temple, but the Ephesians declined, saying "it would be improper for one god to dedicate offerings to gods."

39. See Antipater, *Gr. Anth.* VIII.177, LCL 68.478–79 and IX.58, LCL 84.30–31.

40. See Pliny, *Nat.* 34.53, LCL 394.166–67.

41. See Pliny, *Nat.* 35.92, LCL 394.328–29.

The success of my argument is tied to establishing the influence of Artemis upon the thought world of believers in Ephesus or more specifically in relation to Paul's marital code. This is best accomplished in keeping the letter's audience narrow to just the city of Ephesus, with her abundance of supporting inscriptional evidence, thus steering away from the notion of a circular letter. However, given the fame of the city and her goddess, and the spread of Paul's gospel from Ephesus to "the whole province of Asia" (Acts 19:26), according to Demetrius the silversmith, it would be implausible to say that the Ephesian letter would not have circulated to the churches of Asia Minor, their residents also having knowledge of Artemis plus marriage codes of their own (Col 3:18–19; 1 Pet 3:1–7). Similarly, Paul instructs the Colossian letter to be read to the Laodiceans in 4:16.

The calming words of the city clerk to Demetrius and the riotous crowd, "Citizens of Ephesus, who is there that does not know that the city of the Ephesians is the temple keeper of the great Artemis and of the statue that fell from heaven?" (Acts 19:35 NRSV)[42] testifies to the influential reach of the goddess and offers relevant audience context for the Ephesian epistle. Beyond the abundance of inscriptional evidence about Artemis in Ephesus, literary evidence showing the spread of the cult to cities and towns of Asia Minor such as Adrasteia and Astyra (Troas), Pitane (Aeolia), Mt. Sipylus and Lake Gygaea (Lydia), Magnesia and Miletus (Ionia), Perge (Pamphilia), Byzantium, Phyrgia, and Pylae (Cilicia) support the words of the city clerk.[43] Beyond this, an examination of numismatic evidence illuminates the context of Acts 19 and the recognition of the Ephesian goddess among the cities of Asia Minor. Coins served as an imperial form of influential social media touching all levels of society across the empire.[44] Gold and silver coins were typically minted under the control of empire, but on occasion, in recognition of special service and endorsement by the empire, a city such as Ephesus was granted this privilege. During the reign of Claudius (41–54 CE) two silver coins were minted in Ephesus: one to celebrate Claudius' marriage to Agrippina in 49 CE, which shows the

---

42. "Ἄνδρες Ἐφέσιοι, τίς γάρ ἐστιν ἀνθρώπων ὃς οὐ γινώσκει τὴν Ἐφεσίων πόλιν νεωκόρον οὖσαν τῆς μεγάλης Ἀρτέμιδος καὶ τοῦ διοπετοῦς;"

43. See Strabo, *Geogr.* 13.1.13, LCL 223.28–29; 51, LCL 223.102–3; 65, LCL 223.128–29; 13.4.5, LCL 223. 172–73; 14.4.2, LCL 223.322–25; 14.5.19, LCL 223.354–57; Pausanias, *Descr.* 6.22.1, LCL 272.136–37; 7.6.6, LCL 272.202–3; Callimachus, *Hymn 3 to Artemis*, 183–265, LCL 129.250–61; Herodotus, *Hist.* 4.87, LCL 118.288–91; Aelian, *Nat. An.* 12.39, LCL 449:60–61.

44. For more on coinage, see 3.5 and 4.2.3.

emperor on the obverse and Agrippina on the reverse (50–51 CE); and the second, which shows Claudius and Agrippina on the obverse and Diana/Artemis on the reverse.[45] The second coin is undated but is similar enough to the first that it was likely minted close to the same time as the second and clearly within the dates of 49–54 CE when Agrippina was his wife. A third coin with Claudius on the obverse and on the reverse Diana/Artemis and her temple with polos on her head and fillets hanging from her wrists is also undated but likely minted prior to his marriage.[46] Indigenous issues of coins were often designed for local use and inscribed in Greek; however, these three cistophori issues bear Latin inscriptions, which supports their status and production endorsed by Rome. These coins were in circulation throughout Asia Minor when Paul lived in Ephesus in the shadow of the Artemision bank of Asia and anyone who used them would be reminded that the emperor supported Artemis and she him.[47]

Endorsed by the emperor, the influence of the Ephesian Artemis was not only part of the fabric of everyday life in her patron city of Ephesus, but all of Asia Minor. Accepting the fact that Artemis was renowned throughout the region it is not too much to say that the inscriptional allusions and allegory related to the goddess in the Ephesian letter would not be lost on gentile readers in Asia Minor as it circulated and cohered with Demetrius' fear that "this trade of ours may come into disrepute but also that the temple of the great goddess Artemis will be scorned, and she will be deprived of her majesty that brought all Asia and the world to worship her" (Acts 19:27 NRSV).[48] But what of the Jews? Would allegory and allusion about Artemis in the Ephesian letter mean anything to the Jewish Christ-follower in Ephesus?

Diaspora Jews are very much present in Asia Minor: where Antiochus III instructs the relocation of 2000 Jewish families from Babylonia to Lydia and Phrygia (*Antiquities* 12:148–53; LCL 365.76–79)[49] and Jew-

45. Listed as Claudius #117 and #119, *The Roman Imperial Coinage* 1, rev. ed.

46. Claudius #118, *The Roman Imperial Coinage*.

47. See Kreitzer, "A Numismatic Clue to Acts 19.23–41."

48. This also resonates with the notion of an evangelistic strategy behind the Ephesian marital code which I discuss in ch. 6. MacDonald briefly makes mention of evangelism in her discussion of the Colossian HH code, *Colossians and Ephesians*, Kindle loc. 4171. Also, in her "Was Celsus Right," she comments that the ideal Christian wife could perpetuate the growth of the movement referring to Ephesians 5:22–33, but she has no discussion of the text beyond this, 157–84.

49. The letter from Antiochus III written 212–205/204 BCE. It is unlikely that these Jews settled in Ephesus directly, but likely they relocated to Ephesus in subsequent decades.

ish families emigrate to Asia Minor after the destruction of the temple (70 CE). In Ephesus: where Paul preaches in the synagogue, and hall of Tryrannus (Acts 19:8–10); and the sons of the Jewish chief priest, Sceva, cast out demons (19:13–16); at the riot where Alexander is pushed to the front as a representative of fellow Jews wishing to distance from Paul's message (19:32–34); and Josephus identifies Jews as indigenous citizens (*Against Apion* 2:39; LCL 186.306–7)[50] and notes their exemption from military service by consul L. Lentulus Crus (*Antiquities* 14:228–30, 234, 240; LCL 489.122–25, 126–27, 130–31) and Dolabella (14:223–27; LCL 489.120–23);[51] their request to observe the Sabbath (14:262–64; LCL 489.142–45);[52] Philo's citation of G. Norbanus Flaccus permitting Jews to collect a temple tax (*Embassy to Gaius* 315–16; LCL 379.158–59)[53]—all accounts in support of a sizeable Jewish community living in Ephesus by the time of the Ephesian epistle.[54] Notably, Jews receive mention in the inscriptions of Ephesus, albeit few in number.[55] In Miletus: Josephus identifies a document written by Proconsul Servilius Isauricus, (46–44 BCE) where he finds in favor of Miletus Jews who claimed that Miletus gentiles attacked them and would not let them observe the Sabbath.[56] Miletus also has one Jewish inscription (second/third century CE) where a section of the theatre is reserved for Jews and/or God Fearers.[57] In Pisidian Antioch: where a verse epitaph from Appolonia in Phrygia refers to Deborah an Antiochian Jewish woman.[58]

50. The right would have been received by the Jews from "Alexander's successor" Seleucus Nicator (312–281/280 BCE).

51. Crus (49 BCE) and Dolabella (43 BCE).

52. 42 BCE.

53. Flaccus doc. (31–27 BCE).

54. For more see Trebilco, *The Early Christians in Ephesus*, 37–52 and Levinskaya, *The Book of Acts in Its First Century Setting*, 138–43. Strelan, *Paul, Artemis, and the Jews in Ephesus*, 181, estimates a Jewish population in Ephesus of 25,000 based on an overall population of 250,000 for the city and the consensus that Jews accounted for about 10 percent of any Greco-Roman city during imperial times.

55. The mentions are not extensive and after first century: alter and menorah (IEPH 4130); Ioulios the doctor (his wife Ioulia, and children) entrusts the Jews care of his family tomb (IEPH 1677); as does Marcus Aurelios Moussios (IEPH 1676) a Roman citizen. The lack of Jewish inscriptions is somewhat telling. The volume of inscriptions would testify to who is in power in the city. Among the thousands of inscriptions only a few mentions the Jews.

56. *Ant.* 14.244–46, LCL 489.132–35.

57. *CIJ* II.748, Miletus. See Levinskaya, 63–65, for the debate surrounding this inscription.

58. *CIJ* II.772. For more on Diaspora Jews see Levinskaya, *The Book of Acts in Its First*

THE PROBLEM

Diaspora Jews lived Asia Minor for hundreds of years, their presence providing an important connection between Acts 19 and the Ephesian letter. Luke typically presents Paul as starting his preaching with the Jews in the synagogues, even after he had already identified evangelizing the gentiles as his goal.[59] This suggests that in the cities Paul stopped there were already Jewish communities. Hence, Paul's evangelistic strategy begins with the communities of Diaspora Jews with the intent of his message spreading to their gentile neighbors. According to Luke, this is exactly what has happened in the Ephesus synagogue, the hall of Tyrannus (Acts 19:8–10), even with the Jewish seven sons of Sceva (19:13–16) who are badly beaten by a demon, but with the result that both Jews and Greeks are seized with fear and the name of Jesus is honored among them (19:13–17). Paul's goal is one of unity, bringing those who are apart together under Christ, but when Alexander is pushed to the front of the crowd to reinforce the Jews separation from Paul's gospel message (19:33), the crowd recognizes him as a Jew who believes not in Artemis, and they are filled with fury. The unbelieving Greeks and Jews in Ephesus could not be farther apart in this moment and will remain as such unless they change.

The Ephesian letter represents this change. Both groups, having lived together for hundreds of years, both aware of the chasm that once existed between their beliefs, are now united by the blood of Christ (Eph 2:13), who brings peace between the two by making them one (2:14–15) putting to death their hostility (2:16). Having shared a similar plight in their prior existence (2:1–3) they have been resurrected together in Christ (2:5) because of the power of God's love (2:4). This theme of a uniting transforming identity in new creation is carried-on throughout the letter as the unifying image of God and will stand in opposition to the notion of the independent Artemis in the marital *Haustafel* of the letter which arrives in Ephesus then circulates throughout Asia Minor. "Great is Artemis of the Ephesians" (Acts 19:28, 34) pales in comparison to Christ, who is seated in the heavens above every name that can ever be, and whose goal is that his image-bearers serve each other (Eph 5:21).

Century Setting; also, Trebilco, *Jewish Communities in Asia Minor*.

59. Cf. Acts 13:46; 14:1; 17:1, 10, 17; 18:6, 19.

1.3 WHERE TO BEGIN?

Does the Ephesian marital code begin at 5:21 with mutual submission or 5:22 with wifely submission? Commonly known reasons to argue for beginning the marriage *Haustafel* at 5:21 include that, first, along with "speaking" (λαλοῦντες), "singing and making melody" (ᾄδοντες καὶ ψάλλοντες), and "giving thanks" (εὐχαριστοῦντες) in 5:19–20, "submitting yourselves" (ὑποτασσόμενοι) in 5:21 is part of an uninterrupted string of participles that are all grammatically connected to "be filled with the Spirit" in 5:18. And, second, the earliest manuscripts[60] agree that there is no verb or participle in 5:22, which makes the matron's implied "submit" in 5:22 grammatically dependent on the mutual submission of ὑποτασσόμενοι in 5:21. Hence, Paul's instructions for the matron to submit are not exclusive to her gender (5:22) but one side of the mutual submission expected of both male and female (5:21).[61]

Common reasons to argue for beginning the marital *Haustafel* at 5:22 are, first, one may say that 5:21 is grammatically connected to the preceding participles of 5:19–20 and that the matron's implied "submit" may be grammatically dependent the notion of gender mutual submission, but 5:21 nonetheless remains thematically connected to only the matron's submission of 5:22, not her husband's. Second, being subject to Christ includes the notion of our subordination to him, that is central to the *Haustafeln*, not his mutual subordination to us. Third, the marriage *Haustafel* is best understood as a self-contained unit beginning with 5:22, hence 5:21 is best understood as a transitional introduction to 5:22 that remains part of the preceding section of verses tied to "be filled with the Spirit" (5:18). Fourth, the husband is not directly called upon to submit, only the wife.[62]

In either case, the parsing of Ephesians 5:21 between two sections of verses in hope of assigning it to one section and not the other or identifying it as merely a transitional verse between sections is to miss the point of

---

60. P46, B, Clement, Origen, Greek mss acc. to Jerome, Jerome, Theodore. For extended exegetical and manuscript discussion see Belz, "The Rhetoric of Gender in the Household of God," 87–101.

61. For more, see the following sampling of scholars who begin the household code with 5:21: Thielman, *Ephesians*; Baugh, *Ephesians*; Lincoln, *Ephesians*; Arnold, *Ephesians*.

62. For more, see the following sampling of scholars who begin the household code with 5:22: Miletic, *One Flesh*; Best, *Ephesians*; Tanzer, "Ephesians"; Perkins, *Ephesians*; O'Brien, *The Letter to the Ephesians*; MacDonald, *Colossians and Ephesians*; Hoehner, *Ephesians*.

new creation and the cultural reversal where the husband leaves his parent's house to be joined to his wife (5:31 cf. Gen 2:24).⁶³ Moreover, the notion of the husband's mutual submission goes beyond the grammatical analysis of 5:21. It is manifest by his personal self-sacrifice (5:25), taking on characteristically wifely duties of washing and cleansing (5:26), and loving his wife as he loves himself (5:28). This reflects Paul's intent for the mutual submission of 5:21 to be manifest by both the wife (5:22) and the husband (5:25-26, 28).

1.4 METHODOLOGY

I deploy an interdisciplinary approach, as do other scholars who have combined various methods to clarify Paul's intent behind the Ephesus NT marital code: lexicological, intertextual, rhetorical, socio-grammatical, socio-historical, most recently coupled with new creation language. Lexicology is significant to my discussions on the meaning of κεφαλή for "head" (Sect. 1.1; 1.7; 2.3; 6.3). Lexicology also has some bearing on my Section 4.1.1 discussion of whether to assign social categories or biological categories to איש for "husband," אשה for "wife" (cf. Gen 2:24), זכר for "male" and נקבה for "female" (Gen 1:27) in constructing Paul's frame of reference for understanding of the *imago Dei* and gender.

Although I am critical of the weight scholarship has placed on intertextuality to interpret the Ephesian marital code, especially when so much epigraphical and artefactual evidence is in Ephesus, intertextuality remains an important part of my work. Intertextual conversations are clearly in the landscape in my chapter 2 construction of writer context, including: Paul's ministry leaders (Rom 16; Phil 4:2-3); marriage and celibacy (1 Cor 7); circumcision (1 Cor 7:17-20); sex and marriage (1 Cor 7:2-9); sex and slaves (1 Cor 7:21-24); hairstyles, head coverings, honor, and headship (1 Cor 11:2-16); female prophets and teachers (1 Cor 11:5, 14:34-35), and so forth.

Socio-historical analysis prior to the writing of the Ephesian epistle is most obvious in my chapter 3 discussion of Greek cultural and philosophical influences, Roman political influence, the wealthy women of Asia Minor, and prominent priestesses of the Artemis cult. True, I am critical of scholarship's rather liberal application of literature, culture, and history across

---

63. Typically, the wife would leave her parents for him. See 6.6 discussion of Ephesians 5:31 (cf. Gen 2:23-24), and 1.7.5 discussion of theological reversal, and Lee-Barnewall, *Neither Complementarian*.

hundreds of years and thousands of miles to the specific first-century situation of Ephesus (Sect. 3.3), but even so, such information provides some context for the well-travelled, well-educated author of the epistle. Chapter 5 is also replete with socio-historical analysis: comparing and contrasting the reception histories of Eve and Artemis; the rise of married and celibate traditions for bearing the *imago Dei*; celibate Christian communities; and attitudes toward sex as sinful.

Unique to my methodology is the use of socio-grammatical analysis specific to the artefacts and inscriptions about the goddess Artemis as related to the notoriously long marital *Haustafel* in the Ephesian letter (chs. 4 and 6). This is paired with a rhetorical analysis (ch. 6) of Ephesians 5:21–33 that explains what is happening in the text and reveals the moves Paul makes to persuade Ephesian wives and husbands to adopt a paradigm for their marriage of oneness (5:30) and sacrificial living (5:21–22, 25–29) based on the example of Christ himself (5:25), with Paul's ultimate goal of evangelizing the unbeliever through the believer's marriage.

1.5 CHAPTER OUTLINE

To illustrate the advantage of this method, the book begins with a literature review of scholars who attempt to combine socio-historical research and intertextuality with new creation language for *Haustafel* interpretation (ch. 1). But this combination is non-specific to the *Sitz im Leben* of the Ephesian believer, applying broad socio-historical settings of Greco-Rome to Ephesus, and lacking a close reading of local inscriptional evidence with the marital *Haustafel*. Next, the book develops writer context for the Ephesian correspondence by examining Paul's undisputed letters to work out his new creation attitude toward female ministry leaders, marriage, and women's role in public worship (ch. 2), which he seeks to implement in a world of harsh Hellenistic realities. Chapter 3 defines the *Sitz im Leben* of the Ephesian reader with an examination of inscriptional evidence specific to the reader's prior relationship with Artemis suggesting that Paul borrows prevalent inscriptions about the believer's old identity as an image-bearer for Artemis and repurposes them for the believer's new identity as an image-bearer for Christ.[64]

---

64. Residents of Asia Minor who visited the city would also understand Paul's use of inscriptions in plain sight of anyone.

Subsequently, the question of what the *imago Dei* looked like to the Ephesian reader (ch. 4) is answered in two parts: first, the impasse that emerges from exclusive intertextual use of the Hebrew Bible with Pauline scriptures to define what the image of God looks like in people (Part One), which scholars then bring to bear upon the Ephesian household to define what the *imago Dei* meant to the new Ephesian believer; and second, by comparing how the Ephesian citizens thought of themselves as image-bearers for Artemis with Paul's vision of the Ephesian believer as a new creation image-bearer for Christ (Part Two).[65] But the new believer's notion of what the image of God looks like in them is distorted by their prior relationship as Artemis' image-bearers which had adversely influenced their marital relationship.

Chapter 5 juxtaposes the rise of two traditions for the *imago Dei* in the Ephesian believer, marriage versus celibacy. Part One argues that Eve, as the first female *imago Dei*, is an unlikely candidate for the gentile Ephesian matron to emulate given Eve's tattered reception history. Rather, the matron's pre-conversion experience as a worshipper of the independent goddess presents Artemis as the likely candidate in the matron's mind for emulation as an image-bearer for Christ. Part Two supports the rise of two traditions with a trajectory of celibacy as witnessed in Christian celibate communities coupled with negative attitudes toward sexual intercourse as sinful. Although Paul has endorsed celibate behavior before (1 Cor 7), his concern in the Ephesian letter is that spouses have mistaken their new identity in Christ as one of independence from each other rather than interdependence with each other (ch. 6), which hinders his evangelistic intentions for Ephesus. Chapter 7 presents conclusions, contribution to knowledge, and implications for modern society.

1.6 SCOPE AND LIMITATION

To provide an in-depth investigation of the Ephesian marital *Haustafel* some parameters should be established at the outset. It can be argued that none of Paul's undisputed letters quote the Gospel writers, indicating that his letters either pre-date the codified Gospels or were written at the same time as the Gospels. The teachings of Jesus were clearly in the air during

---

65. Not all Ephesian residents were citizens, albeit the Ephesian church could have a mix of residents and citizens who were former Artemis worshippers. Citizenry and devotion to Artemis went hand in hand. See 4.2.4.

Paul's lifetime but, without the Gospels in written form for comparison, speculating on what Paul knew or did not know about Jesus' thoughts on women and marriage is beyond the scope of this study.[66]

Although I touch on these briefly, since they share geography and a similar audience of gentiles and Diaspora Jews who have knowledge of Artemis, I will not present a side-by-side comparison of the marital codes as they appear in Ephesians, Colossians, 1 Peter, 1 Timothy, and Titus. To harmonize or distinguish the accounts in these letters is not my area of interest. I do not expect Peter to have the mind of Paul or the church of the Ephesian letter to match the unique setting of the (later) Pastoral Epistles.

The evidence considered comes from the near post-Pauline period, within the first few centuries of Paul.[67] To move beyond the horizon of this time frame dilutes the chronological specificity of my argument and invites an entirely new work regarding how the marital code of Ephesians was interpreted across the centuries.

Although I interact intertextually with the Pauline corpus and Genesis creation accounts, I am not interested in revisiting decades-long debates over contested texts.[68] My interest is in the continued influence of Artemis on the thought world of the Ephesian new believer in marriage.

Although I am interested in the influence of Artemis upon the Ephesian thought world, this does not extend in a detailed manner regarding Artemis and the marital code of other NT letters. Both Jews and gentiles throughout Asia Minor knew of Artemis and would understand the references to her in the Ephesian letter but, as she was the patron goddess of Ephesus, my focus will remain on the marital code within the Ephesian letter.

---

66. There is general acceptance among scholarship that Paul's uncontested letters predate the Gospels since, in addition to other items, Paul does not mention the virgin birth, miracles of Jesus, empty tomb, and states that Christ appeared to the twelve apostles (1 Cor 15:5) when Judas had already committed suicide. For more see Brown, on the "Nature and Origin of the New Testament," 1–6; Wenham, *Paul: Follower of Jesus or Founder of Christianity?* Also, Dodd, *The Founder of Christianity*, for when it was a live issue among scholarship.

67. Specifically, to the Cappadocian fathers. See 5.1.4.

68. For examples of the debate see fns. 5–9. For a chronological meta-study of the debate see https://www.cbeinternational.org/resource/meta-study-debate-over-meaning-head-kephale-pauls-writings/, accessed 3/16/2023.

1.7 MARITAL CODE SCHOLARSHIP REVIEW

Whether self-identifying as such or not, scholars who interact with the marriage *Haustafeln* largely adopt beliefs common to one of two diverging interpretative roads from the twentieth century. Beliefs common to egalitarians are:[69] 1) God created men and women with equal stature in all respects;[70] 2) Both Adam and Eve were created in the *imago Dei*; 3) Both are given equal responsibility to rule over creation (Gen 1:26–27); 4) The fall of humankind in Genesis 3 led to sinful gender domination by the male; 5) Galatians 3:28 flattens marital hierarchical relationships; 6) Mutual submission (Eph 5:21) has replaced male dominance; 7) The marital code should be interpreted in light of the gender-neutral totality of Scripture.[71]

Beliefs common to complementarians are:[72] 1) Both genders are equal before God as persons, but differences in male and female are ordained by God in the created order; 2) Adam's headship in marriage was established before "the fall," not a result of sin;[73] 3) At creation, man was given the position of spiritual leadership in the home (Gen 2:16–17); 4) Adam named Eve rather than her naming him (Gen 2:23); 5) She is his helper (Gen 2:18, 20); 6) Galatians 3:28 does not teach that all differences of nationality, status, and sex cease to exist at conversion; 7) The husband is the leader (κεφαλή) of his wife as Christ is the leader (κεφαλή) of the church, hence, as the church is to submit to Christ, so the wife is to submit to her husband (Eph 5:22–33).

Much of the lexical debate over the meaning of κεφαλή was played out on the twentieth-century stage, although it still receives limited discussion in the twenty-first century.[74] Both twentieth-century complementarians and egalitarians focused mainly on lexical exegesis of κεφαλή in biblical and extrabiblical contexts.[75] Consensus over the meaning of κεφαλή in the

---

69. For a detailed description of egalitarianism, see *Christians for Biblical Equality: Statement on Men, Women, and Biblical Equality*.

70. For more see Pierce and Groothuis, *Discovering Biblical Equality*.

71. See Webb, *Slaves, Women, and Homosexuals*; and Stallard, "Gender Neutral Translations," 5–26.

72. See Piper and Grudem, *Recovering*, for a detailed exposition of complementarianism.

73. Council on Biblical Manhood and Womanhood: Danvers Statement.

74. For example, two of the authors reviewed in this chapter touch on the lexical debate; Lee-Barnewall, *Neither Complementarian*, 147–66, and Westfall, *Paul and Gender*, 80–84, although debate over the meaning of κεφαλή has largely played out.

75. The meaning of κεφαλή was not the only topic of twentieth-century scholarship, but the volume of work published on κεφαλή supports its priority.

Ephesian marital code proved elusive.⁷⁶ Meanings emerge, overlap, and fade away in varying contexts, hence, transferring the meaning of κεφαλή from unrelated extrabiblical contexts with different philosophical attitudes from Paul placed too much weight on just one word.⁷⁷ It cannot be primarily a matter of studying the meaning of words and culture throughout Greco-Rome and then imposing them onto Paul's notion of κεφαλή as related to marital relationships in the Mediterranean. The conversation has moved on from lexicology to interpreting the household codes through new kingdom realities and the struggle of the emerging church. But the application of new creation thinking has continued to result in contradictory conclusions about the meaning of the marital *Haustafel*.

In this section, five contemporary *Haustafeln* interpreters are compared, highlighting the range of conclusions about the meaning of the marital code and offering a new way forward.⁷⁸ Why these five as a representative sample among a sea of so many? Each scholar's work presents a recent individual perspective that, when taken together with the others, makes for a formidable summary of the whole of the *Haustafeln* debate. Carolyn Osiek argues that the Ephesian marital *Haustafel* appears compliant while the real message is to separate from the evils of Rome. Elif Karaman argues that just by being Christian the church was already set apart and needed to blend in. Shively Smith's thinks that staying alive is

---

76. For example, see Liddell and Scott, *A Greek-English Lexicon*, which includes more than twenty-five possible metaphorical meanings in addition to the literal meaning of the physical head of a man or beast. Missing from the list are "authority," "superior rank," "leader," or "director." On the other hand, Bauer, *A Greek-English Lexicon of the New Testament*, carries the meaning of "superior rank." Bauer includes examples from classical Greek literature in addition to Septuagint (LXX) usage of κεφαλή to translate ראש which is followed by קצי, meaning "chief" or "ruler." For קצי the LXX uses ἡγέομαι "be a leader" and ἀρχηγός "captain, leader, chief prince." Second to κεφαλή (used 239 times for ראש) in frequency, ἄρχων (used 180 times for ראש), meaning "ruler, commander, leader" surpasses κεφαλή when the intended meaning for ראש is "chief" or "authority." In this context ἄρχων is used 109 times, about 60 percent of its total usage.

77. For examples of the debate, see Perriman's discussion, "The Head of a Woman," where he argues that "neither authority over nor the source interpretation of κεφαλή is as well established lexicologically as their proponents would like to think," 616; and his discussion in *Speaking of Women*, 13–33. Perriman argues for "pre-eminence as a primary sense of κεφαλή. See also Cotterell and Turner, *Linguistics and Biblical Interpretation*, for their discussion regarding the sense of a word and relationships between words and concepts, 151–81.

78. It is noteworthy that all five authors reviewed are female, which at some level reflects the demographic of scholarly interest in the subject matter.

the pressing goal for the emerging church in 1 Peter.[79] Cynthia Westfall reasons that the tangible benefits the church receives from Christ in the Ephesian *Haustafel* is a template for reciprocity between equals in Christian marriage. Michelle Lee-Barnewall reasons we are spending too much effort supporting male authority or female equality and too little on self-sacrifice and a united purpose. Their research is far more relevant a review than the twentieth-century debates over the meaning of κεφαλή.

1.7.1 Carolyn Osiek: The Compliance and Defiance Marital Code

In *A Woman's Place: House Churches in Earliest Christianity*, Carolyn Osiek et al. views the Ephesian marital code as one manifestation of an epistle written deliberately to defy the *Pax Romana*.[80] She sees the *peroratio* section of 6:10–20 as a call to war where believers put on the armor of God to stand against the schemes of the devil (6:11) which are loosed like "flaming arrows" upon the faithful believers (6:16).[81] They must shun evil spiritual powers personified in the Roman way of life (2:2; 6:12) or they will once again walk as the gentiles walk in the futility of their minds with darkened understanding . . . (4:17–24). In Osiek's understanding, Paul thinks that survival of the church depends on creating separation from Roman society. The believers' true "gospel of peace" (εὐαγγελίου τῆς εἰρήνης) in 6:15 must replace the false peace of Rome.

Osiek argues that taken together with the 4:17—5:20 contrast between the repulsive vices of Roman society and the godly virtues of believing society, 6:10–20 reinforces Paul's message for the Ephesian believers to separate from the unbelieving world. Sandwiched between these two bookend passages is the Ephesian marital code (5:21–33) which is designed to encourage cohesion among believers by "submitting yourselves to one another" (Ὑποτασσόμενοι ἀλλήλοις) in reverence to Christ (5:21). This cohesion serves to set Ephesian believers apart from negative outside influences, giving the marital code the appearance of being outwardly compliant although

---

79. Note that Smith's work is in 1 Peter and focused on the master/slave relationship, not the Ephesians marital code, but her work remains relevant to mine as both letters are for believers in Asia Minor.

80. Osiek, MacDonald, Tulloch, *A Woman's Place*, 121–23.

81. See Lincoln, *Ephesians*, who also considers the Ephesians 6:10–20 *peroratio* as a call to battle, similar to a general giving a rousing speech to his soldiers about their superior might, 432–34.

it remains inwardly defiant. Thus, the Ephesian marital *Haustafel* serves to separate believers from Roman society while protecting believers from Roman wrath.[82]

The difficulty with Osiek's understanding of the *Haustafeln* is that it isolates the Ephesian believers from the very individuals they are trying to evangelize, which hardly resonates with Paul's attitude toward the unbeliever, and is not the proper function of the Ephesian text. Although the notion of evangelism is present throughout her book, it does not enter her chapter 6 discussion of the Ephesian marital code. The marital code, as she sees it, is that which ultimately sets believers apart from Roman society. It is a boundary, a safety net of "balance between flight from society and confrontation with society,"[83] which is consistent with a view that the Ephesian text does not have anything particular to support the notion of evangelism.[84] But to what extent does this resonate with Paul's intent "to preach to the gentiles the boundless riches of Christ" and that "now the wisdom of God should be made known" (3:8–10 NRSV)? Beyond this, her work has no significant interaction with the influence of Artemis upon the Ephesian household or mention of inscriptional evidence regarding the dominance of the goddess in the thought lives of her citizens, both deserving thoughtful consideration if one values reader context when interpreting the Ephesian letter. Rather, the context of her research is the wider background of Greco-Roman ethical ideals found in various moralists, political thinkers, and philosophers combined with an intertextual examination of the Ephesians *Haustafel*.[85]

1.7.2 Elif Hilal Karaman: The Good Citizen Marital Code

While Osiek sees the function of the Ephesian marital *Haustafel* as a boundary between the emerging church and secular Hellenistic society, Elif Karaman, *Ephesian Women in Greco-Roman and Early Christian Perspective*, sees the opposite. Karaman argues that the believers' newly manifest faith in Christ was sizeable enough to set them apart from larger society, without

---

82. See Osiek, *A Woman's Place*, 118–31, for additional discussion.
83. Osiek, *A Woman's Place*, 123.
84. In this sense Osiek does justice to her work since separation, not evangelism, would be the purpose of the *Haustafel*.
85. Osiek, *A Woman's Place*, 118–43

the supposed boundary of the *Haustafeln*.⁸⁶ Karaman spends significant energy on reader context by depicting how the wife functioned in the Ephesus household, based on archaeological and inscriptional evidence. She then couches this evidence in the larger setting of the Hellenistic culture of Asia Minor to demonstrate how early Christian writers used the social norms of Hellenistic society to build the social norms of early Christian society in Ephesus as well as other parts of the Mediterranean.⁸⁷ She concludes that it was not the intent of early Christian writers and, for my purpose, the Ephesian marital code to argue for gender equality. Rather, the Christian wife was intended to be the Christianized mirror image of her Hellenistic counterparts as submissive to her husband and a devoted mother.⁸⁸

Karaman makes good use of material artifactual resources to define this submissive role for the matron as one that is admired, with the matron and her husband serving as the respected core of the larger household family of children, uncles, aunts, grandparents, freedmen, servants, and so on.⁸⁹ She deploys these resources to argue that the matron's submission to her husband was in no way servile, but an esteemed role in household management.⁹⁰ Upon marriage she received a societally acknowledged and improved status beyond that of a maiden, plus a domestic space over which to rule. Karaman rightly offers a word of caution for scholars wishing to use our modern standards to evaluate the social conditions of Greco-Roman culture.⁹¹ Hence, she concludes that the Ephesian marital *Haustafel* is a Christianized version of the Hellenistic code designed to communicate that Christians are not a societal threat, but good citizens who are Christians.⁹²

---

86. Karaman, *Ephesian Women*, 85.

87. 1 Corinthians, Colossians, Ephesians, 1 Peter, the Letter of Ignatius to Polycarp, and the Letter of Polycarp to the Philippians.

88. Karaman, *Ephesian Women*, 63.

89. See her ch. 4 discussion of marriage for her use of Terrace House 2 and epigraphic evidence. Her conclusions differ from mine, but her research illumines reader context for the Ephesian letter.

90. Karaman, *Ephesian Women*, 79.

91. Karaman, *Ephesian Women*, 88.

92. Karaman also observes, "The first and foremost characteristic of a woman named in early Christian writing is her faith, whereas in Ephesian inscriptions women were recorded as a source of money," 148. Hence, even if the marital *Haustafel* was not revolutionary, the faith of the Christian wife was. This serves as evidence that a new kingdom had been inaugurated that was already changing what was of value in human relationships.

While Karaman rightly argues that it was not Paul's intent in the Ephesian letter to argue for gender equality, because both Paul and the Ephesian reader knew that equality was part of their new kingdom identity, her conclusion does not account for Paul's admonition that the Ephesian believers are to live out their new identity as ones who no longer "walk as the gentiles are walking" (4:17) and "to put on the new self in the likeness of God" (4:24). A fundamental shift in identity has occurred for the believer in the Ephesian letter that is insufficiently accounted for in Karaman's work. This fundamental shift in identity for both genders has transformed the marital code from that of maintaining the status quo as proof of good Roman citizenry to a marital code intent on evangelizing the skeptical onlooker. Karaman's focus is on the human structure of the marital *Haustafel*, not on the divine structure. Yet the Ephesians marital *Haustafel* is intentionally divine in its depiction of marriage as the relationship between Christ and the church.

1.7.3 Shively Smith: The Survival Marital Code

Albeit authored by different individuals, both the Petrine and Pauline household codes share the common objective to evangelize secular society in Asia Minor with new kingdom realities, making Shively Smith's work on the Petrine *Haustafeln* relevant to my discussion.[93] In *Strangers to Family*, Smith considers the submission passages in 1 Peter, including the marital code (3:1–7), to be short term survival strategy texts for the believers in Asia Minor. Smith argues that the household code of 1 Peter "presents two social arrangements of the household: the human structure and God's structure."[94] "They have no real systemic power in the governing systems around them. All they have is a future hope that a time of triumph, retribution, and restitution will come. But in order to see that they must navigate the world they inhabit and live in—not die in—now."[95]

Smith gives contextual support for her strategy for survival argument: 1) Peter writes to Jewish Christians who have fled Jerusalem to Judea and Samaria fearing persecution (Acts 8:1); 2) After the stoning of Stephen (7:54–60) they flee even further to Phoenicia, Cyprus, and Antioch where their non-participation in the cultic life of these Greco-Roman

---

93. For more discussion on the relationship between 1 Peter and Ephesians, see 6.1.
94. Smith, *Strangers to Family*, 76.
95. Smith, *Strangers to Family*, 169.

communities makes them appear threatening to established societal order (1 Pet 2:11, 18; 3:1, 7);[96] 3) To remedy this, Peter prescribes living lives filled with good deeds (1 Pet 2:12) so believers in Asia Minor can avoid drawing negative attention that leads their death (2:21); 4) They are to "honor everyone" without exception (2:17a), including the emperor as the Roman provincial authority (2:17d). With this strategy believers can navigate the temporal world governed by humans and the eternal cosmos governed by God. They can survive.

Turning to the Petrine marital *Haustafel*, Smith points out that Peter adopts Aristotle's gender hierarchy by echoing the conventional notion that men are stronger than women (3:7a).[97] With this in mind, a wife's silent obedience (3:4) will lead to her non-believing husband's conversion through deeds rather than words (3:1–2). Hence, in addition to survival as the major theme, evangelism is also present in Peter's marital code. Peter then deviates from Aristotle's formula, appearing to flatten the gender power structure in an alternate reality by telling believing husbands to honor their wives as joint heirs in God's household (3:7b).

Smith's work clearly brings out the dangers of being a believer in Asia Minor, a geographic region shared by Ephesus. Twenty-six times in her book she uses the word "survive" (or some form of the word) to make her main point of Peter's letter serving as a survival handbook for the faithful. But beyond acknowledging the obedient wife's role in evangelizing her husband (3:1–2) Smith's work shines insufficient light on the importance of the explicit references to evangelism (2:12; 3:15) in the letter.[98] In her work there is only one mention of evangelize and one of conversion. It is understandable that she wishes to highlight Peter's desire for the scattered believers of Asia Minor to avoid martyrdom. After all, it is the theme of her book. But her laser focus on survival is to the exclusion of the equally important theme of evangelism, of which Smith affords only passing consideration.[99] Evangelism is a theme of importance to the both the Pauline and Petrine *Haustafeln* of Asia Minor, a theme to be explored in greater detail as this work unfolds.

---

96. Smith, *Strangers to Family*, 21–26. The Pliny-Trajan letter, *Ep.* 10.96 (112 CE) states that Christians' refusal to participate in public polytheistic practices is worthy of punishment, LCL 59.286–91.

97. Smith, *Strangers to Family*, 74–80.

98. Albeit, highlighting the notion of evangelism is not the objective of her work, while survival is.

99. See 6.1.

1.7.4 Cynthia Westfall: The Reciprocity Marital Code

In *Paul and Gender*, Cynthia Westfall defines the first-century Hellenistic marriage relationship as one of give-and-take, a subset of the basic building block of Greco-Roman society's reciprocal patronage system "whose scope stretched from the home to the relationship between the Roman emperor and the empire."[100] From her husband the wife receives identity, status, and shares in the household property. She reciprocates by acknowledging her husband's authority, giving him honor, birthing children, and managing his household affairs.[101] Speaking of the Ephesian *Haustafel*, Westfall states that Paul's "husband is the head of the wife as Christ is the head of the church" (5:23) is based on the pragmatic give-and-take of patronage benefits, not on the order of creation or the nature of masculine or feminine.[102] Promoting gender equality, she argues that in saying, "Submitting yourselves to one another in reverence to Christ" (5:21),[103] Paul makes a syntactic link between the matron's submission and mutual submission, thus giving the wife the same level of status as the husband. Hence, 5:22–27 in no way affirms the ontological superiority of men. Instead, it draws a comparison between the tangible benefits that the church receives from Christ and the tangible benefits that the wife receives from her husband.[104]

Continuing her discussion of gender, she observes that male and female roles in the Mediterranean were structured in ways that brought honor to the household for both husbands and wives. Men who displayed feminine emotions and women who displayed masculine behaviors brought dishonor upon their households.[105] Westfall argues that Paul turns this notion on its head with a transformative Ephesian marital code that redefines what is masculine in 5:25–29 by ascribing typically feminine traits (self-sacrificial love, nourishing, cherishing) and domestic chores (serving,

---

100. Westfall, *Paul and Gender*, 101.

101. See also deSilva, "Patronage and Reciprocity," 33; also, his *Honor, Patronage, Kinship & Purity*; and Dudry, "'Submit Yourselves to One Another,'" 27–44.

102. Westfall, *Paul and Gender*, 101. Her conclusion in this instance of "head" not being tied to the order of creation coheres with mine, albeit she equates "head" with patronage while I equate "head" with leading by example in sacrificial love (6.3; 7.2).

103. Ὑποτασσόμενοι ἀλλήλοις ἐν φόβῳ Χριστοῦ.

104. See Westfall, *Paul and Gender*, 100–102, for full discussion.

105. See Westfall, *Paul and Gender*, 15. See also Ben Sira, 26:10–16; 42:9–12; 4 Macc 18:6–8; Thucydides, *Hist.*, 2.45.2, LCL 108.340–41.

cleansing, washing) to the male.[106] In Paul's new paradigm of marital relations men treat women as superior when compared to the Greco-Roman ideal. Thus, by instructing wives to submit (5:22) and respect (5:33), the Ephesian marital *Haustafel* appears to adhere to Hellenistic gender expectations on the outside all the while subverting them from the inside.

Westfall's thinking about the subversive twist of the Ephesian *Haustafel* agrees with Osiek. Westfall's recognition of a decidedly new marital role for the husband demonstrates that transformation has taken place in the marriage relationship of the Ephesian believers, transformation that coheres with the notion of new identity (4:17, 24) and runs counter to societal expectations. However, Westfall's comparison of the Ephesian marital code to the Roman patronage system breaks down at the point where she writes, "Neither partner is entitled or has priority, because every patron is reduced to functioning like a client."[107] By its very nature the notion of patronage is incongruent with the notion of equality. Patronage requires a patron who is in the position of power and a client who is not. Hierarchy is implicit in patronage. Hence, to identify both the husband and wife as equal clients is to do away with the notion of patronage. Applying her analogy of patronage to the relationship of Christ and the church she writes, "Woman draws her life from man, and the church draws its life from Christ."[108] Careful not to push the analogy too far, she wisely stops short of saying that both the church and Christ are now clients thus making them equals. Even so, her application of the Roman patronage system to the marital code would make better sense were she to admit that this human structure of patronage hierarchy is a temporary tool for church survival, while the divine structure of self-sacrifice by all parties is transcendent. Lastly, her notion of patronage in this text dilutes the very message of self-sacrifice displayed by Christ (5:25), which the husband and wife are to emulate.

---

106. Westfall, *Paul and Gender*, adds that Paul "recasts the man as the bride of Christ and the wife as the man's male body," 56. She also argues that Paul uses common Hellenistic masculine and feminine metaphors in ways that are transformational. As the bride of Christ men are clothed in feminine wedding garments (5:26–27) 57. Paul applied masculine metaphors to all believers, he applied feminine metaphors to all believers, 58. Paul applied feminine images to the churches he addresses, as well as depicting them as children, 52. Paul's maternal imagery (childbirth Gal 4:19, breastfeeding 1 Cor 3:1–2; 1 Thess 2:6–7) is similar to how Moses characterized God's expectations of him as a leader (Num 11:2). Isaiah also used similar imagery of a mother's commitment to her children to illustrate God's compassion to Zion (Isa 49:15–16), 52.

107. Westfall, *Paul and Gender*, 101.

108. Westfall, *Paul and Gender*, 102.

Westfall's analysis in *Paul and Gender* is an intertextual approach which involves multiple Pauline letters and multiple aspects of human relationships across a broad Roman empire. This aligns with her purpose to "reframe gender issues in the light of coherence within Pauline theology . . . and carry it to new ground."[109] Her work provides some new thinking about the marital code and Pauline context, but more attention could be placed on Ephesian reader context and inscriptional evidence of the influence of goddess Artemis on the life of her city, to which Westfall gives only a passing mention.[110]

1.7.5 Michelle Lee-Barnewall: The Hierarchical Oneness Marital Code

Michelle Lee-Barnewall in her *Neither Complementarian nor Egalitarian* argues for a theology of reversal where conversations about gender ought to be viewed through the transcendent categories of unity in the body of Christ and the holiness of God's people. She supports this notion of theological reversal by making the point that the kingdom that Jesus announced did not bring about the expected changes in Israel's fortune. Teachings such as: "many who are first will be last, and the last, first" (Mark 10:31; Luke 13:30; Mark 9:35; Matt 20:16) and; "whoever exalts himself shall be humbled; and whoever humbles himself shall be exalted" (Matt 23:12; Luke 14:11; 18:14; cf. Matt 18:4); and "the one who is greatest among you must become like the youngest, and the leader like the one who serves" (Luke 22:26 NRSV) bear an unexpected theological reversal for Israel's concept of a restored kingdom.[111] She spotlights Christ as the prime example of reversal as the one who existed "in the form of God" yet "did not regard equality with God as something to be exploited" and the one who sacrificed himself as a "slave" and was "obedient to the point of death" (Phil 2:6–8 NRSV).[112]

The cross becomes the most prominent paradoxical situation as "foolishness to those who are perishing, but to us who are being saved it is the power of God" (1 Cor 1:18 NRSV). The notion of a victorious, crucified Messiah made no sense to Greco-Roman or Jewish thinking (1 Cor 1:23–24), but through Jesus' self-sacrifice a new kingdom indeed arrives,

---

109. Westfall, *Paul and Gender*, 1.

110. Westfall, *Paul and Gender*, 310, where she mentions Artemis and the Salutaris Inscription of 104 CE.

111. Lee-Barnewall, *Neither Complementarian*, 78.

112. Lee-Barnewall, *Neither Complementarian*, 78.

unique in its continued self-sacrifice and unified purpose (Rom 12:10; Phil 2:1–11).[113] From this platform of theological reversal she challenges egalitarians and complementarians by asking how central can the notion of equality or authority possibly be to the marital *Haustafel* when Paul talks more about not using rights than fighting for rights, or when he speaks of himself as a slave (Rom 1:1; Gal 1:10; 2 Cor 4:5)? She takes this further by asking if we are spending too much time trying to support male authority or female equality and not enough time on Christ's teaching about the first being last?[114]

Turning to Ephesians, she observes that whether 5:21 refers to mutual submission or not, Paul specifically calls on wives to submit in 5:22 but does not say the same to husbands. Hence, if Paul intended only for believers to submit to one another, there would be no need to give specific instructions to the wife.[115] Lee-Barnewall then places the marital code in the context of the Genesis account of "the fall," pointing out that Adam identified Eve impersonally as "the woman whom You gave to be with me," blaming both her and God (Gen 3:12). This, Lee-Barnewall argues, contrasts with the Ephesus believing husband who is to consider the woman as his body and to give himself up for her (5:22) rather than trying to save himself by blaming her.[116] She then points out that the wife is not called to submit to Hellenistic patriarchal authority but to her believing husband's authority, which self-sacrifices on her behalf. Instead of being ruled by her husband as an inferior, they become another example of theological reversal where the one we would expect to serve becomes the one who is served.[117] This reversal of expectations is what leads to the fulfillment of the one-flesh union of Genesis 2:24 in Ephesians 5:31.

There is so much to agree with in Lee-Barnewall. What makes "new creation" people unique is their ability to love one another despite differences in social status. The ability to love and sacrifice for others transcends and ultimately transforms social constructs. Paul knows this, hence, his lasting concern in his letters is not one of equal rights for all in the "here and now" but the inclusiveness of the church which will ultimately transform society and provide equal rights for all in the "then." Issues such as

---

113. Lee-Barnewall, *Neither Complementarian*, 78–79.
114. Lee-Barnewall, *Neither Complementarian*, 66.
115. Lee-Barnewall, *Neither Complementarian*, 162.
116. Lee-Barnewall, *Neither Complementarian*, 163.
117. Lee-Barnewall, *Neither Complementarian*, 163–64.

equality will arise and must be addressed, but to Paul they remain secondary issues to that of unity and inclusiveness among believers who have the same transcendent care for one another (1 Cor 12:25) regardless of temporal social status. It is precisely because of their differences in social status that their commitment to oneness, self-sacrifice, and love would appear so remarkable in first-century life and bear witness to the future promise of the inaugurated new kingdom while it also transforms the here and now.[118]

Lee-Barnewall's contribution to the marriage *Haustafeln* conversation is significant, but should she have taken her argument of theological reversal, with its notions of oneness, love, and self-sacrifice, which are so readily observable in the Ephesian *Haustafel*, a step further in the direction of evangelism? Paul's intent was for the newly inaugurated kingdom of Christ to spread through sacrificial living, but Lee-Barnewall makes no mention of evangelism or intent to convert. Moreover, her observation that, if Paul only intended mutual submission between believers, he would not have given the wife specific instructions to submit (5:22)[119] overlooks that Paul's entreaty for both the husband and wife to mutually submit (5.21) is because the wife is not submitting (5:22, 24) and neither is the husband (5:25–31). Although the title of her work may read *Neither Complementarian, Nor Egalitarian*, such statements reveal a hierarchical inclination.

1.8 SUMMARY

When read in concert, these five scholars represent a well-rounded summary of modern *Haustafeln* scholarship. Osiek argues that the Ephesian marital code may appear as compliant on the surface while underneath is designed to separate the believing community from the worldliness of the empire. Karaman argues that, just by being Christian, the church is already

---

118. Galatians 3:28 (ethnicity, gender, slave, master) does not speak of "equality" so much as that of "oneness." Distinctions are not eliminated. They are just irrelevant. See Lee-Barnewall, where she comments, "The concept that all people are created equal and endowed with certain inalienable rights comes from the Enlightenment and would have been 'thoroughly alien' to the ancient world. The predominant belief instead was that people were by nature created unequal, as evidenced physically (males as dominant and females as inferior), socially (parents would be superior to children, freeborn superior to slaves), and ethnically (Greeks vs. barbarians)," 85. Yet the notion of equality being a post-Enlightenment issue and not a first-century issue is another debate for another time. See my Sect. 7.2 for additional comments.

119. For more see Lee-Barnewall, *Neither Complementarian*, 162.

set apart and needs to work at blending in as good citizens while Christianizing the Hellenistic marital code. Smith argues that survival is the urgent need of the emerging church and living in compliance to the marital code of 1 Peter is quite literally the way to stay alive. Westfall argues that the reciprocal give-and-take between believing spouses as married equals reflects the Roman patronage system where the husband as benefactor is the patron-head, but Paul redefines "head" by assigning feminine qualities of tender care to the husband, making spouses equal. Lee-Barnewall argues that wifely submission is not to a Hellenistic patriarchy but to a husband who sacrifices himself for her like Christ in an unexpected theological reversal. Each offers a unique contribution to the body of scholarship with a different perspective on the purpose of the NT marital *Haustafel*.

The intent of my research is also to contribute by arguing that Paul's evangelistic purpose in revealing to the Hellenistic community the superiority of marriages transformed by the *imago Dei* in believers is to invite them into Christ's kingdom that they too might share in its blessings. This contribution is accomplished by a close re-reading of the Ephesian marital code alongside an abundance of local epigraphical evidence that illumines writer and reader context for the epistle, offers a way forward for the interpreter, and redefines the notion of power relationships in Christ's new kingdom. To this end, chapter 2 examines writer context with a focus on intertextuality. Chapter 3 explores writer understanding of reader context with an examination of literary and inscriptional evidence as the background for reading the Ephesian letter.

2

Writer Context and the Ephesian Marriage Code

AN EXAMINATION OF PAUL'S undisputed letters to work out his new creation disposition toward female ministry leaders, marriage, and a woman's role in public worship offers an intertextual framework for writer context in the Ephesian letter.[1] If Ephesians is authored by Paul in c. 62 CE, the undisputed letters provide background to his thinking as he speaks to the unique *Sitz im Leben* of the Ephesian reader. If Ephesians is authored by a serious student of Paul's in c. 80–90 CE, the undisputed letters become source documents that illumine the Paulinist with the mind of Paul to be applied to unique *Sitz im Leben* of Ephesus eighteen to twenty-five years following the apostle's death.[2] In this chapter Paul's new creation intentions for social equality in the inaugurated kingdom are juxtaposed with the human reality of Hellenistic patriarchy. To illustrate, I have chosen a rhetorical reading of the Corinthian correspondence with full knowledge that my understanding of the text will conflict with that of others. Following an examination of his undisputed letters, we turn to the Colossian letter due to the notable similarity between it and Ephesians. I have taken an agnostic stance regarding authorship of either letter so the question of "who influenced whom" is only relevant if one assumes pseudonymous authorship

---

1. This chapter will not discuss the Pastorals which will receive attention in ch. 5.

2. For example, the Jerusalem temple fell in 70 CE meaning that the near reference for the believer as a holy temple (Eph 2:21) would more likely be the Artemision than the fallen temple in Jerusalem.

of at least one of the letters. What do the undisputed letters communicate about Paul's thinking on gender and marriage in the inaugural kingdom, and how might this information be refashioned for the Ephesian reader?[3]

2.1 PAUL'S MINISTRY LEADERS

Paul understands his transformation on the Damascus Road as a call to announce a new world order to the gentiles (Gal 1:15–16).[4] With unwavering devotion he: 1) lives as a gentile (Gal 2:14; 1 Cor 9:21); 2) distances himself with his Pharisaic past (Gal 1:13–14; Phil 3:4–6);[5] 3) confronts Peter over not eating with gentile Christians (Gal 2:12–14); 4) refuses have Titus circumcised (2:3);[6] 5) and announces the believing community as free from the law that separated Jews from gentiles and men from women (Rom 6:14–15; 7:1–6; Gal 3:28). The old-world order means nothing to him (Phil 3:8) while transforming into the likeness of Christ in the new world order means everything (Rom 13:14; Phil 3:8–11; see also Col 3:10).

The transformed Paul has a leadership team including many women. 1) He calls on Euodia and Syntyche to work out their differences (Phil 4:2–3). 2) Phoebe is commended as a deacon (Rom 16:1–2).[7] 3) Wife–husband

---

3. For a discussion of Ephesians' use of Pauline tradition, see Gese, *Das Vermächtnis des Apostels*. For a list of parallels see Johnston, "Ephesians," 110–11.

4. Paul does not mention his Acts 9 Damascus Road experience per se. But see Kim, *The Origin of Paul's Gospel*, 32–74 for his comments on the pre-conversion Paul, and argument for his apostolic commission and revelation of the gospel at the Damascus event. For more, see Garroway, *The Beginning of the Gospel*, ch. 2.

5. Collaborative testimony of Paul's Jewish roots (Rom 11:1; 1 Cor 15:9; 2 Cor 11:22; Gal 1:13–17; Phil 3:4–6), identify him as a Pharisee (Acts 23:6) educated by Gamaliel (22:3), scholastically trained (Gal 1:13–14; Phil 3:4–6), and life spent in the Jewish community (26:4); is accompanied by an indeterminable level of Greek cultural and Roman political influence.

6. To the charge that Paul is inconsistent by refusing to have Titus circumcised, but circumcising Timothy (Acts 16:3), see Bruce, *Paul: Apostle of the Heart Set Free*, 215–16, where Bruce, fn. 16, cites Emerson, "A foolish consistency is the hobgoblin of little minds, adored by little statesmen and philosophers and divines." See Emerson's "Essay on Self-Reliance," 15. Bruce adds, "Paul's higher consistency appears in his defense and promotion of the law-free gospel, for the sake of which many lower-consistencies may be ignored," 215, which supports the notion of evangelism being a priority in the *Haustafel*.

7. Debate exists over whether she was truly an official deaconess. Dunn, *Romans 9–16*, 886–87, suggests that Paul's readers were likely to think of Phoebe as occupying a position of responsibility within the congregation, a figure of significance whose wealth had been put at the disposal of the church at Cenchraea, basing his conclusion that she

team, Priscilla and Aquila, are co-workers (16:34), with Priscilla named first more often than Aquila.[8] 4) The Jewish woman Marian has ministry opportunities with Paul that she would never have in the synagogue (16:6). 5) Husband and wife Andronicus and Junia are called "outstanding apostles" (16:7).[9] 6) Tryphena and Tryphosa are known to "work hard in the Lord" (16:12). 7) Female slave, Persa, works hard as well (16:12). 8) Paul extends a special greeting to Julia and the sister of Nereus (16:15). These various pairings, greetings, and commendations of women clearly illustrate Paul's use of female leaders in his early ministry years.[10]

2.2 MARRIAGE, CIRCUMCISION, SEX, AND SLAVES

Paul's instructions about "sexual immorality" (πορνεία) illumine the status of new kingdom women in Corinth. Paul personally prefers the ideal of celibacy (7:1, 7, 32–35) to promote male and female unencumbered devotion to God's work. Yet, as a conciliatory alternative to burning with unbridled passion leading to πορνεία and shame (7:2–9), Paul recommends sex within marriage, so that Satan will not tempt celibates through their lack of "self-control" (ἐγκράτεια) in 2:9. Paul's paraenesis is filled with good will and empowering intention for women. A wife can initiate divorce,

---

served in a recognized ministry using "deacon" (διάκονον) together with "being" (οὖσαν). But he considers it premature to think of her as occupying a formally established office of diaconate. Cranfield, *A Critical and Exegetical Commentary on the Epistle to the Romans*, 781–82, suggests that Paul's formulation "deacon of the church" (διάκονον τῆς ἐκκλησίας) indicates a level where deacon (or deaconess) was a recognized ongoing function in charge of charitable work (Rom 12:8). For more see Witherington, *Women and the Genesis of Christianity*, 210–13.

8. Priscilla is named first in Acts 18:18, 26; Rom 16:3; and 2 Tim 4:19. Aquila is named first in Acts 18:2 and 1 Cor 16:19. That Paul uses the naming order interchangeably supports the notion of their shared leadership.

9. "Apostle" has multiple NT designations: 1) the original twelve charter members (Acts 1:21–26; 2:37, 42; 6:2, 6) or; 2) Paul and Barnabas who are selected in Antioch by the Holy Spirit as missionaries (Acts 13:1–3) and identified as "apostles" (ἀπόστολοι) in 14:14 or; 3) other ἀποστόλοις who were part of a large group (1 Cor 15:6) that had seen the risen Christ and like Paul (15:8) were commissioned by Christ as ἀποστόλοις for special ministry (15:7). Andronicus and Junia belonged to this closed group of apostles appointed directly by the risen Christ during a limited time after his resurrection. See Dunn, *Romans 9–16*, 894–95 for further discussion.

10. Some view Paul's references to "co-workers," as missionaries. See D'Angelo, "Women Partners in the New Testament," 73; MacDonald, "Reading Real Women," 207.

remain unmarried, or reconcile (7:10–11).¹¹ She has equal authority in the marital bedchamber (7:3–4). And, like Paul, she can control her passions and remain celibate if she so chooses (7:8). Yet, coupled with these new-world freedoms is a message that should not be missed if one wishes to take seriously Paul's motives in the passage. Wives and husbands should make every attempt to remain with their spouses (7:10–11) even if the spouse is an unbeliever because the believing spouse may have the opportunity to save the non-believer (7:12–14). Paul's objective is evangelism.

Turning to circumcision Paul redefines it as an inward condition (1 Cor 7:17–20) that becomes available to all believing gentile men and, by association, women.¹² Mary Tolbert observes:

> If faith in action was all that mattered to God and physical circumcision played no role in convental relationship, then women gained an equal footing with men in the chosen community of Israel. If "real" circumcision was internal, a circumcision of the heart, then women could participate in that "real" circumcision as fully as did any man. Consequently, the spiritual circumcision Paul proclaimed not only did away with the distinction between "Jew and Greek" but also the distinction between "male and female" (see Gal 3:28).¹³

---

11. Paul's marriage instructions here are a response (7:1a) to the Corinthians' statement (7:1b) "it is good for a man not to have sexual relations with a woman" (καλὸν ἀνθρώπῳ γυναικὸς μὴ ἅπτεσθαι) which may reference first-century debate about the Stoic perspective of the indispensable need of marriage to make the wise man wise versus the Cynic need of free time to pursue philosophy at leisure. See Deming's dialogue in *Paul on Marriage and Celibacy* on Stoic and Cynic marriage discussions as the backdrop to 1 Corinthians 7. Stoic philosopher Epictetus (c. 50–135 CE) appears to have some Cynic marital perspectives when he says that he likes the freedom to pursue philosophy without marriage and family to distract him (*Diss.* 3.45–48, 69–72; LCL 218.146–47, 154–55).

There appears little in first-century literature in support female celibacy. An exception is the *therapeutrides* of Philo of Alexandria's *Contempl.*, 68, LCL 363.154–55, which describes a Jewish monastic community in Alexandria made up of both male (*therapeutae*) and female (*therapeutrides*). Philo describes most of the female members as "elderly virgins" living celibate for the sake of "a zeal and yearning for wisdom." See also Taylor, *Jewish Women Philosophers*. Albeit there may not be abundant evidence for female celibate life in the first century, some can be observed in my discussion in 5.2 regarding a trajectory of celibacy.

12. See Valentine, *For You Were Bought*, 244. Also see Dunn's discussion of "neither circumcision nor uncircumcision" in Galatians with reference to 1 Corinthians 7:19 in his *Theology of Paul the Apostle*, 324–27.

13. Tolbert, "Philo and Paul: The Circumcision Debates in Early Judaism," 404.

Paul's words that physical "circumcision is nothing" (ἡ περιτομὴ οὐδέν ἐστιν) in 7:19 reflects his vision of the new world order where believing gentile men can possess markers of Judaism in their hearts, including "self-control" (ἐγκράτεια).[14] If circumcision (7:17–20) for gentile men was now of the heart, and self-control for both men and women can be attained through the Spirit (Gal 5:22–23), then women circumcised of heart are equal with men before God.[15] But are Paul's empowering intentions achievable for women in the here-and-now of Corinthian life? Would the believing husbands of Corinth agree with Paul's admonitions or is this an overly positive assessment from Paul about the prospects of believing women, considering the realities of life in first-century Hellenism?

Paul's instructions about "sexual immorality" (πορνεία) also illumine harsh Hellenistic realities for slaves in Corinth. Paul wants slaves also to be able to exercise self-control but acknowledges that the presence of abusive masters may mean that avoiding πορνεία is not always possible for slaves.[16] The sexual use of both male and female slaves was common in the ancient world. In Greco-Roman society female slaves were especially vulnerable. Katy Valentine writes, "The slaves in the Christian community faced the double-bind of stigma related to sexuality: as slaves they were unable to control a significant portion of their sexual experiences, yet they were also asked to abide by particular sexual ethics in 1 Corinthians 7, including the avoidance of all πορνεία."[17] Paul may want freedom for slaves so they can abide by the Christian sexual ethics of self-control, but he recognizes that this may not be an option for some (7:21–24). Those who are subject to the sexual advances of their masters may feel shame over their inability to thwart such advances; hence, Paul encourages them to not be ashamed

---

14. See Valentine, *For You Were Bought*, 245–46.

15. See Barclay's discussion "Paul and Philo on Circumcision," 61–80; see also Boyarin's article, "Paul and the Genealogy of Gender," 1–33, where he considers Paul to be more of a benevolent hierarchicalist who has settled for something less than his ideal, maintaining milder Hellenistic structures with moments of ecstatic androgyny, where any possibility of the eradication of male and female with its social hierarchy is only possible on the level of the spirit, 13–15.

16. Although Paul's recommendation of manumission falls short of the total abolition of slavery, manumission for slaves would bring greater sexual autonomy so they could avoid πορνεία and live out their calling. See Valentine, *For You Were Bought*, 147; For more see Osiek and MacDonald, "Female Slaves: Twice Vulnerable," 95–117; Glancy, "Obstacles to Slaves Participation in the Corinthian Church," 481–501; Harrill, *Slaves in the New Testament*.

17. Valentine, *For You Were Bought*, 147.

over that which was out of their control (7:21).[18] Despite Paul's parenesis that an alternate new kingdom reality has invaded the old world order, his instructions to slaves remain a reminder to them of the present human reality, the "not yet" of inaugural eschatology. Similarly, to presume that Paul's words of good will toward women, a new creation reality where women are empowered to take control their passions and possess options apart from marriage and children, were immediately implemented in first-century Corinth without resistance may be asking too much of the text when read in conjunction with other undisputed texts.

2.3 HAIRSTYLES, HEAD COVERINGS, HONOR, AND HEADSHIP

A few chapters later Paul writes, "However, I want you to know that the head of every man is Christ, and the man is the head of the woman, and the head of Christ is God" (1 Cor 11:3).[19] Addressing appropriate clothing and hairstyles in the church, Paul appears to say that men should have heads uncovered and short hair (11:4, 14) and women should have heads covered and long hair (11:5, 15).[20] Paul reasons in 11:7 that any man "being the image and glory of God" (εἰκὼν καὶ δόξα Θεοῦ ὑπάρχων), "praying or prophesying with anything on his head" (προσευχόμενος ἢ προφητεύων κατὰ κεφαλῆς ἔχων) dishonors his head (11:4), meaning both his own head and Christ's as man's head (11:3). Paul continues (11:7) that "the woman, being the glory of man" (ἡ γυνὴ δὲ, δόξα ἀνδρός ἐστιν) who prays or prophesies with her head uncovered dishonors her head (11:5),[21] meaning both her own head and that of her husband who is her head (11:3); because

---

18. By the mid first century CE the virtue of self-control had spread across the Roman East and was associated strongly with elite men—with Augustus and successive emperors as models. Paul is Romanized and accepts, perhaps unconsciously, the value of ἐγκράτεια as a virtue necessary to control the appetites, and he also accepts that the loss of control over these appetites in both the Roman and Jewish worlds is shameful.

19. Θέλω δὲ ὑμᾶς εἰδέναι ὅτι παντὸς ἀνδρὸς ἡ κεφαλὴ ὁ Χριστός ἐστιν, κεφαλὴ δὲ γυναικὸς ὁ ἀνήρ, κεφαλὴ δὲ τοῦ Χριστοῦ ὁ Θεός.

20. This is not to say that the outward manifestation of gender was the same across all cities within the empire. Local custom specific to the residents of Corinth may be different from that of the residents in other cities to whom Paul wrote. For more on how women were viewed in different locales of the empire, see Winter, *Roman Wives*; Osiek and MacDonald, *A Woman's Place*, 194–219; Boatwright, "Plancia Magna," 249–72.

21. See Winter, *Roman Wives*, for discussion on the importance of a wife's veil in Roman law, 83–96.

man did not come from woman but woman from man (11:8) and man was not created for woman, but woman for man (11:9),[22] and for this reason a woman should have authority over her head, because of the angels (11:10).[23]

This text is one of unending debate among scholars, three of which are presented here as representative samples of the wide-ranging scope of the debate. Why these three among a sea of so many? Lone Fatum presents arguably one of the most restrictive interpretations of Paul's intentions for women while Cynthia Westfall presents the opposite, with remaining scholarship largely positioned somewhere in between.[24] Unique to the debate is the voice of Lucy Peppiatt who persuasively argues that a rhetorical reading offers the most clarity for Paul's intentions regarding Corinthian women.

Of relevance to the Ephesian marital *Haustafel*, the use of authorial context for one Pauline passage (such as 1 Cor 11:2–16) to interpret another (such as Eph 5:21–33 or Col 3:18–19) is accepted intertextual practice, meaning if one concludes from the Corinthian situation that Paul thinks woman is not the image of God hence must submit, one will also conclude that wives in Ephesus are not in God's image hence must submit. And if one concludes from the Corinthian situation that Paul thinks woman is the image of God (ontologically or functionally) then the notion of submission in the Ephesian household can be subject to a variety of outcomes, which it has.

---

22. Philo represents the traditional Jewish Hellenistic interpretation of Gen 2:18, "Why was not woman, like the other animals and man, also formed from earth, instead of the side of man? First, because woman is not equal in honor with man. Second, because she is not equal in age but younger.... Third, he wishes that man should take care of woman as a very necessary part of him; but woman, in return, should serve him as a whole. Fourth, he counsels man figuratively to take care of woman as of a daughter, and woman to honor man as a father" (*QG* 1.27, LCL 380.16).

23. Be it human messengers, holy angels, or guardian angels (all being used to seeing women with head coverings) that are present in the worship service, who τοὺς ἀγγέλους are remains unclear. Winter, in *Roman Wives*, 85–91, and *After Paul Left Corinth*, 136–37, suggests that τοὺς ἀγγέλους in 11:10 is a reference to "magistrates" (γυναικονόμοι) responsible to keep watch over appropriate behavior of women in public settings. See also Foster, *Communal Participation in the Spirit*, for his discussion of the presence of heavenly beings in the Corinthian Church, 123–29. Also see Brooke, *The Dead Sea Scrolls and the New Testament*, 195–214, where he compares 11:10 to 4Q270 to suggest that according to Paul what the woman wears on her head is a sign of her *exousia* (authority) that "enables her to participate in the praying community in her proper place so that the worshipping angels are not compromised by any kind of unnaturalness" (214).

24. Space will not permit an exhaustive review of scholarship.

Lone Fatum argues on a pre-Christological and non-eschatological basis that women are not the *imago Dei*, but men are, so the Corinthian women wanting to pray or prophesy in public with their heads uncovered should cover up.[25] Of all situations in the NT, one would expect Paul to bring the new kingdom declaration of Galatians 3:28c to the defense of women in Corinth. Instead, Fatum says that Paul trots out creation theology where man is the image and glory of God; but woman is the glory of man (11:3–9) adding that man did not come from woman but woman from man and man was not created for woman but woman for man (11:7–9) to provide the basis for his restrictions upon women.[26] Paul's aim in Corinth is to maintain gender dominance based on the order of creation. Paul's polemical point in 11:3–9 is that the image of God expresses superiority and hierarchical order. As the "glory of man," woman is not the "glory of God," thus not the *imago Dei*. Likeness to God is an expression of authority which man has as the image and glory of God and which, as the glory of man, she does not.

According to Fatum, man as the *imago Dei* is the qualitative difference between man and woman that represents the fixed order of creation. Paul connects 11:3–9 to Genesis 1:26–27a instead of 1:27b–28, making it clear that a woman is not included in God's image.[27] The focus of 1 Corinthians 11:3 and 11:7 is one of dominion over creation (cf. Gen 1:26). Man was stamped directly by God in his image which defines his inferior relationship both to God and Christ on the one hand, and superior relationship to the rest of the creation (including woman) on the other, as seen in the hierarchic order of 11:3. Man is qualified by the fact that he, as a man, is both subordinate to God and superior to woman, while the woman is only subordinate.[28] Fatum writes, "Summing up, it seems that the consequence of 11:3 and 11:7 is unavoidable: a woman who was not created in the image of God cannot pray or prophesy before God in her own right or by her own status, for she possesses neither."[29]

25. Fatum, "Image of God and Glory of Man," 71–79. Fatum's argument may appear harsh and non-representative of the majority of scholarship, but complementarians who argue that the female is only ontologically equal to the male as the *imago Dei* limit female participation in ministry in a manner consistent with Fatum's interpretation of 1 Corinthians 11.

26. Fatum, "Image of God and Glory of Man," 70–74.

27. 4.1.1 will discuss Paul's view of the *imago Dei* and Genesis 1.

28. Fatum, "Image of God and Glory of Man," 71–72.

29. Fatum, "Image of God and Glory of Man," 79. Clearly, Fatum's position is different from my own and that of Peppiatt's.

Representing the exact opposite interpretation of the text, Cynthia Westfall, raises the question, "How then can we understand 1 Corinthians 11:7 where Paul asserts that man is in the image and glory of God, but woman (in contrast) is the glory of man?"[30] She responds that, like every human descended from Adam, Eve has a multiple identity. She can be made in the image of God plus be the glory of Adam because she was made directly from Adam (Gen 2:23–24). Thus, Paul implies from 1 Corinthians 11:7 that Eve is the "glory of the glory" matching Adam's positive assessment "this is now bone of my bones and flesh of my flesh" (Gen 2:23–24). Woman as the glory of man is something additional that is part of her identity as God's image-bearer, not something less.[31] She goes on to argue that although a woman is man's glory this does not mean that a woman does not bear the image of God, or that she has a lesser glory than the man.[32] Westfall contends that the Pauline corpus maintains that all believers "male and female" are on the same footing in terms of the ontological image and glory of God. Female believers are renewed in the image of God in the same way as men but when it comes to external appearance there is a difference between the glory of men and the glory of women. Long hair was not considered glorious in a man, but it was in a woman (11:14–15).

According to Westfall, "Paul believed that God created women to be more attractive or more glorious, so that she is the glory of man."[33] Woman is the glory of man (11:7) and her hair is glorious too (11:15), revealing her beauty as the fairer sex once uncovered. She says that this translates into a practical problem the moment women prophesy or pray in church worship with unveiled head because the beauty of her glorious, uncovered hair distracts men, magnifies her glory of man, competes with the worship of God, thus detracting from the glory of God. "Eve was created to powerfully attract Adam, which was the point of the positive climax of creation, but worship is not the time or place to experience that dynamic."[34] Her head covering was designed to divert attention away from man's glory to God's glory. Hence, Paul's mandate to veil is not a polemic against women nor meant to subordinate women to men. Rather, veiling protected women (and men) in a culture where veiling was a sign of status and honor (11:5–6).

30. Westfall, *Paul and Gender*, 65.
31. For more see Westfall, *Paul and Gender*, 40–44.
32. Westfall, *Paul and Gender*, 65–70.
33. Westfall, *Paul and Gender*, 69.
34. Westfall, *Paul and Gender*, 68.

To summarize their differences, Fatum argues that Paul wants to subordinate Corinthian women by making them veil since they are clearly not in God's image; while Westfall argues that Corinthian women are clearly in God's image, but Paul wants them to veil because once men see such beautiful hair, they won't be able to concentrate during worship. Fatum's claim that Paul argues on a pre-Christological and non-eschatological basis is problematic, considering that Paul's gospel is abundantly Christological and eschatological throughout the Pauline corpus.[35] The logic of her argument leads clearly to her conclusion, but casts Paul as doubleminded, one who brings to the forefront conflicting aspects of his theology whenever it suits him, wherever it suits him. Her conclusion that the women of 1 Corinthians 11 are not the *imago Dei* runs counter to Paul's appointment of ministry leaders (Rom 16; Phil 4:2–3) and their ability to exercise self-control as circumcised of heart by the Spirit (1 Cor 7; Gal 5:22–23).[36] And, while Westfall presents an interesting perspective on the text that women must cover up or else men will be distracted, the notion that believing men who are supposed to be circumcised of heart by the Spirit empowering them to exercise self-control (1 Cor 7:17–20) are now just a few chapters later so consumed with the glorious beauty of women's luxurious long hair that they cannot worship God in church does not speak well for the ability of the transforming Spirit to change anyone.

Lucy Peppiatt rightly asks, is this voice of Paul the same as 1 Corinthians 7 or is it the voice of another? Paul's letter is written to a group whose meetings appear to hurt more than help (11:17). In contrast to traditional views of 1 Corinthians 11, Peppiatt suggests a rhetorical reading of the text where Paul has entwined Corinthian ideas and phrases with his own to argue against head coverings rather than for them.[37] She continues:

---

35. See 4.1.

36. See 2.1 and 2.2.

37. Peppiatt, *Women and Worship at Corinth*. She admits, "This, of course, is only a hypothesis. It cannot be proven that in 1 Corinthians 11 Paul is using a rhetorical device where he includes the argument of his opponents in order to refute it. The reason that it cannot be proven is that there is no signal given in the text by Paul that this is what he is doing. However, if this is an accepted method of argumentation, it is possible that there are simply clues in the text rather than overt statements of intent" (84). Despite her humble admission, we have precedent for Paul acting in this manner where he quotes the positions of others, sometimes unannounced, as well as uncontested instances in the Corinthian letter where he quotes them (1:12; 3:4; 6:12–13; 7:1; 8:1; 4; 8; 10:23).

> If this is now understood as the voice of the Corinthians, it becomes much clearer why there is a corrupted form of Genesis 1:26–27. The Corinthian prophetic leaders and teachers who claim that they "have the word of God" are teaching that men are the image and glory of God, and that women are merely the image and glory of man— the perfect rationale for the subordination of women and the superiority of men. This theology of glory has superseded any sense of what it means for both men and women to be in Christ.[38]

Peppiatt suggests that the Corinthian church was dominated by a group of overbearing male teachers who reinterpreted a version of Paul's teaching to mean that men and women should display signs, in the forms of head coverings and hair length, of their own status before God. Because women were created second (Gen 2:21–22), the Corinthians were teaching that they hold second place in the created order deriving their glory directly from man, not Christ; hence women need a sign of authority over their heads while men remain bareheaded. Peppiatt then reads 11:6 as Paul poking fun at the misguided logic of the Corinthian men—if you force women to wear head coverings and they refuse you might as well shave their heads because they are behaving like prostitutes (who shave their heads) but then these Christian women will be known to be prostitutes (when they're not) so they should cover their heads.[39]

Paul's intent for 11:2–3, according to Peppiatt, is: "I praise you for remembering the traditions that I passed on to you regarding Christ as the head of man and man as the head of woman. However, I want you to know that when I say that Christ is the head of every man, and man is the head of woman, you must also understand that God is the head of Christ."[40] From here she seeks to clarify what Paul intends to communicate with the

---

38. Peppiatt, *Women and Worship*, 100. See her ch. 3 where she points out the weakness of arguments that suggest Paul's wants head coverings and silent women.

39. Peppiatt, *Women and Worship*, 99. Taking the traditional view, Winter comments, "Paul made a startling statement about the unveiled wife. He said that her behavior was 'one and the same thing as a woman who has been shorn' (11.5). It is known, e.g., that in Cyprus the law prescribed that 'a woman guilty of adultery shall have her hair cut off and be a prostitute,' i.e., like a foreigner or freedwoman who provided sexual favors at a dinner. Therefore, Paul equated not wearing a veil with the social stigma of a publicly exposed and punished adulteress reduced to the status of a prostitute" (*After Paul Left Corinth*, 128). Given Peppiatt's rhetorical reading of the text, Winter's comment that Paul equates an unveiled wife with a prostitute is unconvincing.

40. Peppiatt, *Women and Worship*, 87.

rhetorical phrase by moving to a discussion of the church fathers who consistently conveyed that the Son also is God. A significant amount of her discussion in connection with the church fathers has to do with accepting a polymorphous concept of the meaning of head (κεφαλή) to include "origin" and "relation" where she argues, "Whatever κεφαλή does mean, it does not mean that as God rules over Christ, Christ rules over man, and man rules over woman, because we cannot claim that God rules over Christ in the first place."[41] Christ can rule over man and woman since both are created by God/Christ, whereas Christ is eternally begotten of God/as God. Man cannot rule over woman precisely because he did not create her.[42] Hence, if the Corinthian men have extrapolated from Paul's original teaching in 11:2–3 that man is the ruling κεφαλή of woman which is to be acknowledged in female head coverings, Paul is seeking to correct this misconception of rule with the notion of mutual interdependence, "in the Lord woman is not independent of man or man independent of woman. For just as woman came from man, so man comes from woman, but all things come from God" (11:11–12 NRSV). I agree with Peppiatt that Paul is emphatically making the point that the Corinthians' patriarchal reading of the Genesis 2 creation account is misguided. Hierarchy is not to be endorsed. Independence is not to be endorsed. Interdependence is. This important theme to the Ephesian *Haustafel* of marital interdependence between equals will be detailed in chapter 6.[43]

Notwithstanding Peppiatt's plausible solution, 1 Corinthians 11 remains contested, and I do not expect to resolve the debate here. But one should point out that, despite the notion of equal footing for all as an alternate new kingdom reality, the human reality of female subordination persisted in the teachings of a first-century Corinthian church that read the Genesis 2 creation account through the lens of Hellenistic patriarchy. Beyond this there are similarities to the Ephesian correspondence. Paul replaces the human notion of gender dominance that the Corinthians might have entertained from the creation account (1 Cor 11:7–10) with the divine notion, introduced by his phrase "in the Lord" (ἐν Κυρίῳ), of

---

41. Peppiatt, *Women and Worship*, 91.

42. See Peppiatt, *Women and Worship*, 91–92. Woman is derived from man in that she comes from his side. But this does not mean that man is derived from Christ, rather man is a derivative of the ground.

43. See Peppiatt's additional comments around the Genesis 2 creation account where she writes, "Since woman was taken from (ἐκ) man because his solitude was not good (Gen. 2:18), she is for him and, for Paul, this means that she is to be his δόξα," 102.

interdependence between woman and man (11:11–12). He uses the same strategy in the Ephesian letter by qualifying the seemingly hierarchical notion in 5:23, "for the husband is the head of the wife" (ὅτι ἀνήρ ἐστιν κεφαλὴ τῆς γυναικός) with the interdependence of 5:31, "and the two will become one flesh" (καὶ ἔσονται οἱ δύο εἰς σάρκα μίαν), Paul interpreting the Genesis account in a manner that supplants present Hellenistic human reality with intended divine reality.[44]

2.4 MALE AND FEMALE

In 1 Corinthians 12 Paul expands beyond notions of gender and glory with a parenesis to equally value the diversity of spiritual gifts (12:4–11; 21–24; 27–31) and the diverse nature of those in possession of these gifts (12:13) or unity among the believers in Corinth will fail (12:25–26). Although all gifts and people are to be treated with equal care for each another (12:25) Paul expresses priority for apostles, prophets, and teachers (12:28) in that order, which includes the women prophets in Corinth (11:5), meaning that the women prophets in Corinth possessed a gift that took priority over teaching. It should not be missed that female prophets possessed a gift of higher priority in the new world order than the dominant male Corinthian teachers.

It is noteworthy that Paul adds "male and female" (ἄρσεν καὶ θῆλυ) to the list in Galatians 3:28, while the pairing is absent from 1 Corinthians 12:13.[45] But too much should not be made of this. These two letters go out in a similar timeframe to different locations (Corinth and Galatia) with content matter specific to that location. Paul has already spent two chapters discussing gender relationships (1 Cor 7 and 11) so perhaps he feels no urgency to reiterate ἄρσεν καὶ θῆλυ given his earlier claim that "woman is not independent of man or man independent of woman" (11:11 NRSV).[46]

One may argue that to imply egalitarianism from ἄρσεν καὶ θῆλυ is to move beyond Paul's intent to inform Galatian believers that they need not succumb to the pressure of Torah observance (1:6–7; 2:3, 11–12, 14; 4:10), and that the letter speaks nothing else of gender or marital relations. But, even if Galatians 3:28 was not written with marriage in mind, it reflects

---

44. See 6.6.

45. Consensus exists that Galatians was written in 53 CE and 1 Corinthians in 53–54 CE.

46. Note that this third pairing differs from the two preceding pairs by its substitution of "and" (καὶ), for "nor" (οὐδὲ). This additional third pair hearkens to Genesis 1:27, "male and female he created them" (זכר ונקבה ברא אתם).

Paul's own relationships and those relationships he intends to foster in his churches. Again, the great lengths to which the apostle must go in order to explain basic new kingdom notions of fairness, equality, generosity, and unity to the Corinthians reveal that intended new kingdom realities in Corinth have been supplanted by old kingdom human realities of pride, selfishness, inequality, and division.[47]

2.5 SILENCING WOMEN

Two chapters later we read that women should be silent at church, be in submission, and ask their husbands at home if they have questions, otherwise it is shameful (14:34–35); which is a peculiar statement since women already have the responsibility of prophets (11:5). The text appears to assume that all women are married to believing husbands (14:35) in contradiction of both 7:13 which flatly says that women are married to unbelieving husbands, and 7:8 which makes clear the presence of "unmarried" and "widows."

There are sufficient inconsistencies to argue that 14:34–35 is not written by Paul but is a textual interpolation inserted close to the time when the Pastoral Epistles were written. Philip Payne argues that the earlier Vorlage had 11:34–35 in the margin, then a copyist later placed them after 11:33; and that among the church fathers only Tertullian (160–225 CE) seems familiar with 11:34–35 (*On Baptism* 17, LCL 250.274–77) and that Clement of Alexandria (150–215 CE) quotes from 1 Corinthians 14 with no reference to 11:34–35 (*Paed.* 3.11; *Strom.* 4.19). Payne's assessment is not without criticism. Kirk MacGregor assesses Payne's case for interpolation and argues that "Clement's failure to cite 1 Corinthians 14:34–35 is better explained by the following proposal, which also explains its absence from the Apostolic Fathers: Clement and the Apostolic Fathers before him knew that 1 Corinthians 14:34 35 was not Paul's position but was a quotation of the Corinthians' position that Paul proceeded to refute. So, of course, they did not cite 1 Corinthians 14:34–35 as authoritative."[48]

---

47. This would be clear in the mind of Paul, as well as that of an Ephesian Paulinist with access to Paul's undisputed letters. Old world values as manifest by divisions, (1:10–17; 3:1–21), lawsuits (6:1–11), pride, boasting, and inequality (3:18–21; 4:8–13; 5:6), immorality (5:1–12; 6:12–20), selfishness (11:17–22) are contrasted with love, patience, kindness, humility, generosity, forgiveness, self-sacrifice (13:1–7).

48. See Payne, "Fuldensis, Sigla for Variants in Vaticanus, and 1 Cor. 14:34–35," 240–62, where he calls attention to Codex Fuldensis (545 CE) which instructs the reader

The passage sounds oddly familiar to "Let a woman learn in silence with full submission. I do not permit a woman to teach nor to have authority over a man; she is to keep silent" (1 Tim 2:11–12 NRSV). And the notion that Paul wishes to silence Corinthian women, or at least married ones, from teaching men hardly resonates with the desired mutuality in marriage one finds in 1 Corinthians 7. Does the passage have relevance to the Ephesian *Haustafel*? There are enough challenges regarding its authenticity to make one wonder.

First, if 14:34–35 is an interpolation written at the time of the Pastorals, it would not have been known by an Ephesian Paulinist, thus making it irrelevant to the earlier Ephesian letter. Second, 14:34–35 as an interpolation makes Paul not its author, thus again irrelevant to Ephesians. Third, if, following Peppiatt, we read 14:34–35 as Paul once again quoting his opponents, perhaps in a letter they wrote to him, in order to refute them, then it does not reflect his own attitude toward women but that of the Corinthian men he is refuting.[49] This may present the most attractive alternative given Peppiatt's persuasive rhetorical reading of 1 Corinthians 11 and MacGregor's comment above. However, the presence of women prophets (11:5), women married to unbelieving husbands (7:13), unmarried women and widows (7:8) makes 14:35 an awkward fit. The unmarried and widows would have no husband to turn to for their questions, and the odd familiarity to 1 Timothy 2:11–12 remains. Beyond this, the focus of 14:34–35 is that of silencing women teachers while the Ephesian letter makes no mention of women teachers.

Yet, the women of the Ephesian letter may share common ground with the women of Corinth, which is magnified if 14:34–35 is a scribal interpolation from the era of the Pastorals in Ephesus, suggesting that patriarchal

---

to skip over 14:34–35 in the lower margin. Also see MacGregor's article, "1 Corinthians 14:33b-38 as a Pauline Quotation-Refutation Device." For more see link to the article https://www.cbeinternational.org/resource/1-corinthians-1433b-38-pauline-quotation-refutation-device/, accessed 02/23/22; also Payne's discussion, "Ms. 88 as Evidence for A Text without 1 Cor. 14.34–35," 152–158. For an alternate perspective see Khobnya, "Preparing Women for Ministry in 1 Cor 14:34–35 and 1 Tim 2:8–15," 1–9, where she argues that Paul's prohibition against women teachers was only temporal, until they had become learned.

49. See Peppiatt, *Women and Worship*, 108, 110. These include Allison, "'Let the Women Be Silent in the Churches,' (1 Cor 14:33b-36), 27–60; Flanagan and Snyder, "Did Paul Put Down Women in 1 Cor 14:34–36?," 10–12; Manus, "The Subordination of Women in the Church: 1 Cor 14:33b-36 Reconsidered," 183–95; Odell-Scott, "In Defense of an Egalitarian Interpretation of 1 Cor 14:34–36," 100–103.

attitudes toward women persisted with such vigor that one felt compelled to rewrite the Corinthian letter to make it compliant with 1 Timothy.

2.6 RELEVANCE OF COLOSSIANS TO EPHESIANS

Since both Ephesians and Colossians claim Paul as their author, and Ephesians finds its closest parallels in Colossians, the comparative relationship between the two is relevant for this book. One can appreciate the "who used whom" debate given the letters are filled with similarities: 1) both claim Paul's authorship from prison; 2) both have a developed Christology which enlarges Paul's claim (Phil 2:6-11) that "JESUS CHRIST IS LORD" (ΚΥΡΙΟΣ ΙΗΣΟΥΣ ΧΡΙΣΤΟΣ) of the cosmos; 3) both use language common to first-century conversations about the cosmos, language rarely found elsewhere in scripture.[50] There are also significant differences: 1) Colossians appears to promote marital hierarchy while Ephesians appears to promote mutual subordination; 2) Colossians devotes only two verses to marriage (3:18-19) while Ephesians devotes thirteen (5:21-33); 3) the focus of the Colossian *Haustafeln* is the appropriate actions of slaves (3:22-25) while the Ephesian *Haustafeln* is the appropriate actions of husbands (5:25-31); 4) Colossians offers no explanation for wifely submission while Ephesians adds 5:22-23 to explain wifely submission as ultimately to Christ's headship. Both letters offer explanation for slaves to obey their masters (Col 3:22-25; Eph 6:5-8) while Ephesians also addresses masters (6:9) indicating that perhaps the Colossian church did not have believing masters. Andrew Lincoln speculates that Ephesians was copied by a careful student of Paul who used Colossians as a model.[51] The reverse has also been argued: that, as a co-sender of Colossians, Timothy contributed to Colossians. Hence, it is more credible that Colossians shows the mark of a student of Paul, not Ephesians.[52] Whether authored by Paul himself, one Paulinist, or two, it

---

50. Words such as "fullness" (πλήρωμα) and "all" (τὰ πάντα) are frequently deployed in a cosmic sense (Col 1:16-17, 20; 3:11; Eph 1:10, 23; 3:9; 4:10) but are rarely observed elsewhere (1 Cor 8:6; 15:28; Phil 3:21). For instance, Colossians 1:19, "the fullness to dwell" (τὸ πλήρωμα κατοικῆσαι) and 2:9 "the fullness of the Deity" (τὸ πλήρωμα τῆς θεότητος) and Ephesians 1:23, "the fullness of him who fills everything" (τὸ πλήρωμα τοῦ τὰ πάντα ἐν πᾶσιν πληρουμένου). For more see Mansfeld, "Theology," 452-78; and Todd, "The Stoics and Their Cosmology," 1365-78; Gill, "The School in the Roman Imperial Period," 33-58.

51. See his detailed discussion in *Ephesians*, lx-lxxiii.

52. For example, see Baugh, *Ephesians*, 6-8.

seems clear that the authors of each letter have knowledge of other's work or share a similar corpus of core teachings from Paul which are brought to bear in each letter according to individual style and need.

Relevant to this work are the shared notions of new creation and evangelism in both letters which resonates with Paul's evangelistic attitude toward marriage in the Corinthian letter (7:12–14). Ephesians makes explicit Paul's evangelistic intent to preach the boundless riches of Christ (3:9–10), while Colossians makes explicit Paul's intent to proclaim the mystery of Christ (4:3) and instruction for the Colossians to make the most of evangelistic opportunities with outsiders (4:5). Colossians' invitation to put to death one's earthly nature (3:5) and rid oneself of nefarious practices (3:3:8–9) and put on the new self which is being renewed in the image of its creator (3:10) finds parallel in Ephesians invitation to put off the old self (4:22), to be renewed in one's mind (4:23), and put on the new self, created to be like God (4:24). Paul's notion of new creation and his intent to evangelize Asia Minor is explicit in both letters, and chapter 6 will advance the argument that the household codes in Ephesians and Colossians (in addition to 1 Peter) implicitly sought to evangelize outsiders to a movement that would ultimately transform first century social order including the household codes themselves.

2.7 SUMMARY

This chapter has sought to illumine writer context for the Ephesian letter by examining Paul's undisputed letters to work out his new creation disposition toward women within hierarchical Hellenism. Paul's inaugural kingdom intentions for social equality were juxtaposed with the human reality of Hellenistic social constructs, which yielded the following: 1) Paul's leadership team with a mix of males and females, single and married reveal his intention to replace patriarchal realities with missional equality; 2) His teachings reveal a preference for celibacy for both sexes while also endorsing marriage with equal bedchamber rights; 3) Believing spouses should remain with unbelieving spouses to evangelize the unbeliever; 4) Circumcision is an inward condition of the heart open to all; 5) His instructions about sexual immorality illumine the harsh human conditions for slaves despite his divine intentions. 6) The shared evangelistic intent in the Corinthian, Colossian, and Ephesian correspondence has clearly been compromised in Corinth. The shambles of the Corinthian church, with divided leadership (1:10), jealously and arguing (3:3), incest (5:1), lawsuits (6:6), hurting others while clinging to personal rights (10:23), and meetings which do more harm than good (11:17) has become a missionally ineffective mirror image of the very culture Paul is trying to evangelize. Paul's Corinthian correspondence regarding head coverings, female prophets, and dominant male teachers reveals a writer context of one struggling to implement Spirit-filled evangelistic kingdom values in a resistant world of fleshly human realities. Besides this information gleaned from Paul's undisputed works, much more can be gained about writer context for the Ephesian letter, with its long marital code, by an examination of reader context, the subject of the following chapter.

3

Reader Context and the Ephesian Marriage Code

WHILE WRITER CONTEXT FROM the undisputed letters is informative for the Ephesian letter, writer context coupled with reader context specific to Ephesus has been overlooked. Through the examination of Ephesian inscriptional and analogical evidence I argue that, when interpreting the marital *Haustafel* in light of the transforming *imago Dei*, more emphasis needs to be placed on Paul's knowledge of the prominence of the Artemis cult and the influence of the ubiquitous image of the goddess on the letter's recipients. To this end, the general nature of Greek cultural, philosophical, and Roman political influence, which is frequently used as background to interpret the Ephesian letter, is evaluated and juxtaposed alongside a specific examination of the potential impact of the Artemis deity, wealthy independent women, and prominent priestesses to suggest that a close look at the inscriptional evidence is very important for understanding the Ephesian letter with its thirteen-verse marital code.

3.1 GREEK CULTURAL AND PHILOSOPHICAL INFLUENCE

While *Haustafeln* scholarship has sought for cultural clarity, the record of the status of women in antiquity paints an unreliable picture. In some cultures, women enjoyed more freedoms, in others less.[1] The classical Greek

1. See Pomeroy, *Goddesses, Whores, Wives, and Slaves*, x, where she writes, "One woman

period reveals Athens as a city of more rigid gender boundaries with its classifications of companions, concubines and wives;[2] while gender boundaries for Spartan women, with more equality in attire,[3] politics,[4] morality,[5] property rights,[6] and mixing freely with men[7] appear porous. Some Macedonian men named cities after their wives.[8] Macedonian women ate at the same table as their husbands and shared in their activities.[9] Macedonian women occupied public office.[10] Coinage depicts the head of Queen Arsinoë II (c. 316–270 BCE) individually and with her husband, Ptolemy II.[11] Arsinoë II was also known for her love of culture and correspondence

---

who rules as queen may enjoy the highest status, but her position does not empower her female subjects." See also Corley, *Private Women, Public Meals*; Kraemer, *Her Share of the Blessings*; Dover, "Classical Greek Attitudes to Sexual Behavior," 59–73; Richter, "The Position of Women in Classical Athens," 1–8; and de Ste. Croix, "Some Observations on the Property Rights of Athenian Women," 273–78.

2. Demosthenes (384–322 BCE), *Neaer.* 59.122, LCL 351.446–47, writes "We have companions for our pleasure, concubines for the daily needs of the body, and wives so that we may have legitimate children and a faithful steward of our houses." Thucydides (c. 400 BCE) spoke for this period in Athens when he had his story hero Pericles say that the glory of a woman is greatest "of whom there is least talk among men, whether in praise or in blame." See his *History of the Peloponnesian War*, 2.45.2, LCL 108.340–41.

3. See Pomeroy, *Spartan Women*, 25, where she comments that Spartan women wore more comfortable clothing, their tunics open on the side during athletic contests. See also Ibycus, *fr.* 339, LCL 476.288–89, and Euripides, *Andr.* 595–602, LCL 484.328–29.

4. Plutarch, *Mor.* 240.1, LCL 245.455

5. Plutarch, *Mor.* 240.5–6, LCL 245.457.

6. Aristotle records that the women owned a sizeable percent of all the real estate of Sparta (*Pol.* 1270a20–29, LCL 264.138–39).

7. Plutarch, *Par. Liv., Lyc.* 14, LCL 1.245–46; *Mor.* LCL 245.362–63. Unfortunately, this gave men the opportunity to select a "strong" woman that would give him sons that were ideal for military service, discriminating against "weaker" women who were then prohibited from marrying and producing "weaker" children (*Lyc.* 14.2–3, LCL 46.244–49).

8. Thessalonica was named by Cassander after his wife, Thessalonice, daughter of Philip (Strabo, *Geogr.*, 7.21–24, LCL 182.342–43).

9. See Herodotus, *Hist.* 5.19–20, LCL, 119.18–23.

10. Macedonian queens Arsinoë II (c. 316–270 BCE) and Berenice (c. 340–275 BCE) ruled in Egypt while Eurydice of Macedon (c. 407–369 BCE) and Olympias (c. 375–316 BCE), mother of Alexander, ruled in Macedonia; see Tarn and Griffith, *Hellenistic Civilization*, 56; Macurdy, "Queen Eurydice and the Evidence for Woman Power in Early Macedonia," *AJP* 48.3:201–14; Pausanias, *Descr., Attica* 6.8–7.2, LCL 93.34–35.

11. See Thompson, "A Portrait of Arsinoe Philadelphos," 199–206.

with scholars.¹² Coming to the throne in 51 BCE, Cleopatra VII, Philopater (69–30 BCE) disposed of her rivals and won over both Mark Antony and Julius Caesar as Roman allies.¹³ Egyptian women were buyers, sellers, borrowers, lenders, and could initiate divorce.¹⁴

From here, modern scholarship has implied that the diverse history of women's status in various places such as Egypt, Macedonia, Sparta, and Athens would have been in the air and the cosmopolitan Paul would have at least been aware of this, and perhaps even influenced by this. Although informative, such generalized background on the status of women across various cities and hundreds of years speaks little to the *Sitz im Leben* of the Ephesus audience (or Asia Minor) and fails to take into the account the everyday life of the common household matron without wealth, power, or public office. The level of influence of what was in the air upon the Ephesian author (and reader) is significant, but unquantifiable.

The role of women in ancient philosophy paints an equally unreliable picture for the context specific of Ephesus. Clearly, women were active in philosophy throughout Greek pre-Classical, Classical, and Hellenistic periods.¹⁵ The Pythagorean School¹⁶ of Pre-Classical Greece included female

---

12. See Diogenes Laërtius, *Strato* 5.60, LCL 184.512–13, "Letters beginning Strato to Arsinoe Greeting." See also Carney, *Arsinoë of Egypt and Macedon*.

13. Pomeroy, *Goddesses*, 124.

14. See Grenfell and Hunt, *The Oxyrhynchus Papyri Part II*, POxy 266 for a fragment of a Deed of Divorce (c. 96 CE) between Thaësis (wife and principal party in the agreement) and late husband Petosarapis (husband); see Grenfell, *An Alexandrian Erotic Fragment and Other Greek Papyri Chiefly Ptolemaic*, *PGrenf* 18–20 (38–44) on women as sellers and lenders (c. 127–132 BCE with Appolonia [wife of Dryton] being the lender); *PGrenf* 27 (54–57) on women being ceded land (c. 132–109 BCE, Sebtitis cedes cornland to her daughter Naamsesis); *PGrenf* 25 (51–53) on land sold by a priestess and her priest husband (c. 114 BCE, Naomsesis and her husband Stotoetis sell waste-land); *PGrenf* 18 (38), on a woman lending without interest; *PGrenf* 21 (44–48) on women inheriting land (the Will of Dryton has his daughters inherit land, c. 126 BCE), and *PGrenf* 33 (62–65) on women selling land (sisters, Senchnoubis the elder and Senchnoubis the younger, c. 103–102 BCE). For more see Witherington, *Women in the Earliest Churches*, 277, fn. 90.

15. This listing of female philosophers is only a representative sample of a larger corpus. Many of the writings of ancient philosophers were lost, so our limited understanding of them is often based only on fragments of their work and insights gleaned from historians writing about them centuries later.

16. Named after Pythagoras (c. 570–495 BCE). Iamblichus (c. 245–325 CE) in his *Vit. Pyth.*, trans. Taylor, 138–39, lists the names of seventeen renowned Pythagorean women. Ménage (1613–92 CE) in 1690 published *Historia Mulierum Philosopharum*, a supplement to the work of Diogenes Laërtius, where Ménage lists twenty-six women Pythagoreans; see his *The History of Women Philosophers*, trans. Zedler, 92.

philosophers Theano (possible wife of Pythagoras), Myia, Damo, and Arignote (possible daughters), Perictione (c. fifth century BCE) the mother (or sister) of Plato, Melissa (c. third century BCE), and Phintys (c. third century BCE). There are fragments and letters attributed to Theano, fragments attributed to Perictione and Phintys, and letters attributed to Myia and Melissa. Whether these writings were actually authored by these women is debated. Of the writings of the women philosophers from antiquity the only ones extant are attributed to Pythagorean women.

In the Classical period, Socrates (c. 470–399 BCE) instructs his friends to send his sons to Aspasia (c. 470–410 BCE) because of her intelligence.[17] He adds that female philosopher Diotima of Mantinea (c. 440 BCE) educated him about love, and that she was the inspiration for his Socratic method.[18] The Hellenistic period (c. 323–33 BCE)[19] names several women philosophers: Arete was the head of the Cyrenaic school of philosophy after her father Aristippus died in 350 BCE; Hipparchia of Maroneia (c. 325 BCE) is known for forsaking a life of riches to live the simple life of a Cynic; Pamphile was a disciple of Theophrastus (c. 371–287 BCE) and she headed the Lyceum after Aristotle.[20] Leontion (c. 300 BCE), who wrote arguments against Theophrastus,[21] was the most famous of the women Epicurus (c. 341–270 BCE) allowed into his philosophic school.[22] The Stoic, Diodorus Cronus (d. 284 BCE), had five daughters who were logicians: Menexene, Argeia, Theognis, Artemisia, and Pantacleia.[23]

17. Aspasia of Miletus, a "companion" woman, instructed Socrates in affairs of the heart and also opened her home to Sophocles, Euripides, Phidias and Socrates as a place for debate and discussion; see Xenophon, *Mem.* 2.6.36, LCL 168.156–57.

18. Plato, *Symp.* 201D–212C, LCL 166.172–209.

19. Typically considered between the death of Alexander the Great (323 BCE) and the battle of Actium (31 BCE) with the emerging Roman Empire and the fall of Ptolemaic Egypt (30 BCE).

20. See Wider, "Women Philosophers in the Ancient Greek World," 21–62; also, Swindler, *Women in Judaism*, 19.

21. No works of Leontion are extant. Cicero (106–43 BCE) in *Nat. d.* 1.93, LCL 268.90–91, of her writes, "Leontium, a loose woman, to write a book refuting Theophrastus—Her style is in the neatest of Attic, but all the same!—such was the license which prevailed in the Garden of Epicurus." Pliny the Elder (c. 23/24 CE–79 CE) *Nat.* speaks negatively of her as well (*Praefatio* 29, LCL 330.18–19).

22. Whether women were physically present in Epicurus' Teaching Garden is of some debate. See Gordon's ch. 3 discussion in *The Invention and Gendering of Epicurus*, 188–93.

23. Diodorus Cronus was part of a branch of the Megarian school founded by Euclid (c. 435–365), a follower of Socrates. This branch included of Eubulides, Apollonius Cronus, and Philo (20 BCE–c. 50 CE).

Contrasting attitudes toward females, even by females, accompanied the presence of female philosophers. Pythagorean philosopher Perictione teaches a woman to shape herself into something unintelligible from her husband, "In the company of her husband, she will live in conformity to the opinions of a common life with him; she will adapt herself to the parents and friends who esteem her husband and will regard as sweet and bitter the same things as her husband."[24] Writing about the ideal state, Plato (c. 428–348 BCE) argues for the equality of women with men, "Therefore, if we wish to engage the women in the same work as the men, they must also be allowed to learn the same things. The men receive intellectual and physical education. Thus, the women must also learn and appropriately employ these two disciplines and the art of warfare."[25] But he also wished to limit freedom for women by curtailing their lifestyles,[26] omitting them from funeral processions,[27] choral competitions,[28] and offering them exemption from military service.[29] Like Plato, Aristotle trumpeted democratic freedom of women, but not so much as to make it a "political evil."[30] Women have the subordinate role[31] because "the male is by nature superior and the

---

24. Attributed to Perictione, *On the Harmony of Women* is considered pseudonymous Pythagorean literature dating to fourth or third cent. BCE). See Thesleff, *The Pythagorean Texts of the Hellenistic Period*, 142–46 for the Greek texts. See also reference to Perictione in *Stobaeus Anthology* 4.28.19, LCL 527.436–37.

25. *Rep.*, V, 451d ff, LCL 237.454ff. See also *Laws* 804e-806b, LCL 192:58–63. Diogenes Laërtius (third cent. CE), *Lives of Eminent Philosophers* 3.46, LCL 184.316–17 listing Plato's disciples identifies two women, "Lastheneia of Mantinea and Axiothea of Phlius, who is reported by Dicaearchus to have worn men's clothing," as evidence that there were female students in the renowned schools of Plato's Academy and Aristotle's Lyceum. For more on female Greek philosophers, see Wider, "Women Philosophers," 21–62.

26. *Laws* 806c, LCL 192.62–63, "The lawgiver ought to be wholehearted, not half-hearted—(*not*) letting the female sex indulge in luxury and expense and disorderly ways of life."

27. *Laws* 947b-d, LCL 192.492–95. Women past the age of childbearing were included.

28. *Laws* 764e, LCL 187.434–37. Girls and boys are mentioned in choir competitions with adult, male umpires, but no mention of women.

29. *Laws* 794c-d, LCL 192.22–23. ". . . and when it is necessary for them to begin lessons, the boys must go to teachers of riding, archery, javelin-throwing and slinging, and the girls also, if they agree to it, must share in the lessons . . . ."

30. *Pol.* 1269b, LCL 264.134–35; 1319b, LCL 264.506–7.

31. *Pol.* 1259b, LCL 264.258–59; 1260a-b, LCL 264.62–67.

female inferior."[32] Although Plato and Aristotle failed to "practice what they preached," their selected writings affirm the intelligence and skill of women to equally exercise a superior level of reflective thought.

One may say that, even if the study of philosophy in antiquity did not fully free women from the chains of social custom, the seeds of equality were sown in all three patriarchic periods.[33] From here one may attempt to argue that Paul would have been mindful of the gentile recipients of his letter[34] in cosmopolitan Ephesus who were also exposed to (and some perhaps adhering to) the genesis of more progressive philosophical thinking about gender; and from here to argue for mutual marital submission in Ephesians 5:21–33 (cf. 5:21). But again, the gathering of philosophical data across multiple centuries fails to speak directly to the daily life of the Ephesus household and remains unquantifiable for both author and reader. The canvas on which Paul paints his Ephesian letter is a variegated one rich in history, philosophy, privilege, wealth and diversity. And the specific scene that Paul paints on this variegated canvas is his portrait of the Ephesian matron who rises out of *Sitz im Leben* of the letter's recipients. Perhaps then, the immediate presence of Roman political influence in Ephesus might strike closer to home for both Paul and the Ephesian matron.

3.2 ROMAN POLITICAL INFLUENCE

While the Republic marched toward the first century with the birth of the empire under Augustus Caesar (27 BCE), the status of Roman women, in limited ways, did as well. A woman's consent was necessary for marriage.[35] Education was designed to help women grow, albeit as Roman citizens and

---

32. *Pol.* 1254b, LCL 264.20–21. Reinforcing gender superiority, he adds, "A man would be thought a coward if he were only as brave as a brave woman, and a woman a chatterer if she were only as modest as a good man; since even the household functions of a man and woman are different—his business is to get and hers is to keep (*Pol.* 1277b, LCL 264.192–95)."

33. Pre-Classical, Classical, Hellenistic.

34. Ephesians 2:11–22; 3:1–13.

35. See Alan, *The Spirit of Roman Law*, 173; and Treggiari, *Roman Marriage*, 258–59, 500–502, especially 259 where she remarks that "falling in love is (at least from the time of Augustus) proper for a couple who are to marry each other," then gives the example of Arruntius Stella who has to resort to gifts, prayers, and tears before he wins Violentilla (Statius, *Silvae* I.2.1–275, LCL 206.18–41; cf. I.2.195, LCL 206.34–35).

mothers.³⁶ Wives of emperors, such as Augustus' Livia (58 BCE–29CE) and Claudius' Messalina (c. 17/20–48 CE) had significant impact in the realm.³⁷ By the end of the Republican period the image of leading women appeared on coins.³⁸ Yet, advances such as these were largely enjoyed by those of privileged economic status and social position, while most matrons continued to spend the bulk of their time in the home, responsible for its proper working.³⁹ And the proper working of the Roman home was important to the proper working of the Roman state.

Augustus (63 BCE–14 CE) was convinced that Rome's social ills (lack of patriotism, population decline, financial disparity) were due to a movement away from patriarchalism and the national religious cults that supported stable traditional family structures.⁴⁰ Life-long marriage became rare among Roman aristocracy.⁴¹ In response, Augustus sought to revive national religious cults by restoring or building anew eighty-two temples.⁴²

---

36. See Pliny the Younger, *Letters* 5.16, LCL 55.378–81, recounting the death of Fudanus' daughter who loved her books and her teachers; Plutarch, *Par. Liv., Pomp.* 55, LCL 87.260–61, Pompey's marriage to the highly educated Cornelia.

37. Livia counselled Augustus on affairs of state while Messalina has a rather nefarious reputation of promiscuity, conspiring against her husband, and poisoning her adversaries. See Suetonius, *Aug.* 84.2, LCL, 31.272–73, where Augustus reads from a manuscript in his conversations with Livia regarding affairs of state; Seneca the Younger, *Mor. Ess., Clem.* I.9.6–10, LCL 214.382–85 (where Livia advises Augustus to pardon Lucius Cinna); Suetonius, *Galb.* 5.2, LCL 38.190–91, where Galba owes his success to Livia's influence, and she almost makes him a rich man by naming him in her will; Tacitus, *Ann.* 1.8.2, LCL 249.256–57, where Livia is adopted into the Julian family and the Augustan name; and 1.14.3, LCL 249.270–71, where one party of the Senate wished to title her "Parent of her Country" and another "Mother of her Country." For Messalina see Suetonius, *Claud.* 5.36–37, LCL 38.66–67; *Claud.* 5.26, LCL 38.52–53; and *Nero* 6.6, LCL 38.92–93; Dio Cassius, *Hist. Rom.* 60.14.3, LCL 175.402–403; and 60.22.5, LCL 175.424–25.

38. Mattingly, *Roman Coins*, 145.

39. Tacitus, *Agr.* 4, LCL 35.32–33; and *Dial.* 28–29, LCL 35.304–9; Petronius, *Satyr.* 44.15–18, LCL 15.148–49.

40. In response to this see Augustus' *Leges Juliae* (18–17 BCE) making adultery a public crime, and *Lex Papia Poppaea* (9 CE) designed to encourage population expansion with incentives to marry and disincentives to remain celibate.

41. See Plutarch, *Par. Liv., Pomp.* 9, LCL 87.134–37 (where Sulla persuades Pompey to divorce his wife and marry Sulla's stepdaughter). Quintus Lucretius Vespillo, Consul in 19 BCE thought the longevity of his own marriage as unique, "So long a marriage as ours ended by death and not divorce is rare; it has been our to have prolonged for 41 years without a quarrel" (*Laud. Tur.*, CIL 1527 [1876] VI: I, 332–36).

42. The most dominant, female led, native cult of the Republic was the cult of Vesta, which included female virgins as spiritual leaders. For a description of their duties, see

Worried about the growth of foreign deities he enacted legislation to extricate particular Egyptian and Jewish rites.[43] While Roman national cults waned, the growth of eastern religions that worshipped Isis, Serapis, Cybele, or Attis waxed with autonomy for women. By the first century foreign gods had won over so much of the female populace that the historian Petronius (c. 27–66 CE) mourns that few Roman matrons worship the traditional gods at all.[44]

Like Petronius, well-travelled Paul knew of the plethora of religious influences throughout the empire (Acts 17:23). He knew the background of Caesar's discomfort with the "insidious pollution" of Roman family values by foreign deities. He knew Caesar did not take kindly to threats against the stability of Roman state. But would fear of Roman political consequence be enough to make Paul, a devout Jew now living in the promise of Jewish Second Temple eschatological hope, "toe the line" with *Haustafeln* that pacified the Roman state?[45] Caesar's concerns may in part inform the background of his thinking as he picks up his pen to write the Ephesian letter, but this pales in comparison to his thinking about the dawning of a new day and how best to express this in language that will appeal to the Ephesian listener.

In addition to Artemis worship and other deities, the early church in Asia Minor was surrounded by emperor worship, which may also be alluded to in the Ephesian letter.[46] Fredrick Long argues that Ephesians represents a mature political theology for Paul where, like the imperial cult, the church of Christ brings heaven and earth together to meet the socio-political needs of Christians in Asia Minor. He argues that the author does this by drawing

---

Tacitus, *Ann.* 4.1, LCL 312.30–31 (primary duty was tending the flame); and Livy, *Hist. Rom., From the Founding of the City* 1.20.3, LCL 114.70–71. See also Tacitus 11.32.5, LCL 312.302–3; Seutonius, *Caes., Jul.* 83, LCL 31.140–41; Pliny the Younger, *Let.* 7.19, LCL 55.524–25; Plutarch, *Par. Liv., Ant.* 58.3–5, LCL 101.268–71; and *Par. Liv., Numa* 10, LCL 46.340–43.

43. Tacitus, *Ann.* 2.85, LCL, 249.516–17, where they were shipped off to Sardinia.

44. Petronius, *Satyr.* 44, LCL 15.148–49, where he says, "No one now believes that heaven's heaven, no one observes the fast, no one thinks that Jupiter's worth a damn . . . ."

45. Jewish teachings about women were important to the devout Jew eagerly awaiting the arriving KOG. 5.1.1 argues that they also may influence an Ephesian gentile audience.

46. For examples of allusions see Long, "Paul's Theology in Greco-Roman Political Context." For more on the imperial cult in Asia Minor see Das, "A Narrative of the Imperial Cult in Asia Minor"; Miller, "The Imperial Cult," where he argues from archaeological evidence that the emperor cult was marginal in the cities where Paul visited; also, Trebilco, *Early Christians*, 30–36; and especially Wizenburg, *Ephesians and Empire* for an in depth treatment.

on political concepts such as benefactors, temple building, head-body and military imagery in an economy of human relationships that are central to the life of the polis: city-state, husband-wife, parent-child, master-servant.[47] Although the widespread image of Caesar and presence of the imperial cult in Ephesus may strike closer to home as an ominous reminder of Roman authority in the minds of the reader, it was a more recent development that remained second to the cult of ancient Artemis, and third to the powerful new kingdom of Christ.[48]

3.3 SUMMARY OF SOCIAL AND POLITICAL INFLUENCES

Greco-Roman literature offers positive and negative traditions about women's status and roles. Cities are named after her. She is a businessperson. She owns property. She advises on public policy. She disposes of rivals. She is a philosopher. She has no opinion other than her husband's. She is naturally inferior, weak, and a busybody. Immersed in Hellenistic culture, Paul is an intellectual who might know all of this, as well as disparaging Jewish teachings about women,[49] but this does not ensure that the Ephesian believers are intellectuals as well. Modern scholarship has made heroic efforts to reconstruct the influences of his thought world as the key to unlock the meaning of his *Haustafel* for spouses. While authorial context is important, has too much emphasis has been placed on this and too little emphasis on the thought world of the letters' recipients: Jews aware of Artemis, and gentile former Artemis worshipers who have lived under the overwhelming dominance of the goddess in all aspects of life?[50] The volume of clear infer-

---

47. See Long, "Paul's Theology in Greco-Roman Political Context," 264.

48. See 4.2.3 for more. The imperial cult experienced rapid growth from 35 BCE-60CE. Artemis is first mentioned by Homer of Greece in his *Iliad* and *Odyssey* c. 800 BCE-c. 700 BCE. See *Hom. Hymns 9, To Artemis*, LCL 496.190–91; and *Hom. Hymns 27, To Artemis*, LCL 496.208–9.

49. For example, *Testaments of the Twelve Patriarchs* (109–106 BCE) warns: "And now I command you, my children, not to . . . gaze upon the beauty of a woman" (*T. Jud.* 17:1); and "For women are evil my children; and since they have no power or strength over man, they use wiles by outward attractions, that they may draw him to themselves. And whom they cannot bewitch by outward attractions, him they overcome by craft" (*T. Reu.* 5:1–3); and Philo of Alexandria (c. 20 BCE-50 CE) writes that a wife is a selfish creature, excessively jealous and adept at beguiling the morals of her husband and seducing him by her continued impostures (see *Hypoth.* 11:14–17, LCL 363.442–43), and intellectually subordinate since she is easily deceived (see *QG* 1:33, LCL 380.20).

50. This is not to say that Ephesian believers were uninfluenced by Paul's teachings

ences to the cult of Artemis in the letter, without naming her specifically, shows that Paul was quite knowledgeable of her history with the city.[51] He knows his audience, so he selects themes, language, allegory, and allusion to make clear to the Ephesian reader, in a common everyday Ephesian household, that the world as they know it has changed, as have they.

3.4 ARTEMIS IN INSCRIPTION AND ANALOGY

Ephesian inscriptional and analogical evidence furnish a first-hand account of the influence of Artemis upon daily life in ancient Ephesus, constructing a far more specific background for the letter and its marital *Haustafel* than Hellenistic literary evidence. *Die Inschriften von Ephesos*,[52] the most comprehensive collection of the Ephesus Inscriptions, is the primary source for this research.[53] Some inscriptions can be dated to the time of Paul, some predate him, and some postdate. All such references to Artemis testify to her prominence in the city and dominance in the thought world of the Ephesian residents.[54] The Ephesian marital code must be read closely in tandem with Ephesian inscriptional evidence to appreciate the way Paul's *Haustafel* is empowered by the transforming work of the image of God in the believer as a response to the adverse influence of Artemis upon Christian marriage.[55]

---

from his three-year stay in Ephesus (Acts 20:31), albeit one might argue that the believers in receipt of the letter were unknown to Paul or the Paulinst (Eph 1:15); or that there were no Jewish believers in the city. Acts 18:24–28 implies a sizable Jewish community in Ephesus which is affirmed by Josephus in his *Antiquities*, 14.10.13, LCL 489.122–25.

51. It was unnecessary for Paul to name her since the readers we're already well familiar with Artemis.

52. Henceforth referred to as IEPH.

53. Die Inschriften von Ephesos, Komission für die Archchäologische Erforschung Kleinasiens bei der Österreichischen Akademie der Wissenschaften, *Die Inschriften von Ephesos*, vols. 1–10 (1979–84), eds. Engelmann, et al. The available artefacts now number nearly 6,000 texts and fragments that date from the sixth century BCE to the Byzantine Middle Ages, with most during the first three centuries CE.

54. In this section my discussion is built upon the work of Immendörfer and Karaman where they provide a much larger corpus of inscriptional research on daily life in Ephesus than I require for my purposes. See Immendörfer, *Ephesians and Artemis*; and Karaman, *Ephesian Women in Greco-Roman and Early Christian Perspective*. For additional detail see Strelan, *Paul, Artemis, and the Jews*. For more see Rogers, *The Mysteries of Artemis of Ephesos*; Oster, *A Bibliography of Ancient Ephesus*; Horsley, "The Inscriptions of Ephesos and the New Testament," 105–68; Arnold, "Festivals of Ephesus," 17–22; Trebilco, *Early Christians in Ephesus*.

55. See ch. 6 for detailed discussion.

Recognizing the importance of Ephesus to maintaining Roman power in the region, in 40 BCE Proconsul Marc Antony starts building the State Agora in the upper city. In 29 BCE Octavian names Ephesus the capital of the province of Asia.[56] The Artemision temple was built southwest of the State Agora, a magnificent, awe inspiring symbol of beauty and strength. Other deities (notably the imperial cult) are worshipped in Ephesus, but none so eminent as Artemis worship.[57] Ephesus applies to build an imperial temple in 26 CE, but the Roman Senate rejects the application since Artemis is already so prominent.[58] Legend tells of the birth of Artemis and her brother Apollo to Leto in Ephesus.[59] The Ephesians celebrated her birth every year on the 6th day of the month of Thargelion.[60] She was *Artemis Ephesia* with a very special relationship to the inhabitants of the city where she was born.[61] Her relationship with the Ephesians was divinely initiated, her image in the temple having fallen from heaven to earth (Acts 19:35),[62] and the prosperity of the city inextricably linked to the level she was worshipped.

Because of Artemis' blessing the city was "glorious" (IEPH 24B.9–11),[63] and Artemis was a glorious deity because the city "nurtured" her

---

56. Multiple buildings continue being erected during the reign of Domitian (81–96 CE). Construction continues under Trajan (98–117 CE), Hadrian (117–138 CE) and beyond, which is not relevant to the Ephesian letter, but could be for the Pastorals.

57. As with other cities of the Greek east, many Greco-Roman and some Anatolian gods were worshipped. See Trebilco, *Early Christians*, 19, fn. 47 where he lists Aphrodite, Apollos, Asclepius, Athena, Cabiri, Demeter, Dionysus, Hecate, Hephaestus, Hercules, Hestia, the mother goddess, Pluton, Poseidon, Zeus.

58. Tacitus, *Ann.* 4.55; LCL 312.98–99; also, Pausanias, *Desc. Gr.* 4.31.8, LCL 188:344–45, where he says that Artemis of Ephesus is the most worshipped of all the deities.

59. Tacitus, *Ann.* 3.61.1, LCL 249.618–19; Strabo, *Geogr.* 14.1.20, LCL 223.222–25; Callimachus, *Hymns* 3.30, LCL 129:62–62 and 3.240–47, LCL 129.104–5.

60. May 24 or 25.

61. Albeit her influence grew well beyond the city into Asia Minor.

62. Inscriptional verification for this is lacking. Euripides provides a literary parallel where in his play, *Iphigenia Among the Taurians,* he writes the image of the Taurian Artemis as fallen from heaven (lines 86–87, LCL 10.160–61; 977, LCL 10.254–55; 1384–85, LCL 10.300–301).

63. "Because the goddess, Artemis, leader of our city is worshipped not only in her hometown, which she has made the most glorious (ἐνδοξοτέραν) of all cities but also among the Greeks and the barbarians" (ἐπειδὴ ἡ προετῶσα τῆς πόλεως ἡμῶν θεὸς Ἄπτεμις, οὐ μόνον ἐν τῇ ἑαυτῇ πατρίδι τειμᾶται, ἣν ἁπασῶν, τῷ πόλεων ἐνδοξοτέραν διὰ τῆς ἰδίας θειότητος πεποίν, κεν, ἀλλὰ καὶ παρὰ Ἕλλησίν τε καὶ βαρβάροις, ὥστε παν).

(IEPH 24B.22–23).⁶⁴ Artemis and the Ephesians were joint catalysts in a love story that spanned thousands of years where nurturing flowed from the city to the goddess and back again.⁶⁵ "Glorious" (ἔνδοξος) and "nurture" (τροφός) highlight this, appearing together in IEPH 24B. Paul knows this, so he tells a new love story of glory and nurturing (Eph 5:1–2; 25–33), one much more empowering and fulfilling than the first; by crafting his letter with familiar analogy and terminology. Both ἔνδοξος and τροφός are found in one pericope of the NT (Eph 5:27, 29).⁶⁶ That Christ nourishes and cares for (ἐκτρέφει καὶ θάλπει) the church (5:29) so that he might present a glorious (ἔνδοξον) church to himself (5:27) is more than mere coincidence. The context of the pericope (Eph 5:21–33) is a marriage analogy where the husband is to nourish and cherish his wife, as Christ does the church, to present his wife as glorious. This, in light of Ephesus nourishing and cherishing Artemis to present her as glorious is important to this work and will be discussed in chapter 6. It could well be intentional, and relevant to understanding the Ephesian marriage *Haustafel* in the minds of its readers.

It is doubtful that Paul could possibly know every Ephesian inscription written before or during his lifetime, and Paul certainly did not know those written after. But more than enough inscriptional evidence from past and present is in plain sight of him and the emerging Ephesian church⁶⁷ to support the claim that the primary backdrop of the Ephesian letter is not general Greco-Roman culture or Roman Politics but Artemis and the city of Ephesus itself. And inscriptions such as the lengthy IEPH 24B Salutaris inscription of 104 CE reflect attitudes in and around the time of Paul that

---

64. "Especially in our city, the nurturer (τῇ τροφῷ) of its own Ephesian goddess . . ." (διαφερόντως ἐν τῇ ἡμετέρᾳ πόλει τῇ τροφῷ τῆς ἰδίας θεοῦ τῆς Ἐφεσίας). The last sentence of the inscription (IEPH 24B.32–34) echoes this, by worshipping the goddess the city continues to be glorious (ἐνδοξοτέρα) and blessed, "This way with better worshipping of the goddess, our city will continue to be more glorious and blessed forever" (νου τῇ θεῷ οὕτω γὰρ ἐπὶ τὸ ἄμεινον τῆς θεοῦ τιμωμέ, νης ἡ πόλις ἡμῶν ἐνδοξοτέρα τε καὶ εὐδαιμονεστέρα, εἰς τὸν ἅπαντα διαμενεῖ χρόνον).

65. IEPH 24B.22–23, 33. See fn 64.

66. See fn. 64. The verb form ἐκτρέφει in 5:29 has linguistic similarity and coherence with τροφῷ in IEPH 24B.32–34.

67. Muddiman, *Ephesians*, 35, estimates the population of Ephesus at 200,000 with 500 Christians in various house churches. Other population estimates for the city range from 150,000–250,000.

persisted after his passing.[68] In addition to terminology focused on nurturing and glory that ties inscriptional evidence to the *Haustafel*, the following examples show that Paul continues to connect various parts of his letter to the immediate context of the Ephesian reader with more inscription, allegory, and allusion to the goddess.

First, "temple" (ναός) building terminology is abundantly used in Ephesians 2:20–22 with seven building terms[69] that are widespread in the inscriptions of Ephesus[70] supporting the notion that this an allusion to the building history of the Artemision. During the thousand years before Christ, five different temples of Artemis were built in Ephesus, each one more magnificent than the one before. The fourth temple alone, the Temple of Croesus, took 120 years to build, showing how much the topic of temple construction was rooted in the thought world of the Ephesians. One might attempt to argue that the Ephesian writer had the Jerusalem temple in mind, but it is doubtful that gentile Christians in Asia Minor would associate temple building terminology with the Jerusalem temple,[71] especially if one accepts a late date of 80–90 CE for the authorship of Ephesians, in which case the Jerusalem temple would have already been destroyed by Titus (70 CE).[72] Here, building the church of Christ is supplemented by "holy" and "dwelling" and, apart from 1 Corinthians 3:16 (notably written

---

68. The Salutaris inscription is very large, in five square blocks, across six columns, with 568 lines.

69. Foundation (Θεμέλιος), cornerstone (ἀκρογωνιαῖος), building (οἰκοδομη), temple (ναός), dwelling (κατοικητήριον), to build on (ἐποικοδομέω), to build together (συνοικοδομέω).

70. θεμέλιος: IEPH 438; 448; 455; 491; 1073; 2260. οἰκοδομή: IEPH 475; 672.15. ναός: IEPH 22.4, 48, 63; 24B.12; 26.18; 27.107; 212; 232; 234; 235; 237; 238; 239; 241; 279; 428; 617; 618; 619; 626; 627; 637; 642; 664B; 671; 686; 692; 710B; 710C; 714; 721; 722; 736; 742; 792; 810; 814; 823; 897; 921; 958; 987; 988; 994. κατοικία: IEPH 3221; 3223; 3233; 3237; 3239A; 3245; 3247; 3249; 3250; 3251; 3252; 3256; 3262; 3263; 3272; 3274; 3287A; 3327; 3701; 3713; 3719; 3757; 3817; 3850; 3854; 3833; 3856; 3857; 3858; 3863A; 3864; 3865; 3868. οἰκοδομέω: IEPH 462.4; 1246.4; 1384.6; 1656; 1939A; 2433.

71. One may attempt to argue that the Jerusalem temple is in reference in Ephesians 2:14–15, "For he is our peace; in this flesh he has made both groups into one and has broken down the dividing wall, that is, the hostility between us. He has abolished the law with its commandments and ordinances, that he might create in himself one new humanity in place of the two, thus making peace (NRSV)," speaking of the four-and-one-half foot wall in the Jerusalem temple precincts that separated the court of the gentiles from the court of the Jews. But it seems unlikely that such a wall would be familiar to the everyday gentile believer living in Ephesus and is likely a metaphorical wall of hostility between Jews and gentiles. See Hoehner, *Ephesians*, 354–55 for more.

72. See Josephus, *JW* 7.1.1, LCL 210.306–7.

from Ephesus), this is the only passage in the NT letters where God dwells in the temple.[73] The Artemision was the dwelling of Artemis because it contained her cult image which fell from heaven. Bearing new identity, the Ephesian Christians have become the temple, the dwelling, and the *imago Dei* all in one (2:22).[74]

Second, "greatness" (μέγεθος) of the temple and goddess is extolled in the inscription IEPH 18B.0–4, "Many temples, through fire or collapse, are in ugly ruins. The sanctuary of Artemis itself, which is the pride of the entire province due to the μέγεθος of the building and the antiquity of worship for the goddess."[75] This inscription dates to 44 CE and is part of a group of inscriptions (IEPH 17–19) that are an edict of the proconsul Paullus Fabius Persicus, addressing financial misconduct by Artemision and city officials. Inscriptions were placed at several locations in the city to emphasize the importance of the edict. A Greek and a Latin version were commissioned also. Archaeologists discovered two copies of the Greek version (IEPH 17; 18), and two copies of the Latin version (IEPH 19A-B). IEPH 17 was placed at a staircase of the Great Theatre, IEPH 18 at the Commercial Agora, which a main entrance to the market square. IEPH 19A slabs were found around the theatre in multiple locations. IEPH 19B was found near the Magnesian Gate. With an inscription date of 44 CE, the group of inscriptions already existed when Paul was in Ephesus and when Ephesians was written. Since the inscriptions were in prominent places in the city it is very likely that Paul knew them.[76] It should not be missed that, unique to the NT, Paul's use of μέγεθος in Ephesians 1:19 is a *hapax legomenon* in the NT[77] that

---

73. Ephesians 2:20–22 is congruent with 1 Corinthians 3:9–17. In contrast to Ephesians, building terminology plays no significant role in Colossians (a letter often compared with Ephesians) with Colossians 2:7 containing only one of the seven building terms, the verb ἐποικοδομέω.

74. In the NT letters, apart from Ephesians 2:21, ναός occurs in seven other locations (1 Cor 3:16, 17; 6:19; 2 Cor 6:16; 2 Thess 2:4). The combination of ἅγιος and ναός as "holy temple" in 2:21, also occurs in 1 Corinthians 3:17 supporting the notion of linguistic parallels of building and temple terminology between Ephesians 2 and 1 Corinthians 3. However, 1 Corinthians 3 makes no mention temple construction, so Ephesians 2:21 is the only passage in all NT letters which mentions the *construction* of a temple. A likely explanation for this is the lengthy construction process of Artemision.

75. Trans. Immendörfer. Note that Pausanias, *Desc. Gr.* 4.31.8, LCL 188.344–45, said one reason for the fame of Artemis was "the size of the temple surpassing all buildings among men."

76. For more see Immendörfer, *Ephesians and Artemis*, 193, 287.

77. Despite being similar to Colossians 1:11, only Ephesians 1:19 uses the term μέγεθος.

trumpets the magnitude of God, "and what is the surpassing μέγεθος of his power toward us, those according to the working of his strong might."

Third, "riches" (πλοῦτος) occurs five times in Ephesians 1:7, 18; 2:7; 3:8, 16 as it does in Romans (2:4; 9:23; 11:12a/b; 11:33), and more frequently in these two letters than any other NT book. Ephesians 1:7 and 2:7 describes the πλοῦτος of God's grace; 1:18 and 3:16 the πλοῦτος of his glory; 3:8 the πλοῦτος of Christ; and in 2:4 of God who is πλούσιος in mercy. Dio Chrysostom (c. 40–c. 115 CE) describes the Artemision as "the bank of Asia." Strabo (64/63 BCE–c. 24 CE) and Xenophon (c. 430–354 BC) also attest to the prominence of the bank.[78] The readers of the Ephesian letter would not have missed the analogy between the goddess, the bank of Asia, and the repetition that the believer is πλοῦτος in Christ.

Fourth, "inheritance" (κληρονομία) is frequent in the Ephesus Inscriptions.[79] Artemis was the heiress (κληρονόμος) of Ephesus whose wealth was immense from faithful donations (IEPH 731; IEPH 669; 3076). Hence, the notion that God receives an "inheritance" (κληρονομίας) in 1:18 was a short walk across the bridge to Ephesian thinking.[80] Ephesians 1:14; 3:6; 5:5 speaks of the κληρονομίας that God bestows on believers, the seal of the Holy Spirit as down payment (ἀρραβὼν) on this inheritance.[81] Thus, Paul uses the well attested concept of inheritance to communicate to the Ephesian readers that they are not only the image of God and temple of God; they are also inheritors with God.[82]

---

78. Dio Chrysostom, *Disc.* 31.54, LCL 358.58–59; Strabo, *Geogr.* 14.1.22, LCL 90.400–401; Xenophon, *Anab.* 5.3.4–6, LCL 223.224–27.

79. Κληρονομίας: IEPH 8.43; 27.285; 274; 627; 660C; 822. Κληρόω: IEPH 4.8, 9; 27.237, 252; 712B; 717; 958; 969.

80. Whether God or believers in Ephesians 1:18 are the recipient of an inheritance continues to be contested in scholarship. See Immendörfer, *Ephesians and Artemis*, 201–2 for a description of the debate. For God as the recipient see Lincoln, *Ephesians*, 59; O'Brien, *Ephesians*, 135; Muddiman, *Ephesians*, 86; Hoehner, *Ephesians*, 266–67; Arnold, *Ephesians*, 135. For the believer as the recipient see Best, *Ephesians*, 167; and Thielman, *Ephesians*, 99, who interprets 1:18 in the sense of 1:14.

81. Κληρονομία occurs fourteen times in the NT, three times in Ephesians (1:14, 18; 5:5) making Ephesians its most frequent use within a NT book. There is only one instance in Colossians (3:24). Ephesians 3:6 speaks of the gentiles as being joint heirs (συνκληρονόμα).

82. Note that Ephesians does not contain the verb "to inherit" (κληρονομέω) used in 1 Corinthians 6:9; 10:15; 15:50 or the noun "heir" (κληρονόμος) used in Romans 4:13, 14; 8:17). Both are missing from Colossians.

Fifth, "Lady/Lord," as in "our Sovereign Lady Artemis" (ἡ κυρία ἡμῶν Ἀρτέμιδος), reveals the reverence the Ephesians had for her.[83] Paul uses this to draw a close analogy with the worship of "our *Lord* Jesus Christ" (τοῦ Κυρίου ἡμῶν Ἰησοῦ Χριστοῦ) in 1:3, 17; 3:11, 5:20, 6:24.[84] "Savior" (Σώτειρα) Artemis offered help and salvation[85] while designation of Christ as "himself Savior of the body" (αὐτὸς σωτὴρ τοῦ σώματος) in 5:23 is analogous to her title.[86] The superlative "Holiest Artemis" (τῆς ἁγιωτάτης Ἀρτέμιδος)[87] in IEPH 467 is met with "holy" (ἅγιος) fifteen times in the Ephesian letter (1:1, 4, 13, 15, 18; 2:19, 21; 3:5, 8, 18; 4:12, 30; 5:3, 26, 27). The worshippers of Artemis are not identified as holy, but the Ephesian believers are (1:15; 2:19; 3:8; 4:12).[88]

---

83. The chant of the Ephesians, "Great is Artemis of the Ephesians" (Μεγάλη ἡ Ἄρτεμις Ἐφεσίων), in Acts 19:28 points this way as well. It is worth noting that this title is used in combination with the possessive ἡμῶν in three inscriptions (IEPH 1078; 3059; 3263) testifying that the Ephesians trusted her and that she ruled the city. For more inscriptions where she is worshipped as Lord, see IEPH 27.110–12; 724; 892; 985. Κυρία for "Lord" is frequently deployed in a thanksgiving phrase (IEPH 940; 943; 957; 958; 960; 961; 962; 963).

84. Jesus as "Lord" (κύριος) appears in the Ephesian letter twenty-six times, and in the New Testament in twenty-three of twenty-seven books (excluding Titus and 1–3 John). Of these twenty-six times, eight of them occur in combination with the name Jesus, while eighteen times κύριος stands alone in an absolute sense. On the other hand, Artemis is never referred to as κυρία in inscriptions in an absolute sense, but always combined with her name. It appears Paul went to some pains to make this distinction.

85. IEPH 1255 reports of an altar dedicated to Artemis "Savior" (Σώτειρα). IEPH 26, a decree of the Ephesian council of elders, occasioned by a donation given by Nikomedes (between 180 and 192 CE), twice calls the goddess Σώτειρα (IEPH 26.4, 18). IEPH 1265 is an honorific inscription for Gaius Iulius Atticus, a priest of Artemis Σώτειρα. IEPH 2928 is a thanksgiving to Artemis Σώτειρα by Marcus Aurelius Hortensius. See also 1578B.2–4.

86. "Savior" (Σωτήρ) as a Christological title is uncommon in the Pauline letters. The parallel wording of Ephesians 5:23 "himself the savior of the body" (αὐτὸς σωτὴρ τοῦ σώματος) and Colossians 1:18 "and himself the head of the body, the church" (καὶ αὐτός ἐστιν ἡ κεφαλὴ τοῦ σώματος τῆς ἐκκλησίας) is notable because of the Paul's apparently intentional use of σωτήρ instead of ἡ κεφαλή, which clearly sets the Ephesian passage apart from its Colossian counterpart.

87. See also IEPH 304; 441; 467; 617; 624; 645; 669; 731; 980; 990.

88. This is with much more frequency than the six occurrences in Colossians (1:2, 4, 12, 22, 26; 3:12), again setting the Ephesian letter apart from Colossians. "Holy" (ἅγιος) occurs 223 times in the NT.

Artemis, Eve, and the Image of God

Sixth, "flaming arrows" are part of the huntress Artemis' arsenal,[89] her reputation renowned in Homer's *Iliad*[90] and *Odyssey*.[91] According to Hera, Queen of the Gods and wife (and sister) of Zeus, Artemis dispatched Ariadne, the daughters of Niobe, the mothers of Sarpedon and Andromache, and the wife of Eumaios.[92] The "flaming arrows of the evil one" (τὰ βέλη τοῦ πονηροῦ τὰ πεπυρωμένα) in Ephesians 6:16 are a theme unique to the letter, a theme missing from Colossians, the remainder of the Pauline corpus, and the rest of the NT.[93]

Seventh, "citizenship" (πολιτεία) in Ephesus meant status, with the names of new citizens inscribed in the Temple of Artemis.[94] A clear distinction was made between the "haves" and "have-nots" as reflected in the frequent use of πολιτείας in inscriptions,[95] citizenship decrees[96] and citizenship conferrals.[97] The Ephesian readers, all identified as "alienated from citizenship" (ἀπηλλοτριωμένοι τῆς πολιτείας) in 2:12, and picked up in 2:19 as "fellow citizens and saints of the household of God" (συμπολῖται τῶν ἁγίων καὶ οἰκεῖοι τοῦ Θεοῦ) would have understood the allusion to Ephesian citizenship specifically, and Roman citizenship generally.[98]

Eighth, "purity" is plainly important to the Ephesian letter (Eph 4–5) the clearest reference found in 5:26, "so that he might sanctify (ἁγιάσῃ) her

---

89. Callimachus, *Hymn* III.1–3, LCL 129.60–61; III.116–28, LCL 129.70–71; III.259–68, LCL 129.82–83.

90. *Il.* 5.51, LCL 170.210; *Il.* 21.470, LCL 171:438–439; Il. 21.464–514, LCL 171.438–43; see also Hom. *Hymn* 9, LCL 496.190–91 and Hom. *Hymn* 27, LCL 496.208–9.

91. *Od.* 6.100–109, LCL 104.226–29.

92. Ariadne: *Od.* 11.324, LCL 104.422–25; the daughters of Niobe: *Il.* 24.606, LCL 171.608–9; the mothers of Sarpedon and Andromache: *Il.* 6.205, LCL 170:288–89 and 6.428, LCL 170.304–5; the wife of Eumaios: *Od.* 15.478, LCL 105.110–11.

93. One might wish to argue that 6:16, "with which you will be able to quench all the flaming arrows of the evil one" (ἐν ᾧ δυνήσεσθε πάντα τὰ βέλη τοῦ πονηροῦ τὰ πεπυρωμένα σβέσαι) refers not to Artemis, but to the devil, since "evil one" (πονηροῦ) is masculine; however, if Paul is of the opinion that Artemis supports the old world order of the devil, then her partnership with the devil makes her arrows his.

94. IEPH 1442.

95. IEPH 1352; 1389; 1405–10; 1412–13; 1417; 1421–22; 1426–28; 1438; 1440–43; 1447–58; 1460; 1465; 1471; 1473.

96. IEPH 1405–10.

97. IEPH 1414–16.

98. In 2:12, ἀπαλλοτριόω (to alienate from) and ξένος (stranger; also found in 2:19) are found in the inscriptions: ἀπαλλοτριόω in IEPH 2212C; 2419; 2471; 2522; 2549; 3224; 3236; 3300; 3473A; 3829; 4127, and ξένος in IEPH 8.44; 453; 947.4; 1625A; 3214.6; 3445; 4330.7.

having cleansed (καθαρίσας) her by the washing of water by the word."⁹⁹ This could be a bridal bath reference to Ezekiel 16:8–14 and God's marriage covenant with Israel.¹⁰⁰ But it is notable that καθαρίζω is also found in the Ephesus Salutaris Inscription (104 CE) describing the purification of Artemis statues at processions, where the image of Artemis was bathed, anointed, and adorned with a wreath.¹⁰¹ This would clearly be better understood by former Artemis worshippers than a Jewish rite.¹⁰²

Ninth, "mystery" rituals united cult initiates with Artemis.¹⁰³ The frequent use of "mystery" (μυστήριον) in the Inscriptions of Ephesus verifies the presence of mysteries in the cult of the goddess.¹⁰⁴ An inscription in honor of the priestess Aurelia who was ordained devoutly, renewing "all the mysteries of God" (πάντα τὰ μυστήρια τῆς Θεοῦ; IEPH 3059) testifies that such rituals occurred. According to Strabo, during the Artemis birthday festival in Ephesus known as "the mysteries of Artemis" (τὰ μυστήρια τῆς Ἀρτέμιδος) the *curetes* executed mystic sacrifices.¹⁰⁵ The often combined "mysteries and sacrifices" (τά τε μυστήρια καὶ τὰς Θυσίας) in inscriptions supports a close relationship between the mystery festivals and sacrifices of incense, drink and animals.¹⁰⁶ In the NT μυστήριον is also widespread, occurring twenty-seven times in nine books,¹⁰⁷ and most fre-

99. Similar verses exist (Acts 20:32; 26:18; 1 Cor 1:2; 6:11; 1 Thess 5:23; Heb 2:11; 10:10, 14; 13:12) but the flow of thought and marital context in 5:26 is unique.

100. O'Brien, *Ephesians*, 422–24, sees 5:26 as a reference to Ezekiel 16:8–14 and the prenuptial Jewish bath; while Schnackenburg, *Ephesians*, 249, sees 5:26 as a reference to baptism; and Batey, *New Testament Nuptial Imagery*, 28, equates the bridal bath with baptism; as does Sampley, "And the Two Shall Become One Flesh," 41–51, 131, 139.

101. IEPH 27.28 directs that the statues be cleaned before they were returned to the vestibule of the Artemision should be paid 30 denarii each.

102. It should be noted that the theme of baptism in the Ephesian letter was earlier introduced in 4:5 and that Paul may allude to baptism again here (see 1 Cor 6:11) as a salvation reference. Purity and the Ephesian matron will receive detailed discussion in ch. 6.

103. See Immendörfer, *Ephesians and Artemis*, 176, 237, 268, 270–71; and Thielman, *Ephesians*, 68. Ephesians 5:32 is a unique OT and NT interpretation of Genesis 2:24, which declares the union of Christ and the church an unfathomable mystery. This statement is particularly potent considering that the initiates of Artemis sought to unite with her.

104. IEPH 26.3; 213.3; 667A.10; 702.13; 987.11; 988.14; 989.10; 1060.7; 1069.5; 1077.6; 1080A.6; 1597.1; 1600.11; 2913.1; 3059.4; 3072.29; 3252.7; 4330.6.

105. Strabo, *Geogr.* 14.1.20, LCL 223.224–25.

106. IEPH 26.3; 213.3; 987.11–12; 988.14–15; 1077.6. Nocturnal cult activities and mystery celebrations are also found in inscriptions (IEPH 10.14; 3860.10).

107. Three times in the Gospels (Matt 13:11; Mark 4:11; Luke 8:10) where Jesus

quently in Ephesians.[108] However, Paul emphasizes a superior μυστήριον which was not made known in other generations (3:5) but was revealed to Paul himself by God (3:3) and which he fearlessly has made known (6:19). This greatest of mysteries unites all inhabitants and all of heaven and earth under Christ (ἀνακεφαλαιώσασθαι τὰ πάντα ἐν τῷ Χριστῷ) fulfilling the ultimate destiny of the cosmos (1:9–10).[109]

3.5 THE UBIQUITOUS IMAGE OF ARTEMIS

In addition to the vast testimony of inscriptional evidence, the image of Artemis was present everywhere in numbers almost inconceivable for modern readers to imagine. Philo wrote that statues and images were set up in the most conspicuous places in cities "to adorn them"[110] and that pride in one's city meant taking pride in the sculpture and painting of countless images for the temple shrines and altars.[111] Numismatic evidence includes 850 years of Ephesian minting.[112] Coins from the reign of Lysimachus (306–281 BCE) show him or his wife on the front while the back shows the deer or bow and quiver, which are the weapons of Artemis.[113] Artemis— her head with mural crown, or her entire figure—appears for the first time on coins dating back to the middle of the second century BCE. A golden minting from 120 BCE shows the bust of Artemis on the front and her figure on the back. During the reign of Claudius (41–54 CE) a new image was added, the front of the Artemision. During the reign of Nero (54–68 CE)

---

speaks in parables, so that the disciples could understand the secrets of God; four times in Revelation (1:20; 10:7; 17:5, 7); and twenty times in the letters (1 Cor 2:7; 4:1; 13:2; 14:2; 15:51; Eph 1:9; 3:3, 4, 9; 5:32; 6:19; Col 1:26, 27; 2:2; 4:3; 2 Thess 2:7; 1 Tim 3:9, 16).

108. Ephesians 1:9; 3:3, 4, 9; 5:32; 6:19.

109. According to 3:3–10, the mystery is the union of Jewish and gentile believers in one body and should be seen as an aspect of 1:9–10. In 5:32, another aspect is revealed, the union of Christ and the church. Ephesians 6:19 refers to God's acceptance of the gentiles in 3:3–10. Each passage reveals an aspect of the larger mystery of 1:9–10.

110. *On the World* (πρὸς κόσμονο, *Abraham*, 267, LCL 289.130–31.

111. *Decalogue* 2.6–9, LCL 320.8–9. It is worth noting that not all statues were of Artemis but, due to her prominence, the majority would have been.

112. For more on Ephesian coinage, see Head, *On The Chronological Sequence of the Coins of Ephesus*; Robinson, "The Coins from the Ephesian Artemision Reconsidered," 156–67; Keil, "Die erste Kaiserneokorie von Ephesos," 115–20; Karwiese, *Die Muünzprägung von Ephesos*.

113. These coins depict the image of a sovereign for the first time, see Immendörfer, *Ephesians and Artemis*, 143; and Karwiese, "Ephesos: C Numismatischer Teil," XII.297–364.

the term "Guardian of the Temple" (ΝΕΩΚΟΡΩΝ) appears for the first time, referring to the Artemis cult.[114] Hence, when examining the notion of the restored *imago Dei,* one would be remiss to overlook how Ephesians 4:24 "to put on the new self in the likeness of God" (ἐνδύσασθαι τὸν καινὸν ἄνθρωπον τὸν κατὰ Θεὸν) might be understood by former Artemis worshippers where the influential, ubiquitous image of the female goddess was seen every day in the money they handled, in the multitude of her statues in the temple and throughout the city, and the colossus of the Artemision itself, all a reminder of her constant presence. However, the ubiquitous, constant presence of the *imago Dei,* transforming the Ephesian believer into the likeness of God as new selves would bear witness to everyone what true deity was to look like.[115]

3.6 WEALTHY WOMEN AND PROMINENT PRIESTESSES

To suggest that there was equality in marriage in the Ephesian *household* because all or most women in Ephesus had wealth and status is a bridge too far. The majority of Ephesian women were without wealth, played no part in the affairs of the city, and rarely travelled beyond their neighborhood. Even so, the volume of inscriptions and literary evidence from Asia Minor pointing out wealthy women benefactors who provided meat, grain, and oil suggests that there was an unusual number who owned large estates capable of such generosity.[116] Following are three such examples. 1) Cicero's *Pro Flacco* (59 BCE) mentions estates near the city of Apollonis[117] that belong to the mother-in-law of Amyntas, a wealthy landowner and "the most important man in his city."[118] 2) In Achilles Tatius novel, *Leucippe and Clitophon,*[119] the widowed Ephesian, Melite, is wealthy in her own

---

114. See Keil, "Die erste Kaiserneokorie von Ephesos," 115–20. Coinage during the reign of Domitian (81–96 CE) shows that ΝΕΩΚΟΡΩΝ was applied to both the Artemis cult and imperial cult.

115. Chs. 4 and 5 will discuss the image of God in detail.

116. See van Bremen, "Women and Wealth," 223–42, especially her focus on examples from the first century BCE and first and second centuries CE, 228–30; see also her *The Limits of Participation* where she continues with the conservative view that female freedoms came with wealth and were the exception to the rule.

117. Apollonis (city of ancient Lydia) was destroyed in 17 CE by the great earthquake that destroyed the cities of Asia Minor (see Tacitus, *Ann.* 2.47, LCL 249.458–59).

118. Cicero, *Flac.* 72, LCL 324.520–21. This is an extortion case against L. Valerius Flaccus, who Cicero defended in his speech *Pro Flacco*.

119. Circa first or second century CE. Achilles Tatius, *Leuc. Clit.,* trans. Whitmarsh.

right with a large, well-appointed house, a country estate, and servants all of which she will share with Clitophon if only he will marry her.[120] Melite encounters Clitophon in Egypt, which further discloses that she had the financial means to experience culture and travel. 3) Inscriptional evidence reveals *Claudia Metrodora* as a mid-first-century patron of the Greek island of Chios[121] who uses her wealth and social prominence to improve the lives of her fellow citizens. During her life she holds the highest magistrate position in Chios as "crowned" (στεφανηφόρος). She finances the construction and adornment of a public bath, distributes oil to the whole city for the Heraklea games and throws a banquet for the city. She also serves as *Basileia* (Βασίλεια) of the religious federation of thirteen Ionian cities.[122] She then marries and lives in Ephesus with her husband where she continued her work as a generous benefactor there.[123]

Ephesian women were prominent in the Artemis cult as priestesses, in the running of the temple, and holding important offices in the many cults of Asia Minor that helped cement their social identity.[124] From very early days of the Artemis cult, the Amazon women resided in the temple and performed rituals to Artemis there.[125] Callimachus (310/305–240 BCE) attributes the first ever foundation of the temple to these Amazon women.[126] The Artemision was a holy place, a sanctuary for virgins, a place of prayer

---

120. 5.11.5–6, LCL 45.258–61; 5.17.1–2, LCL 45:270–73. See additional detail in Karaman, *Ephesian Women in Greco-Roman and Early Christian Perspective*, 110–11.

121. Located just off the west coast of Asia Minor near Ephesus.

122. See Robert, "Inscriptions de Chios du Ier siècle de notre ère," *Études épigraphiques et philologiques*, 128–34. The Chiot texts referring to her are what remains of three civic decrees in six fragments. Emperor Nero's name is found in one of the civic decrees which would then date Claudia Metrodora sometime during Nero's reign of 54–68 CE.

123. From Ephesus, there is a building inscription bearing her name. See *Die Inschriften von Ephesos* 17/1, VII.1.3003. For more on her see Kearsley, "Women in Public Life in the Roman East," 189–211.

124. IEPH 617 and 3072 lists the names of several women who were female priests "of Holy Artemis" (τῆς ἁγιωτάτης Ἀρτέμιδος) and "of Asian Temples" (τῆς Ἀσίας ναῶν). See also IEPH 3059 for an honorific inscription for the Artemis priestess Aurelia. Also note that in the cult of *Hestia Boulaia* in Ephesus, the influential position of "rector" (πρύτανις) was held by Claudia Trophime (IEPH 1012), while Faviona Flaccilla was both "rector" (πρύτανις) and "principal" (γυμνασίαρχος) in IEPH 1060.

125. See Pausanias, *Desc. Gr.* 7.2.6–9, LCL 272.174–77; Strabo describes the Amazons as the earliest inhabitants of the city (*Geogr.* 14.1.4, LCL 223:200–205). The identity of the founders remains a debated issue.

126. Callimachus, *Hymn III to Artemis*, 237–50, LCL 129.256–59.

where maidens sacrificed to Artemis daily before marriage.[127] But the Artemis cult was not exclusive to women. The virgin goddess who roamed the mountains, hunting with bow and spear (traditional male roles), made it easy for men to identify with her. Ephesian men would have appreciated her role in preparing women for marriage and childbearing since marriage and family created status for men. Both men and women worshipped a virgin female goddess who was not beholden to any man but could also identify with the world of men.

3.7 SUMMARY

While authorial context from the undisputed letters and literary context from Greco-Roman life are worthy aspects to consider for understanding the Ephesian marital *Haustafel*, emphasis should be placed on the nearer context of inscriptional evidence, common to all Ephesians, that reveals the influence of the Artemis cult upon the daily lives of the letter's audience. Paul, knowing his audience, borrowed terms prevalent in the Ephesus inscriptions about the cult of Artemis, applied them to Christ to announce his superiority over the Ephesian goddess, and applied them to the Ephesian gentile believer to announce a new identity that surpasses that of Artemis worshippers and even the goddess herself.[128] This new identity is based on a union with Christ as God (2:5–6) where both Jews and gentiles are joined together as one new "person" (ἄνθρωπος) forming a fresh identity (2:11–22). The use of inscriptional evidence about Artemis as the background for the Ephesian letter is further supported by the fact that Paul makes it a point to express to the Ephesian gentile believers that they are now joint heirs with the Jews in Israel's inheritance (2:11–16). This suggests that they may have been unaware of these Jewish roots, or lacking respect for them, and had to be told so, since their frame of reference was so steeped in Artemis worship. This fresh identity is highlighted in the distinction between the old self (τὸν παλαιὸν ἄνθρωπον) in 4:22 and the new self (τὸν καινὸν ἄνθρωπον) in 4:24. For Ephesus' citizens, who once saw their identity wrapped up in the great goddess, under the shadow of the Seventh Wonder of the Ancient World, to now be the

---

127. See Aristophanes, *Clouds*, 598–601, LCL 488.88–89; and Xenophon, *Anthia and Habrocomes* 1.5.1, LCL 69.222–23.

128. For more on new identity see O'Brien, *Ephesians*, 57; Arnold, *Ephesians*, 45; Lincoln, *Ephesians*, lxxxv; Hoehner, *Ephesians*, 106.

citizens of a newly inaugurated kingdom, a new world order, where they personally and corporately (4:13) are the temple, the dwelling place, and the image of God's reign over earth was an enormous truth to digest. The statue fallen from heaven of Artemis in the Artemision was not the image of God, nor were the multitude of statues, paintings, and coinage, but *they* were. What might an image-bearer look like in the mind of Paul? What might it look like in the mind of the Ephesian gentile believer, and were their two perspectives aligned? The following chapter address these questions in two parts. Part One examines texts frequently used by scholarship to answer the first question, while Part Two examines local epigraphy and literary evidence to answer the second.

4

Competing Concepts of the Image of God

WHAT DID PAUL THINK the image of God (*imago Dei*) looked like in people intertextually, and in terms of gender? Do the Ephesians have the same frame of reference? Part One of this chapter begins with what the image of God looks like in people from Paul's perspective.[1] Highlighting the scope of the intertextual debate, one must ask if scholarship has unduly emphasized the dimension of "rule" (רדה) in the *imago Dei* (Gen 1:26) to the exclusion of other aspects, and then asked which gender is most like God (Gen 1:27) in order to decide who gets to rule. If the dimension of רדה in the *imago Dei* has been overemphasized, then one must ask if the emphasis of Paul's lengthy Ephesian marriage *Haustafel* lies not with the intertextual debate of who gets to rule, but elsewhere. Given the abundance of epigraphical and artefactual evidence from the Ephesians' relationship with Artemis, which is in plain sight of both Paul and the Ephesian audience, the city of Ephesus itself is a nearer frame of reference for what the Ephesians thought the image of God looked like in people than the literary context of Genesis. Part Two suggests that any interpretation of the Ephesian marital code must acknowledge that the believers of Ephesus once viewed themselves as the *imago* of Artemis, and that this influenced how they now thought of themselves as the *imago Dei* in marriage. To acknowledge this is to begin to appreciate Paul's sensitivity to reader context, and how his marital code is empowered by the transforming *imago Christi* in the believer to correct their misunderstanding of who they are now.

1. Note that *imago Dei*, *imago Christi*, image of God, and image-bearer will be used interchangeably.

4.1 PART ONE—PAUL'S CONCEPT OF THE IMAGE OF GOD

What does Paul think the "image" (צלם) of God looks like in people? What literature might have informed his understanding? The scarcity of explicit biblical references to the *imago Dei* in the Hebrew Bible (Gen 1:26–27; 5:1; 9:6), even when supplemented by nonbiblical sources, has yielded multiple views of what it means to be made in God's צלם.[2] Psalms 8:4–6 alludes to the

---

2. From OT and NT sources, scholarship has generally agreed upon four primary ways that humanity has understood the image of God in people. First, people can be substantively the *imago* of God in that they possess a divine capacity for reason that separates people from the rest of creation. Second, the *imago* in people shines when in harmonious relationship with God and each other. Going well beyond the literal male and female relationships Karl Barth moved the notion of relationality forward by saying the connection between the divine plural in Genesis 1:26 and creation of male and female in 1:27 constituted the *imago Dei*. Harmonious relational duality of male and female in physical and spiritual union (Gen 5:1–2) reflects the *imago* of God. Third, people are functionally the image of God as agents of God's rule over creation. Based on ancient Near eastern thought, where kings and queens represent the rule of the gods, the *imago Dei* of Genesis 1:26 designates humans to be functional rulers. Accepted as the "correct view" by the majority of biblical scholarship, this view juxtaposes "in our image" (בצלמנו) with "let them rule" (וירדו) as what defines "in our image" and is supported by the explanation of Sumerian, Babylonian, and Egyptian texts that label rulers as the *imago* of their gods. A fourth, composite view, suggests that one view should not be emphasized over another, that all are constitutive of "likeness and image" (דמות and צלם), that the entire person is the *imago Dei*, and that if the Genesis text does not precisely specify an aspect of human nature that is the *imago* of God, then neither should scholarship. Rather, people are finite representations of God's nature who, when in relationship with him and each other, exercise his rule by carrying out responsibilities he has given them. See also Towner's insightful article, "Clones of God: Genesis 1:26–28 and the Image of God in the Hebrew Bible."

For more on Barth see his *Church Dogmatics 3: The Doctrine of Creation*, part 1: *The Work of Creation*, 194–97. Barth was met with both enthusiasm and skepticism as to if relationality came from Genesis 1:27 or was being read into 1:27 by Barth in light of the emerging social sciences. For more on the relational view, see Westermann, *Genesis 1–11*; and Trible, *God and the Rhetoric of Sexuality*, 16–21, where she takes "male and female" and uses Barth's model as a foundation for examining the feminine aspects of God in the Hebrew Bible. See also Bird's critique of the Barthian position, as well as of Trible and Westermann, in her "Male and Female He Created Them," 129–59, where she argues that sexuality is not connected to the image of God, but dominion is. For a detailed explanation of the royal functional view, see Middleton, *The Liberating Image*. For more on the composite view, see Hoekema, *Created in God's Image*, 73; and Ware, "Male and Female Complementarity and the Image of God," 14–23. For a wide range of views on the *imago Dei*, see Tarus, "Imago Dei in Christian Theology," 18–25, where he identifies the categories of substantial (structuralist), relational, royal functional, performative, Christocentric, anthropomorphites, and composite along with scholars throughout history who have supported these views.

צלם of God though it does not directly mention the phrase "image of God." The Apocryphal writings allude to the image of God in Wisdom of Solomon (c. 50 BCE) 1:13–14 and 2:23–24 and Ecclesiasticus (200–175 BCE) 17:1–12 which mirrors the language of Genesis 1:26–28, both connecting humanity as the "likeness" (דמות) and "image" (צלם), and having "rule" (רדה).³ Second Enoch (c. late first century) describes humankind as made by God's hands in his image with the ability to think and reason (65:2), and whoever insults a person's face insults the Lord's face (44:1–3). It is likely that well-read, well-educated Paul was aware of much of the above, some of which is reflected in his thinking that humans are the "image of God" (εἰκὼν τοῦ Θεοῦ) in 1 Corinthians 11:7, Jesus is the εἰκὼν τοῦ Θεοῦ (2 Cor 4:4; Col 1:15), and the image of God is restored in believing humans (Rom 8:29; 1 Cor 15:49; 2 Cor 3:18; Eph 4:22–24; Phil 3:21; Col 3:10).

Paul's robust understanding of the image of God in people as a new humanity conformed to the *imago Christi* (who is the *imago Dei)* goes well beyond the handful of references in the Hebrew Bible and extrabiblical sources.⁴ In 2 Corinthians 4:4–6 Paul says Christ's glory is the image of God (4:4) and his face shines with the glory of God (4:6). Paul then refers to the creation of humankind (4:6; cf. Gen 1:26–27) which he views through Christ as the second Adam (1 Cor 15:45).⁵ In Colossians 1:15–20 Paul praises Christ's pre-eminence over everything as "the image of the invisible God" (1:15), "firstborn of all creation" (1:15) and "firstborn from the dead" (1:18). In Romans 8:29 Paul presents new humanity as "conformed to the image of his Son," language hearkening back to "Let us make humankind in our image" in Genesis 1:26–27. In 1 Corinthians 15:49 he links the *imago Christi* with the new humanity using an Adam-Christ typology with Jesus' resurrected body as the model for everyone who will bear his image. In 2 Corinthians 3:18 he proclaims that those who behold the glory of Jesus are being transformed into his divine image by a progressive process that will culminate at the eschatological resurrection.⁶ Since the believer has been raised with Christ (Col 3:1) Paul calls the believer to set one's heart on things above (3:2), put to death one's earthly nature (3:5), and rid oneself

---

3. See also, 2 Esdras 8:44 (70–218 CE) for similar language.

4. For a more detailed rendering of the subject matter in this paragraph see Grenz, "Jesus as the Imago Dei," 617–28.

5. For a defense of this connection, see Ridderbos, *Paul*, 70–76.

6. The verse contrasts believers who now see the Lord's glory, although indirectly, and Israelites who in Moses' day could not look upon God's glory (Exod 34:29–35).

of odious relational practices (3:8–9). Instead, he calls the believer to put on the new self with no distinction between gentile or Jew, circumcised or not, barbarian, Scythian, slave or free (3:10–11), to be composed with compassion, kindness, humility, gentleness, patience, forgiveness, love, peace, gratitude (3:12–17). In Ephesians Paul calls the believer to put off the old self (4:22), to be renewed in one's mind (4:23), and put on the new self which is created to be like God (4:24), to speak truthfully, to not harbor anger, to be honest, to use uplifting language, to rid oneself of bitterness, to be compassionate and forgiving (4:25–32). This resonates with Paul's message in 2 Corinthians 5:16–21. Believers in Christ are a "new creation" (καινὴ κτίσις), who have been reconciled to God and charged with helping others do so as well (2:17–18) as Christ's ambassadors for a new humanity (2:20); and in Galatians 6:12–16, where old world values of circumcision and uncircumcision are replaced with "new creation" (καινὴ κτίσις) values.[7] As a modern interpreter of scripture for his day, this full-bodied description of what Paul thinks the *imago Dei* looks like in people is far more developed than the limited references of the Hebrew Bible to which scholarship often turns as the primary source for his thinking about the *imago Dei* and gender.

Intertextual research by modern scholarship agrees that Paul thinks the work of the Holy Spirit in people produces a community of new humans in the *imago Dei* that can transform the world. But intertextual research by modern scholarship disagrees in attempts to define Paul's understanding of the *imago Dei* and gender. Does Paul believe that women are the restored image of God as much as men and can participate in the transformation of humanity just like men, but as women, as equals? Do women have a seat as equal image-bearers at Paul's table? Intertextuality fails to provide consensus in this instance, as illustrated in the following.

4.1.1 Paul, Genesis 1, and the Image of God

Albeit references to God are largely patriarchal in the Hebrew Bible, multiple feminine and maternal allegorical references exist: Genesis 1:26–27;

---

[7]. 2 Corinthians 5:16–20 and Galatians 6:12–16 receive additional attention in ch. 6. Paul is the only NT author to use the term "new creation" although Isaiah 65:17 and 66:22 introduces the concept of "new heavens and new earth" which likely is a frame of reference for Paul and broadens the concept of "new creation" out from the individual believer to the cosmos.

Psalm 123:2–3; 131:2; Deuteronomy 32:18; Isaiah 66:13; 49:15; 42:14. Hence, might his Galatian correspondence lead one to conclude that Paul thought the essence of the *imago* was neither male nor female (3:28)? To understand the mind of Paul regarding the image of God and gender, *Haustafeln* scholarship has relied on the critical examination of key terms such as image (צלם), likeness (דמות), male (זכר), female (נקבה), man (איש), woman (אשה)—unfortunately with conflicting conclusions—in both Hebrew Bible and NT texts. The following section examines selected scriptures to demonstrate that, in this instance, an intertextual approach alone has proven insufficient to provide acceptable results for Ephesus. Also, though one may say they endorse a Pauline message of new humanity in the *imago Dei* as universal to all believers regardless of gender, scholarship continues to debate over who gets to rule even when the dimension of rule alone is woefully insufficient to describe the scope of Paul's understanding of the *imago* in people as that which can transform individuals once divided by race, religion, and gender, into the united household of God.[8]

The scholars of this section are a representative sample that illustrates the scope and chronology of the unresolved Genesis 1 debate across the twentieth and twenty-first centuries. I do not expect to resolve the debate highlighted here, but to point out its breadth, to question its relevance for Paul's gentile audience, and to ask what was in the air regarding the image of God in people at the time of Paul in Ephesus. It seems unlikely that the gentile Ephesian believers were debating the finer nuances of Genesis 1 when discussing the image of God in them, yet intertextual study of Genesis 1 continues to fill the scholarly landscape of the Ephesian marital *Haustafel*.

Can it be unequivocally said that an ancient text such as Genesis 1:26–28, written in a patriarchal society using androcentric language such as "dominion" and "rule," teach that men and women are equally made in the image of God,[9] or would this be lost on the reader of long ago who thought of the *imago Dei* as applying only to men?[10] Does "in the image of

---

8. Space will not afford the opportunity to address all such scriptures, but the samples provided in Genesis 1 are frequently deployed by scholarship are sufficient to illustrate my point.

9. Both complementarian and egalitarian scholars agree that at the very least women and men in equal parts share ontology. From here their scholarly paths diverge, one to ontological equality with functional hierarchy, and the other to ontological and functional equality, each path terminating with conflicting interpretations of the marital *Haustafeln*.

10. It is troublesome that right after Genesis 5:1–2 reiterates the claim of 1:26–27 that both male and female are made in God's image the very next verse (5:3) begins the

God He created him, male and female He created them" (בצלם אלהים ברא
אתו זכר ונקבה ברא אתם) of Genesis 1:27 present a vision of gender equality or gender patriarchy in the mind of Paul which he imparts to the Ephesian church?[11] Scholarly consensus has remained elusive when it comes to how the ancient reader and Paul understood such language. The use of *imago Dei* language in Genesis 1 appears to function as a tool to undermine the hierarchal social constructs of Near Eastern religions and to affirm all people as God's image-bearers, but did this include women too?

Maryanne Cline Horowitz (1979)[12] thinks so, "The 'image of God in man and woman' opens us to transcend both the masculine and feminine metaphors for God which abound in the Bible and to transcend our historical selves and social institutions in recognition of the Holy One."[13] Likewise, Westfall (2016) argues that "In Genesis 1:26–27 and 5:1–2, male and female are explicitly created in the image of God, and in Genesis 2:21–22 woman triply bears the image of God by being formed directly by God, by her extraction from man rather that from the dirt, and by being one flesh with the man in marriage."[14] Lee-Barnewall (2016) agrees, albeit with a more nuanced understanding of "like" in Genesis, where the woman is "like" Adam as his female counterpart made in God's image. However, Lee-Barnewall prefers the terms of "sameness" and "unity" with Adam over that of relational "equality" with Adam.[15]

---

genealogy of Adam and appears to limit the propagation of the image to the male line, not female.

11. Historically, Genesis 1:26–28 came to be understood as universal in intent and thus functioned as a basis for human equality, including gender equality.

12. The publication date by each author's name illustrates that the debate over equality from Genesis 1 has traversed the twentieth and twenty-first centuries.

13. Horowitz, "The Image of God in Man: Is Woman Included?," 175. Her statement is generally accepted by most feminist and modern biblical scholarship.

14. Westfall, *Paul and Gender*, 40.

15. Lee-Barnewall, *Neither Complementarian*, 135, 162. Lee-Barnewall is to be recognized for the great length she goes to in her attempt to avoid a label of egalitarian or complementarian, hence her book title. See also Frame, "Men and Women in the Image of God," 225–32, where he writes, "Women and men equally image God, even in their sexual differences, even in their differences with regard to authority and submission. The reason is that the image of God embraces everything that is human. Both men and women, therefore, resemble God and are called to represent Him throughout the creation, exercising control, authority, and presence in His name. This doctrine is not at all inconsistent with the subordination of women to men in the home and in the church. All human beings are under authority, both divine and human. Their submission to authority, as well as their authority itself, images God" (231–32).

On the other hand, Rosemary Radford Ruether (1995) argues that "Christian feminist anthropology has taken for granted the claims of recent Christian theology that Genesis 1:27 is an egalitarian text in which woman, equally with man, is in the image of God. It is also assumed that Galatians 3:28 parallels this modern individualistic reading of Genesis 1:27."[16] Ruether argues that the notion of woman sharing equally in the *imago Dei* with man originates not from the text itself but from modern feminism. She writes, "The phrase 'male and female created he them' does not refer to the divine image, but rather to the bisexuality which humans share with animals, but not with God."[17] In her view the patriarchal sociology of the writer of Genesis 1 assumed that sovereignty over creation was exercised by the male head of the family. Since Adam was the representative of the collective family of humanity that made him the male head of it. Hence, the idea of the male and female as equal images of God is only so because democratic individualistic assumptions from modern societies are mistakenly read into the text while the patriarchal sociology of the writer is overlooked. Modern egalitarian assumptions are foreign to the social context of the ancient author.

To support her conclusion, Ruether cites the literary examination of Genesis 1 by Phyllis Bird (1981),[18] who argues that sexual difference and reproduction (1:27) are not connected to the idea of the image of God (1:26) but simply pave the way for the blessing of reproduction (1:28).[19] Rather, the idea of dominion is what is connected to the *imago Dei*.[20] Bird argues that the third line (1:27c)—"male and female he created them" (זכר ונקבה ברא אתם)—is to be dissociated from the idea of the divine image in the first two lines (1:27a and b). Instead, she views the statement of "male and female" (זכר ונקבה) as a necessary step to receive the blessing of fertility that follows.[21] According to Bird, 1:27c "male and female" is stating more how humans are like animals (Gen 1:22) than like God. Yet she believes Genesis

---

16. Ruether, "*Imago Dei*, Christian Tradition and Feminist Hermeneutics," 284. See also her reference to Daly, *Beyond God the Father*, 73.

17. Ruether, "*Imago Dei*," 272.

18. Ruether, "*Imago Dei*," 272.

19. See Bird, "Male and Female He Created Them," where she critiques the Barthian position (including Trible's and Westermann's variations on it) 125–59.

20. See also Middleton's *The Liberating Image*, for more on this consensus among scholarship with Bird that dominion is the content of the *imago Dei*, 25–29.

21. Bird, "Male and Female He Created Them," 148–50.

1:26–28 can still be a foundation for egalitarian anthropology since the text recognizes no hierarchy in the created order.²²

In agreement with Bird, Richard Middleton (2005) argues that on syntactical grounds it is unlikely that "male and female" define a social or relational nature of the *imago Dei*. While the creation story of Genesis 2 uses the social categories איש for "husband" and אשה for "wife" (cf. Gen 2:24), in 1:27 זכר for "male" and נקבה for "female" are biological, not social, terms that also identify the animals that Noah lead into the ark (6:19; 7:9) as pairs able to reproduce. Not only does the phrase "male and female" in 1:27 fail to define the content of the *imago* in relational terms but its role is anticipatory, preparing the reader for 1:28, where human beings are blessed with fertility and commissioned by God to reproduce in order that they might fill the earth and subdue it.²³ Bird's conclusion that 1:27c should not be connected to 1:27a and b as *imago Dei* but to 1:28 as fertility for procreation is not without debate.

David Clines (1990), agreeing with Bird, writes that "male and female" has nothing to do with the *imago Dei* per se but refers to the kinds of humans there are just as "male and female" describes the kinds of animals there are:

> When we turn to the third clause of 1.27, male and female he created them (*ōtām*), there is nothing in the present text that has anticipated this element. There has been no suggestion, for example, that it is in the existence of male and female that the image of God will consist, for the conceptualization male-female has not been present when the idea of the image of God has been introduced in v. 26. And, in any case, it seems evident that being in the image of God is to be related, if anything, to humankind's having rule over the animals. Where does the specification male-female arise from, then? It can

---

22. See Bird, "Sexual Differentiation and Divine Image in the Genesis Creation Texts" 19. Here is Bird's full quote, "Genesis 1 invites, and demands, renewed reflection on the meaning of sexual differentiation as a constitutive mark on our humanity and the meaning of God-likeness (image) as the defining attribute of humankind. And it contributes to this constructive task by its silences as well as its assertions. Genesis 1, in contrast to most interpreters, does not link its two fundamental statements about *adam*, just juxtaposes them as parallel holistic assertions, ordering them, however, so that the *imago*-dominion statement is prior and encompassing. Nor does the text establish any hierarchy within the species, either of gender or function; all of its statements pertain to the species as a whole. Thus, it may serve as a foundation for a feminist egalitarian anthropology since it recognizes no hierarchy of gender in the created order." See also, Bird, "Male and Female He Created Them," 133, for similar.

23. See Middleton, *The Liberating Image*, 49–50.

only be by correspondence with the report of the creation of other living creatures that they are created "according to their kind" (1.21 [*bis*], 24 [*bis*], 25 [*ter*]). The "kinds" according to which humanity is created are: male and female. That is the most obvious and pervasive line of discrimination among members of the human race: male and female are the "kinds" of humans there are.[24]

In his view, for one to say that women as well as men are created as the *imago Dei* is to move beyond the horizon of the text. Rather, the most that can be said of Genesis 1 is that it does not exclude the idea of the gender equality.

In disagreement with Bird (and Clines), Paul Niskanen (2009) writes that 1:27c, "male and female He created them" (זכר ונקבה ברא אתם) continues the poetic parallelism of the 1:27a and b.[25] The use of both singular and plural pronouns for "male" (אדם) as "him" (אתו) in 1:27b, and "them" (אתם) in 1:27c "is a deliberate two-pronged development of the assertion in Gen 1:27a that '*ĕlōhîm* created *hā'ādām* in his image.'"[26] The third line does not so much develop the second, but both second and third lines taken together are enlargements of the first. The author has used the double meaning of *hā'ādām* (אדם) as a singular and collective noun by using the singular and plural pronouns of "him" and "them."[27] The creation of "humans" (אדם) as male and female in "male and female he created them" should not be separated from the creation of "male" (אדם) in the image of God. The internal logic of the mini poem in 1:27 reinforces this where the phrase "male and female" structurally corresponds to the image of God. The context of 1:26–28, also supports this where the double blessing of 1:28 "be fruitful and multiply" and "fill the earth and subdue it" follows double development of the image of God in lines 1:27b "in the image of God he created him" and 1:27c "male and female he created them" which parallels human procreativity with God's creativity. Niskanen concludes that Genesis 5:1–3 supports this further where the procreativity of "male and female" in the genealogy of אדם corresponds with the image of God.[28]

To Middleton's biological definition of terms as "male and female" (זכר and נקבה) Niskanen responds that they are as relational if not more

24. Clines, *What Does Eve Do to Help?*, 43–44.
25. Niskanen, "The Poetics of Adam," 422.
26. Niskanen, "The Poetics of Adam," 429.
27. Niskanen, "The Poetics of Adam," 428–29.
28. Niskanen, "The Poetics of Adam," 435–36.

than "husband and wife" (איש and אשה). He argues that if the writer had used "husband and wife" (איש and אשה) in 1:27, instead of "male and female" (זכר and נקבה), perhaps this would provide a stronger connection between the relational duality of gender and the image of God, but to do so comes with a cost of using איש and אשה in a very narrow restrictive sense as "husband and wife" rather than the broader sense of "male and female" since the primary understanding of איש and אשה is "husband and wife." He goes on to say that to define זכר and נקבה as only biological and not relational terms is to separate the blessing of fertility from the notion of God's image. The power to bring forth life by creation and procreation is a remarkable relational parallel between God and humans which the Genesis writer repeats in Genesis 5:1–2.[29]

4.1.2 Conclusions

It is a stretch to think that gentile believers in Ephesus possessed a detailed understanding of the Hebrew Scriptures (or even the LXX) that informed them of the finer nuances of "husband and wife" (איש and אשה), or "male and female" (זכר and נקבה) as relational terms verses biological terms, or perhaps even relational nuances within biological, terms.[30] It is unsafe to say that the Genesis 1 account, so familiar to Hellenistic Jewish believers, was now the Ephesian gentile believers' immediate "go to" when thinking of being the image of a god. The Ephesians may require identity reorientation as the *imago Dei* where, as we shall see, it appears more likely that the fragrance of *imago Artemis* continued to linger "in the air" as a reminder of the image-bearers they once were, and polluting their notion of the image-bearers they now are.[31] Daily they saw her statues, coins, paintings, and sculptures, had danced at her festivals, marched in her processionals, celebrated her birthday, sacrificed and prayed to her, and put money in her bank. She had infiltrated every aspect of their lives for their lives. In view of

---

29. Niskanen, "The Poetics of Adam," 431.

30. This is not to say that Greek-speaking Ephesian Christians had no knowledge of scripture. Albeit not being well versed in Hebrew, they could have had access to the Greek translation of Torah and been aware that the LXX (c. third cent. BCE) uses the "biological terms" ἀρσεν καὶ θῆλυ for "male and female" in Genesis 1:27 and "relational terms" ἀθροπος and γυνή for "husband" (or man) and "wife" in 2:24.

31. Albeit one may not be able to say that all gentile believers in Ephesus were former Artemis image-bearers, inscriptional evidence in addition to Acts 19, supports the notion that Artemis worshippers were a sizeable population of Ephesus.

the fact that Paul had to remind them of their new identity and new unity with the Jews throughout all of Ephesians 2, of the plight they had been in as gentiles being dead in their "trespasses and sins" (2:1–3), of the love, grace, kindness, and mercy that both they and the Jews received from God (2:4–10), and that Christ made them one with the Jews (2:11–18) leads in the direction that Ephesian gentile believers suffered from old identity intrusion that required instruction about new identity formation.

It is noteworthy that, despite Clines' conclusions regarding the author's intention of Genesis 1, gender equality is the ultimate outworking of God's intention for humanity:

> If I am right in my understanding of the text, the text is in conflict with a principle that is not a passing fashion of the modern world but has become a fundamental way of looking at the world. It is not only people who would call themselves feminists who want to insist that women are fully human, in every sense that men are, that the issue of the equality of the sexes is not a joke but something we really have to get right if we want to be serious people. What is more, feminist principles are, for many of us, not some godless philosophy wished upon us by the spirit of the age, but an application of the Christian gospel. The equality of the sexes is a cause explicitly promoted by the Christian teaching that "in Christ . . . there is neither male nor female" (Gal. 3.28). It is not a principle that I for my part can give up, not even for the Bible's sake, if that is what it is, without a loss of personal integrity.[32]

If a patriarchal reading of Genesis 1 is incongruous with the application of the Christian gospel to the modern world, then the same can be said for Paul as a modern interpreter for his day with a robust understanding of the *imago Dei* in people, applying the Christian gospel to his modern world.[33] Even if a patriarchal reading of the Genesis text is correct for the ancient world, this does not make it the correct application of the Christian gospel to Paul's modern world of first-century Ephesus, especially in light of Paul's robust understanding of the *imago Dei* when compared to the scarcity of such texts in the Hebrew Bible. Scholarship's undue emphasis on the dimension of "rule" (רדה) in the *imago Dei* (Gen 1:26) and determination to answer which gender is most like God (Gen 1:27–28), so to decide who gets to rule in the Ephesian household, has overlooked the weight of

32. Clines, *What Does Eve Do to Help*, 46.
33. See 2.1–5.

epigraphical evidence in Ephesus indicating that Paul's interests lie elsewhere. Perhaps the more important question is not what Paul thought the image of God/Christ looked like in people, but what did Paul think the image of God/Christ looked like in people living in the context of the church in Ephesus. This will provide a more satisfying explanation for the purpose of the letter and context for the long marital code.

4.2 PART TWO—THE EPHESIANS' CONCEPT OF THE IMAGE OF GOD

Just who do the Ephesians think they are? Paul thinks that the process of the Holy Spirit substantively transforms believers into God's divine image (1 Cor 15:49; 2 Cor 3:18; Col 3:5; Eph 4:22–24) raising them up with Christ (Col 3:1); influencing their relationships vertically (Col 3:2; Eph 4:24) and horizontally (Col 3:8–9; 12–17; Eph 4:25–32), with no functional distinction in social status (Col 3:10–11; Gal 3:28), as new creatures (2 Cor 5:16–21; Gal 6:12–16). But is this how the Ephesian believers thought as well? To know what the Ephesians understood or misunderstood about what the image of God was supposed to look like in them offers a more satisfying explanation for the purpose of the letter, including Paul's instructions for how a believer is to behave as an image-bearer for God.

To this end, Part Two explores the extent to which the citizenry of Ephesus thought of themselves as image-bearers for Artemis, supported by the riot in Acts 19 as coherent with the picture that emerges concerning Artemis in non-biblical sources. But what exactly does this mean to the Ephesians? How might they define what an image-bearer is to be and, in Paul's opinion, is this sufficient to describe who they are now?[34] Since Artemis and Caesar represented the ruling deities among the many gods and goddesses of Ephesus, Part Two will offer a brief survey of the Artemis and imperial deities, followed by how the Ephesians saw themselves particularly in relation to Artemis, which is then contrasted with how Paul saw them in relation to Christ. Part Two will draw conclusions from the data presented, focusing on the idea that the Ephesians thought of themselves

---

34. Going forward the terms "image-bearer" and "representative" will be used interchangeably to describe how the Ephesians saw themselves in relation to Artemis. A distinction must be made between this and Paul's description of their new identity as God's image-bearers, indwelt and being transformed by his Holy Spirit, for which we have no comparison in inscription or literary evidence.

as image-bearers for Artemis rather than the imperial cult, and that Paul's idea of them as image-bearers for Christ was set against their understanding of being image-bearers of Artemis.

4.2.1 Greek Artemis

Greek Artemis was known as the Olympian goddess of hunting, wild animals, vegetation, chastity, and the protectress of women and girls. Regarding the origins of her name Socrates recounts the thoughts of Plato:

> Let us inquire what thought men had in giving them [the gods] their names. . . . The first men who gave names [to the gods] were no ordinary persons, but high thinkers and great talkers. . . . Artemis appears to get her name from her healthy (*artemes*) and well-ordered nature, and her love of virginity; or perhaps he who named her meant that she is learned in virtue (*aretê*), or possibly, too, that she hates sexual intercourse (*aroton misei*) of man and woman; or he who gave the goddess her name may have given it for any or all of these reasons.[35]

As twin sister to Apollo, Artemis appears to be a female version of Apollo. Like her brother, she is armed with a bow, quiver, and arrows, and can visit death upon humans and animals. Her arrows bring sudden death especially to women.[36] She also at times acts in tandem with her brother.[37] As Apollo could be a destructive god, who was also able to stave off the havoc he could wreak, so Artemis could also lighten the sufferings of people.[38] Like Apollo, she remained unmarried, loved by many and once perhaps in love, but still a virgin who never married.[39] Her priests and priestesses were

---

35. Plato, *Crat.* 400d, LCL 167.62–65; 406a, LCL 167.76–79.

36. Homer, *Il.* VI. 205, LCL 170.288–89; VI.427, LCL 170.304–5; XIX.59, LCL 171.338–39; XXI.483, LCL 171.440–41; *Od.* XI.172, LCL 104.412–13; 324, LCL 104.422–25; XV.478, LCL 105.110–11; XX.61, LCL 105.284–85.

37. Homer, *Od.* XV.410, LCL 105.106–7; *Il.* XXIV.606, LCL 171.608–9.

38. See Callimachus, *Hymn to Artemis III*, 129, LCL 129.246–47, where the man, whom she looked graciously, prospered in his fields and flocks and died in old age.

39. Sophocles, *Electra* 1240, LCL 20.288–89. The notion of the never married Artemis is significant to my ch. 6 discussion. Also there exist multiple versions of her relationship with Orion the hunter. In one version she loves him, but jealous Apollo tricks her into killing Orion, while in another version Artemis kills Orion for raping her handmaiden named Oupis. Hence although love is possible for Artemis, she remains an unmarried virgin.

bound by vows of chastity with severe punishment for their violation.[40] Upon reaching maturity a girl eventually wed, passing from the protection of Artemis to the goddesses of womanhood and marriage, Aphrodite and Hera. Prior to the wedding ceremony, maidens sacrificed to Artemis in thanks for the protection the goddess offered them through childhood;[41] and virgins about to have sex dedicated their virginal undergarments to her.[42] Beyond this, it is worth noting that only maidens were permitted in the Artemision temple until marriage. Once married, matrons appear to be no longer welcome within its walls.[43]

The Artemis cult was often merged with the cults of other indigenous local goddesses.[44] The Romans identified their goddess Diana with the Greek Artemis and transferred to Diana all the peculiar features of the Greek Artemis. New elements and attributes were added in various places to the ancient local myths and the worship of one deity would be identified with that of another. Thus, the myths of the two are mixed up into one, or those of the one mapped onto the other. Such too is the case of Ephesian Artemis.

---

40. Pausanias, *Desc. Gr.* VII.19.1, LCL 272.278–79; VIII.13.1; LCL 272.408–11.

41. See Aeschylus, *Suppl.* 1030, LCL 145.422–25, (c. fifth cent. BCE): "May pure Artemis look upon this band [of unwed maidens] in compassion, and may marriage never come through Kythereia's [Aphrodite] compulsion."

42. *Suda* 3.302.859. Suidas s.v. Lysizonos gune, *Byzantine Greek Lexicon* (c. tenth cent. CE), trans. Suda online, "Lysizonos gune: She who has drawn near to a man. For virgins about to have sex dedicated their virginal lingerie to Artemis." See also King, "Bound to Bleed," 109–27; and Strelan, *Paul, Artemis, and the Jews,* 48, where he comments that Artemis is sometimes referred to as Lysizonos, the releaser of the girdle.

43. For her sanctuary being closed to married women see Achilles Tatius, *Leuc. Clit.* 7.13.3, LCL 45.380–81. See also Strelan, *Paul, Artemis, and the Jews,* 72–73, for his discussion on Artemidorus, *Onir.* 4.4 where a prostitute dreams that she enters the temple, is set free and gives up her profession; and 2.12 where a married woman has a dream that she enters the temple, eats there, and dies. The generally accepted notion that married women were no longer welcome in the temple is not without question. See Kirbihler, "Les prêtresses d'Artémis à Éphèse," 21–79, where he suggests although it may appear that the Artemision was closed to matrons at the end of the first century, widows and even celibate matrons at times served as priestesses and that other non-priestess functions could be open to wives.

44. This is largely accepted among scholarship as a common Hellenistic syncretistic practice. See Strabo, *Geogr.* 13.1.13, LCL 223.28–29; 51, LCL 223.102–3; 65, LCL 223.128–29; 13.4.5, LCL 223.172–73; Pausanias, *Desc. Gr.* 6.22.1, LCL 272.136–37 and 7.6.6, LCL 272.202–3 for examples.

4.2.2 Ephesian Artemis

With her many breasts Artemis of Ephesus is often thought of as a fertility goddess or a goddess of nourishment and nurturing.[45] It has been argued that this view of Artemis derives from Christian teachings against Artemis by Minucius Felix, *Octavius* 22.5 (c. 197 CE), which identifies the egg-shaped objects as fertility symbols. Richard Oster believes this view is just part of his Christian polemic against Artemis and not in the primary sources.[46] Lynn LiDonnici argues that the objects are breasts, but that they demonstrate that Artemis was a symbolic wife, protector, and nursing mother to Ephesus rather than a fertility goddess.[47] Other suggestions have been bull testicles, eggs, nuts, or gourds, but these do not conjure up the same notions of nurturing as breasts, which coheres with Paul's description

---

45. For example, Finegan, *The Archaelogy of the New Testament*, 156, writes, "Although the Greek Artemis was primarily a huntress, the Ephesian Artemis was primarily a deity of fertility and in this capacity, her symbol was the egg." For more on this discussion see Trebilco, *Early Christians*, 22–23.

46. See, Oster, "Ephesus was a Religious Center under the Principate," 1725–26; see also Baugh, "Cult Prostitution in New Testament Ephesus," 452–53; and Trebilco, *Early Christians*, 23, fn. 78 for more.

47. See LiDonnici, "The Images of Artemis Ephesia," 391–411. Scholarship has yet to reach consensus about what these breast-like objects are, some saying the weight of evidence makes it unlikely that they are breasts and that, given the silence of primary sources linking the objects with fertility, a true connection with fertility is doubtful. Per my discussion above, the notion that they are indeed breasts makes the most sense. For a review of the suggestions of what the objects are see Trell; "The Temple of Artemis at Ephesos," 87–88; Mussies, "Pagans, Jews, and Christians at Ephesos," 182–85. See also Glahn's detailed discussion in *Nobody's Mother*, 104–10, where she sets out to eliminate egg shaped breasts as an option in favor of tear-drop shaped jewelry with magical properties. Her elimination of breasts as an option certainly resonates with her book title, *Nobody's Mother*, where she argues that Artemis is neither a fertility goddess nor nurturing (105–6, 113, 116). Yet one must ask if multiple breasts are the litmus test to qualify as a nurturing goddess, or if fertility and giving birth is prerequisite for nurturing? Several deities of the Greek pantheon (Athena, Demeter, Persephone, Hera, Aphrodite) qualify as *kourotrophos* (child nurturer) yet do not bear multiple breasts. One might also argue that Apollo nurtured his children (Asclepius, Anius, Lamus) and nurtured others that were not his (Chiron and Carnus), albeit without breasts. For more examples of nurturing deities, see Price, *Kourotrophos: Cults and Representations of the Greek Nursing Deities*, 1–13. Multibreasted or not, Artemis takes on the role of *kourotrophos* for the young sweethearts Anthia and Habrocomes who, upon being rescued by the goddess through shipwrecks, pirate attacks and slavery, offer sacrifices to her (see 5.1.2). Similarly, Artemis offers the young maiden, Leucippe, personal protection and the promise of marriage to her sweetheart Clitophon; see Achilles Tatius, *Leuc. Clit.*, 4.1.4, trans. Gaslee, 191. Her virginity should not exclude her from that of being *kourotrophos*.

of Christ nurturing the Church (Eph 5:25–30). Apart from Oster's speculation, the lack of primary sources makes for an unresolved discussion, yet the pairing of Artemis as the virgin daughter of Leto with notions of fertility is an odd combination. Likely, she was an ancient Asiatic divinity that the Greeks found well established in Ionia, and to whom they applied the name of Artemis due, in their thinking, to her similarity to their Greek Artemis. Thus, features of the Greek Artemis were transferred to her, such as being called a daughter of Leto, who gave birth to Artemis and her twin Apollo in the region of Ephesus.[48] Her priests were eunuchs, and that her image in the Artemision represented her with *many* breasts, it is likely she became a synthesized version to include the influence of the Anatolian mother goddess, Cybele, or Mesopotamian Ishtar, or Canaanite/Phoenician Astarte.[49]

Additional syncretistic influence can be observed in that before the Roman period, and then in the second century, Artemis of Ephesus appears on coins as the huntress with stags. The Salutaris Inscription (104 CE) of Ephesus also speaks of her as accompanied by two stags.[50] By this time Ephesus was in regular contact with non-Anatolian influences so while the many-breasted Artemis resided in the Artemision temple, her identity as the virgin huntress remains part of her story, supporting the notion of

48. Specifically, Ephesian Artemis would have been born on the island of Ortygia while Greek/Roman Artemis/Diana would have been born on the island of Delos. The celebration of the Mysteries of Artemis (fourth cent. BCE–mid third cent. CE) at the least displays her 500 yearlong venerations, albeit she was worshipped far longer than this. According to tradition, the *curetes* (young, divine warriors) helped Leto at the birth of Artemis and Apollo. The pregnant Leto was in search of a safe place to hide from the jealous eye of Hera (wife and sister of Zeus) where she could give birth to these children of Zeus. She found refuge in the floating island of Ortygia, and was protected from Hera by the *curetes*, making loud noise with their weapons to distract from the birth of the twins. For more see *The Mysteries of Artemis*, Roger's study dedicated to her mysteries.

49. Oster, "Ephesus was a Religious Center under the Principate," 1728, notes that some scholars opt for an Anatolian view of Artemis during the Roman period, with Artemis having a strong connection to the mother goddess. Yet, by this time Ephesus had been in regular contact with non-Anatolian influences for a long time so the process of Hellenization had affected the cult of the goddess. Noteworthy also is that the Mesopotamian Ishtar wore necklaces adorned with egg-shaped beads, perhaps the inspiration for the egg-shaped breasts of Ephesian Artemis, see Hill, "Ancient Art and Artemis," 93–94.

50. Deer, buck. For more on the coins, see Immendörfer, *Ephesians and Artemis*, 143; and Karwiese, "Ephesos: C Numismatischer Teil," col. 316, 337; for the Salutaris inscription see IEPH 27.157–59. In *Xenophon of Ephesus* 1.2.4 the horses and dogs were part of Artemis' festival procession which included hunting weapons. On the probable change in the form of the Artemis statue in the mid-second century BCE see Brenk, "Artemis of Ephesos," 157–71.

both a nurturing yet independent virgin goddess with no need of a man's protection. Artemis and her beloved city lived in a reciprocal nurturing relationship which made both parties glorious. The beloved goddess possessed multiple titles of veneration and was honored at multiple festivals. She was the hero of novels and poems who could manifest herself in human form.[51] She answered prayers.[52] She helped women in childbirth. She was admired by both men and women. Caring Artemis helped maidens transition to womanhood. Her statues were everywhere, as was coinage bearing her image.[53] Artemis indeed has much to offer her residents albeit the relationship is a transactional one of reciprocity, not a relationship of self-sacrifice. Without nurturing, the goddess will not nurture in return, which is the opposite of Paul's gospel, where the king of the universe is a self-sacrificing Savior who wants his image-bearers to do the same.

4.2.3 Caesar and Artemis

The cult of Artemis had existed for thousands of years, but on day one of 42 BCE the unimaginable happened. The Roman State declared that the murdered Julius Caesar had survived assassination and now lived on as a god, declaring him to be *Divus Iulius*. Octavian, his grand-nephew and heir, could now enhance his claim as the young Caesar by designating himself *Divi filius*, "Son of the Divine."[54] In 31 BCE, Octavian, defeated Mark Antony at Actium and acceded to the throne as emperor. In 29 BCE the Roman Senate dedicated a temple to honor Octavian, and Octavian granted permission to Ephesus and Nicaea to build temples to his granduncle.[55] Two years later (27 BCE) the Senate declared Emperor Octavian "Augustus," continuing the notion of "divine, exalted, sacred, magnificent."[56] This

---

51. See IEPH 24.B (c. 162–164 CE) which speaks of shrines, sanctuaries, temples, and alters being established everywhere because of "the visible manifestations being effected by her." Noteworthy also is that Emperor Caracalla (r. 211–217 CE) declines Ephesus the right to be *neokoros* for the imperial cult but instead grants it for the goddess who is "most powerful in her appearances" (IEPH 212).

52. IEPH 940, 943, 957, 960.

53. See 4.2.3.

54. See Syme, *The Roman Revolution*, 202.

55. See *Dio Cassius* 51.20.6–7, LCL 83.56–57.

56. Suetonius, *Aug.* 7.2, LCL 31.158–59; Greek Σεβαστός meaning "majestic" or "venerable." Both words, Augustus and Σεβαστός understood as "divine, exalted, sacred, magnificent," had the potential to conjure up notions of what it means for a human to

began the provincial imperial cult in Asia Minor. Upon Octavian's death, it became the official title of his successor, and continued to be used by subsequent emperors.[57] The feminine form "Augusta" was then used for Roman empresses and other female imperial family members.[58] An inscription from the island of Cos, off the western coast of Asia Minor (5/4 BCE), praised Augustus' generosity, "Emperor Caesar, son of god, god Augustus (Θεοῦ υἱὸς Θεὸς Σεβαστός) has by his benefactions to all people outstripped even the Olympian gods" (*I. Olympia* 53.2–3).[59]

Temples, altars, and monuments spread throughout the empire to honor Augustus. From 14–19 CE, statues of Augustus, Julia Augusta, Tiberius, Germanicus, and Drusus adorned the imperial sanctuary at Apollonia. In 23 CE Tiberius granted permission to Asia for a second provincial imperial cult, this one being for Tiberius, his mother Livia who was also the widow of Augustus, and the Senate.[60] Competition was fierce between the cities of the Asian province with Smyrna ultimately being selected by the Roman Senate in 26 CE.[61] Ephesus was rejected because it already had the renowned cult of Artemis. Miletus was similarly rejected since it was the city of Apollo. By the mid-80s CE Ephesus was selected for a third provincial imperial cult, and the imperial temple in Ephesus was dedicated 89/90 CE. This third cult was necessary to show allegiance to the new ruling line of the Sebastoi including Flavian emperors Vespasian, Titus, and Domitian, with the possible inclusion of Domitia, the first two temples having been

---

be godlike in the mind of the everyday gentile. One might wish to argue that the average gentile in no way considered oneself to be on the level of a Caesar, or aspired to be divine, but this misses the point of seeds being sown in the mind of the worshipper, where the average gentile might begin to believe in the potential to be much more than one's present state, a point which Paul capitalizes on by identifying the gentile believer as though once dead in trespasses and sins, has been made alive in Christ and seated in the heavenlies (Eph 2:5–6).

57. This is not to say that every Roman emperor was deified, but enough Roman emperors were deified in and around the first century (Julius, Augustus, Claudius, Vespasian, Titus) to influence one's thinking that humans had the potential to become godlike. For a detailed accounting of the deification of the Caesars see "A Narrative of the Imperial Cult," 179–216; Chalupa, "How Did Roman Emperors Become Gods?," 201–7; Price, "From Noble Funerals to Divine Cult," 56–105.

58. The masculine and feminine forms originated during the Roman Republic in connection with things considered divine in traditional Roman religion.

59. Dittenberger and Purgold, *Die Inschriften von Olympia*, 5.110–11.

60. Tacitus, *Ann.* 4.15, LCL.312.28–29; 37, LCL 312.64–65.

61. Tacitus, *Ann.* 4.55–56, LCL 312.98–99.

for the Julio/Claudian line. During the reign of Domitian (81–96 CE), son of Vespasian and younger brother to Titus, two Ephesian coins were minted where the Ephesians identify themselves twice ΝΕΩΚΟΡΩΝ referring to their esteemed status as temple warden for both the Artemis and imperial cults.[62]

Keeping with what was now tradition, within a year of his elevation to emperor, Claudius (r. 41–54 CE) venerated his grandmother, Livia Drusilla (Julia Augusta),[63] and issued a new coin with his grandparents, Divus Augustus on the obverse and Diva Augusta on the reverse.[64] In Acts 19 a riot occurs 55/56 CE because Artemis is purportedly disrespected by Paul and his team. Close to time of the riot, during the reign of Claudius, he mints three coins in Ephesus: one to celebrate his marriage to Agrippina in 49 CE, which shows Claudius on the obverse and Agrippina on the reverse (50–51 CE); and a second, which shows Claudius and Agrippina on the obverse and Diana/Artemis on the reverse; and a third with Claudius on the obverse and on the reverse Diana/Artemis and her temple. Minting Roman coinage in a city other than Rome was uncommon, but Claudius is a clever emperor. One cannot say that Claudius mints coins in Ephesus with his image on one side and Artemis on the other in response to the Acts 19 riot, but one can say that Claudius had his finger on the pulse of the city and knew that money minted in Ephesus with his image and that of the goddess would win Ephesian "hearts and minds" to his rulership, remind them with every monetary transaction that Claudius was pro-Artemis, and deftly tie his imperial cult to hers, perhaps with the hope of turning the city of Artemis into the city of Artemis and Caesar.

The emperor cult continued to be mingled with the worship of indigenous gods. At Ephesus the imperial images were kept in the porch of the Artemision.[65] For important occasions the busts of the imperial family and the images of Artemis were all carried from the Artemision to the theatre and placed on special bases.[66] Yet, in contrast to this sense of shared rever-

---

62. See Keil, "Die erste Kaiserneokorie von Ephesos," 115–20.

63. Suetonius, *Claud.* 11.2, LCL 38.20–21; Tacitus, *Ann.* 1.8, LCL 249.256–59. See Ramsay, "Early History of Province Galatia," 209–26.

64. Hekster, *Emperors and Ancestors*, 127, fn. 39.

65. See Price, *Rituals and Power*, 189; also, Das, "A Narrative of the Imperial Cult in Asia Minor," 182.

66. Important occasions could be the meeting of the assembly, the new moon sacrifice, the festivals of Sebasta, the Soteria, or the quadrennial Great Ephesia. See Price, *Rituals and Power*, 104, 188–89; Fishwick, "The Imperial Cult in the Latin West," 492; cf. Acts 19:23–40.

ence, the Augustan imperial temple was prominently constructed as the centerpiece of the upper square of the city rather than in the lower plain by the Artemision.[67] Despite their best efforts to continue the promotion of the emperor cult with prominent temples and synthesis with Greek, Roman, and local gods, it had a short shelf life, growing for roughly ninety years then slowing dramatically with only four imperial family members venerated after mid-first century CE.[68] In return for veneration by its cities, the imperial cult could offer beautiful construction, money, protection, and esteem to its cities. Caesar's deification might even sow seeds in the worshipper's mind that a human could become godlike, but try as they may the imperial cult could never offer the level of intimacy and care to the citizens of Ephesus as that of Artemis.[69] And intimacy translated into longevity.[70] Also, a message of intimacy, the imperial cult was no match for Paul's gospel of loving self-sacrifice, manifest in the tender care of Christ for his church and the husband for his wife in united identity. Intimacy was a notion Paul could work with in bridging the gap between who the Ephesians thought they were as image-bearers for Christ and who Paul wanted them to be.

67. See Friesen, *Twice Neokoros*, 59–75.

68. However, temple construction continued into the third century. See Price, *Rituals and Power*, 57–58.

69. It is worth pointing out that the distance between the divine and the human in the Roman notion of what it meant to be godlike was infinitely smaller than modern notions of the all-knowing, all-wise God of Christian theism. Rather, the absolute power of the emperor over his kingdom, equivalent to that of any of the gods, informed the first-century worshipper what it meant to be godlike. The emperor, at the pinnacle of political greatness and deified by the Roman Senate, stands in stark contrast to the doctrine of the deity of the crucified Jesus as the pinnacle of purity and divine love. Suggesting that belief in the divinity of Jesus is due to the influence of the imperial cult is highly unlikely considering that hostility to emperor worship emanated especially from the Jews and Christians. But it is likely that acceptance of Jesus as divine by converts from pagan religion was aided by familiarity with emperor worship along with the hope that the believer, transformed by the Holy Spirit living in them, might also possess a godlike nature destined to live on after one's physical death. For more see Burton, "The Worship of the Roman Emperors," 80–91. See also the PhD thesis of Callahan, "Living Off the Dead."

70. See Arnold, where he writes, "The coins of the city show that the Ephesians did boast of having a temple *neokorate*, but the temple they boasted in was that of Artemis. The imperial cult was essentially political and thus differed from the cult of Artemis and the other religions of the city. It served more to enhance the status of cities and its more influential citizens. There is no evidence that people came to these cults seeking oracular advice or an answer to prayer, to take a vow, to seek a blessing on their crops or animals, or to gain protection from curses or evil spirits" (*Ephesians*, 50). See also Mellor, ΘΕΑ ΡΩΜΗ, 16; and Steven, "The Cult of the Roman Emperors in Ephesus," 231.

4.2.4 Image Bearers for Artemis

The Ephesian citizens understood themselves to the embodiment of Artemis to the watching world. More than just a special relationship with the goddess, I have identified them as image-bearers of her successful rule over the city, and that Paul uses their shared identity with the goddess in writing the Ephesian letter. Inscriptional evidence is lacking that explicitly calls the Ephesians image-bearers but their role as such is implied in the following.

The city of Ephesus used the term "Temple Warden" (νεωκόρος) to describe her divine appointment by Artemis as keeper and protector of the goddess in "the city of Artemis" (τῆς πόλεως Ἀρτέμιδι)[71] and recipient of her many blessings.[72] The Ephesians enjoyed a 500+ year history in the sacred community of the goddess where the city was glorious because she blessed them (IEPH 24B.9–11) and she was glorious because they nurtured her (IEPH 24B.22–23), both parties sharing in the glory of the other. IEPH 24B.21–23 identifies Ephesus, as the "nurturer" (τροφός) of Artemis who is responsible for her well-being, "particularly in our city, the nurturer of its own Ephesian goddess" (διαφερόντως ἐν τῇ ἡμετέρᾳ πόλει τῇ τροφῷ τῆς ἰδίας θεοῦ τῆς Ἐφεσίας).[73] The final sentence of the inscription repeats thought of 24B.9–11 that by worshipping the goddess, the city remains glorified and blessed echoes its importance by extending the holy days of Artemis out to a full month (IEPH 24B.20–34).[74] They believed that their essential

---

71. IEPH 1398.3, 14. Ephesus as "Neokoros" is found on coins minted during Nero's reign (54–68 CE), in Acts 19:35; and Domitian's reign (81–96 CE), where Ephesus is even referred to as "twice Neokoros," being temple warden both of Artemis and the imperial cult of the Sebastoi. Bearing the title of "twice Neokoros" of two of the major religious cults of the Roman empire. Even with the title "twice Neokoros" Ephesus was still first and foremost "Temple Warden" for Artemis.

72. IEPH 24B.22.

73. See ch. 3, fns. 63–64 for the inscriptions.

74. See IEPH 24B.28 setting aside the month, "ὅλον τὸν Ἀτεμισιῶνα εἶναι ἱερὸν πάσας." Here is the translation of IEPH 24B by Oster, "It was decreed by the council and people of the patriotic city of the Ephesians, first and greatest metropolis of Asia, temple-warden of the Augusti two times, concerning the things about which the patriotic. Laberius Amoenus, secretary of the people, made the motion. The patriotic strategoi of the city voted upon it. 'Since the goddess Artemis, leader of our city, is honored not only in her own homeland, which she has made the most illustrious of all cities through her own divine nature, but also among Greeks and also barbarians, the result is that everywhere her shrines and sanctuaries have been established, and temples have been founded for her and altars dedicated to her because of the visible manifestations effected by her. And this is the greatest proof of the reverence surrounding her, the month named after her, called

wellbeing was directly tied to revering the goddess. They even made it a point to inscribe that Roman Proconsul of Asia, Pompillius Carus Pedo had not been honoring the festivals, the implication being that he put them all at risk (IEPH 24A.1–20).[75]

The goddess is identified as "Artemis of the Ephesians" (Acts 19:28, 34), and "the Ephesian Goddess" (τῇ Ἐφεσίᾳ θεῷ),[76] not just "Artemis." She is the personification of the city. She is called the founder of the city (ἡ ἀρχηγέτις),[77] the guiding influence of the city (προκαθηυεμών),[78] and the guardian of the city (ἡ προεστῶσα τῆς πόλεως).[79] Her name appears on official documents and coins. Buildings were dedicated to her.[80] Ephesus was passed over in 23 BCE for an imperial temple because the Roman Senate discerned that Ephesian worship was so focused on Artemis that other cities in Asia Minor with a less devout populace toward one deity were better

---

Artemision among us, and Artemisios among the Macedonians and among the other Greek nations, and among the cities within their borders. During this month festivals and sacrifices are performed, particularly in our city, the nurturer of its own Ephesian goddess. The Ephesian people regard it as appropriate that the entire month named after the divine name be sacred and dedicated to the goddess, and through this decree approved that the religious ritual for her be stipulated. Therefore, it is decreed that the entire month Artemision be sacred for all its days, and that on the same (days) of the month, and throughout the year, feasts and the festival and the sacrifices of the Artemisia are to be conducted, inasmuch as the entire month is dedicated to the goddess. For in this way, with the improvement of the honoring of the goddess, our city will remain more illustrious and more blessed for all time." For the Greek inscription accompanied by translation of IEPH 24B see Oster, "Holy Days in Honor of Artemis," 74–76.

75. Here is the translation of IEPH 24A by Oster, "The proconsul Gaius Popillius Caro states: 'I learned from the decree which was sent to me by the most illustrious council of the Ephesians that the honorable proconsuls before me regarded the days of the festival of the Artemisia as holy and have made this clear by edict. That is why I considered it necessary, since I also have regard for the reverence of the goddess and for the honor of the most illustrious city of the Ephesians, to make it known by decree that these days shall be holy, and the festal holidays will be observed on those days.' (This edict was promulgated) while Titus Aelius Marcianus Priscus, son of Aelius Priscus, a man very well thought of and worthy of all honor and acceptance, was leader of the festival and president of the athletic games." For the Greek inscription accompanied by translation of IEPH 24A see Oster, "Holy Days in Honor of Artemis," 74–76.

76. IEPH 678.12; 3077.9; 3078.11; cf. 24B.22.

77. IEPH 27.20

78. IEPH 26.8; Pausanias, *Desc. Gr.* 10.38.6, LCL 297.600–601.

79. IEPH 24B.8

80. IEPH 4.24

candidates.[81] The names of new citizens were inscribed on the walls of the Artemision temple.[82] Inscriptions in the temple demonstrate that citizenship was a sacred act presided over by the priests (ἐσσῆναι) and consisted of a process of banquets, sacrifices, and conferral of citizenship[83] with the names of new citizens recorded on three large blocks of stone in the Artemision.[84] To be a citizen of Ephesus was to have your name in the temple of the goddess. You belonged to and represented both, such was the notion of image-bearer in the mind of the Ephesian.[85] Apollonius of Tyana (c. 3 BCE–c. 97 CE) reinforces this notion of belonging to and representing the goddess where he writes, "To the Ephesians in Artemis" (Ἐπεσίων τοῖς ἐν Ἀρτέμιδος), which Paul appears to confront with the phrase "in Christ" (ἐν Χριστῷ) or "in him" (ἐν αὐτῷ) or "in whom" (ἐν ᾧ) as image-bearers for Christ.[86]

Artemis is born just outside Ephesus and is the hometown goddess. The wealthy Salutaris Foundation constantly reminded Ephesians "to look to the birth of the goddess Artemis at Ephesos, for a theological sense of how Ephesian social and historical identity was grounded in a sacred reality, which was impervious to all humanly wrought challenges."[87] On procession day, which happened at least every two weeks, thirty-one statues and images were paraded from the temple of Artemis to outside the city wall,

81. Tacitus, *Ann.* 4.55, LCL 312.96–99; Cassius Dio, *Rom. Hist.* 59.28.1, LCL 175.350–53.

82. For example, IEPH 1405.12; 1408.5, 15; 1440.607; 1441.8–9.

83. IEPH 2005; see also where Strelan, *Paul, Artemis, and the Jews*, 31, cites SEG (1989) 1165, 1167.

84. See IEPH 1418–38 for citizenship bestowals, and IEPH 1447–76, 2001–16 for citizenship decrees. It is noteworthy that Paul's language in Ephesians being "excluded from citizenship" (2:12) and "fellow citizens" (2:19) could be an allusion to this practice, albeit the epistle's phrase is Jewish in origin.

85. This is not to say that all Ephesians were citizens of Ephesus. Citizenship within the Roman empire as well as within individual cities such as Ephesus was a prized possession that eluded many (cf. Acts 2:22–29). For those excluded from citizenship in the city of the goddess, this makes the Ephesian believers' citizenship in Christ's universal kingdom all the more valuable (cf. Eph 2:12, 19). At the very least, the non-citizenry of Ephesus was aware of the value and privilege placed on citizenship, hence the implication of their superior value as citizens of Christ's kingdom.

86. See, Apollonius of Tyana, *Let.* 65, LCL 458.60–61 compared with Ephesians 1:1, 4, 7, 9, 10, 11, 12, 13, 20; 2:7, 10, 13, 15, 21; 3:6, 11, 12, 21; 4:21, 32. See 4.2.6 for more on old identity compared with new.

87. Rogers, *The Sacred Identity of Ephesos*, 69; see also pages 112–15; 145–47. In his book Rogers gives a detailed accounting of the Salutaris Foundation. The Salutaris Inscription is dated 104 CE, but it is likely that the processional existed before this time.

then south where the procession was joined by the ephebes,[88] then on to the theatre, to the Koressos Gate and back to the Artemision. The statues were to be carried for everyone to see and the procession route was designed to remind everyone of the shared history of Ephesus and Artemis.[89] Through the twice monthly performance of such rituals the Ephesians were consistently reminded of their shared sacred identity with the goddess.[90]

Artemis with her temple is the guardian of legitimate marriage who oversees the birth of the next generation and protection of the young. Maidens transitioning to womanhood, marriage, and ultimately motherhood would run to the temple, cling to the image of Artemis only to be pulled away from the statue by their future husbands, symbolic of Artemis' involvement in the transitions of a female's life from maiden, to married, to mother.[91] Items purchased at the market were paid with coinage bearing the images of Artemis and her temple.[92] New citizens are inducted by the priests and their names inscribed on the walls of the temple. Youth and adults march in parades for the goddess. She was central to the identity of the city and the individual. Our Western notions of separating our private life from public religion was not an alternative for the Ephesian. The presence of an inscription that precisely says "image-bearer" for the Ephesian citizen is not required, considering the abundance of inscriptional testimony that implies this is something everyone already knew.

4.2.5 Paul Versus the Hometown Goddess

More than a just a synthesized Greek, Roman, Ionian goddess, Ephesian Artemis was "our hometown goddess." IEPH 24B.9 reveals that the Ephesians heralded their city as the "hometown" (πατρίς) of Artemis (οὐ μόνον ἐν τῇ ἑαυτῆς πατρίδι τειμᾶται).[93] IEPH 2026.16 calls her the local goddess (ἡ

---

88. Young man of eighteen to twenty years, in military training.

89. IEPH 27.91. For a detailed description of the processional see Rogers, *Sacred Identity*, 84–85 for the types of statues and 85–107 for the route.

90. See Rogers, *Sacred Identity*, for a detailed discussion of the various rituals.

91. For more see Strelan, *Paul, Artemis, and the Jews*, 48–50; and LiDonnici, "Images of Artemis," 409.

92. In addition to shared coinage with Caesar, Artemis has a robust history of coinage of her own. See Head, *On the Chronological Sequence of the Coins of Ephesus*.

93. The term πατρίς occurs eight times in the NT, all in the Gospels, with the meaning "hometown" or "fatherland."

πάτριος ἡμῖν Θεὸς Ἄρτεμις).[94] Artemis, the city of Ephesus, and the people of Ephesus were "identified as a sacred community" all wrapped-up together with the image which fell from heaven.[95] In hometown vernacular Artemis is one of us and we are one with her. Their sacred identity was fastidiously maintained by civic rituals and religious processionals, especially the Mysteries of Artemis birthday celebration.[96] Beyond this, the goddess could be understood as the "wife" of the city of Ephesus, protector of the city as the matron is the protector of the home, nourisher of the city as the mother nourishes her children.[97] Some might argue that the Acts 19 riot is just about money, tourism, and trade, but this overlooks notions of identity, community, the future of our hometown, our hometown goddess, and perhaps the loss of all of this. Concern for such notions, pride in one's city, pride in one's goddess, and our identity intertwined with her begins to define what makes one an image-bearer in the mind of the Ephesian, and why the riot of Acts 19 is so important to the Ephesian letter.

The Acts 19 account of Artemis and Ephesus is in line with external sources. A close reading reveals that the Ephesian citizens thought of themselves as one with the goddess and that any offence against her was an offence against them all. In 19:21–41 Luke carefully marks out Artemis' religious, political, and economic significance for her city, for her people, and just how perilous it is to disparage the *imago* of the goddess that has "fallen from heaven" (Acts 19:35).[98] Inscriptional verification for this is lacking,

---

94. See also IEPH 669.

95. See Rogers, *Sacred Identity*, 146.

96. Regarding the processions, Rogers, *Sacred Identity*, concludes that "Artemis with her torch lit the way to the Ephesians' ultimate sense of identity," 115.

97. For more see LiDonnici, "Images of Artemis." LiDonnici writes, "Nearly all of the roles of Artemis of Ephesus suggest that the goddess could be understood as the legitimate wife of the city of Ephesus itself: protectress and nourisher; 'trusty warden' not only of the things in people's houses, but also of the financial resources on deposit at the Artemision; guardian of legitimate marriage; overseer of the birth of the next generation, κουροτρόφος. These are categories of power, intimately connected with the stability and continuation of the family, the city, the empire, and, conceptually, the universe. They are not, however, primarily erotic categories, and the figure of Artemis Ephesia in her role as city goddess was not eroticized. This feature may, in fact, be connected with her symbolic role as the legitimate wife, a figure to be respected and generally not represented in art in erotic context," 409.

98. "Luke" as the implied author, with the understanding that the authorship of Acts is debated.

however, Euripides provides a literary parallel where, in his play *Iphigenia Among the Taurians,* he writes the image of the Taurian Artemis as fallen from heaven.[99] The riot in 19:28–41 is a lesson that a challenge to her image is a challenge to all of us, their identity so inextricably tied up in hers that it is difficult for them to imagine themselves as separate from her.[100]

After hearing from silversmith Demetrius that Paul has turned many away from her (19:26–27), for two hours (19:28) the enraged crowd cries out "Great is Artemis of the Ephesians" (Μεγάλη ἡ Ἄρτεμις Ἐφεσίων). As members of the city that was divinely appointed "keeper and protector" (νεωκόρος) of the cult of the goddess her citizens shared a responsibility to represent her glory to the rest of the world. It is clear from the phrase Μεγάλη ἡ Ἄρτεμις Ἐφεσίων that she is theirs and they are hers. It's more than about money for Demetrius and the guild of silversmiths when he acknowledges his concern that "our trade will lose its good name." He is worried the Artemision "will be discredited" and Artemis "who is worshipped throughout Asia and the world, will be robbed of her divine majesty" (19:27). His words stand in stark contrast to Paul gaining converts among "all the residents of Asia" (19:10) coupled with "the word of the Lord grew and prevailed" (19:20) and Paul's message that "gods made with hands are not gods" (19:26).[101] Demetrius claims responsibility to protect her divine majesty as one of her image-bearers on earth who fears for her future. Hence, the city clerk attempts to offer a soothing reminder that her *imago* and their city which represents her remains intact (19:35): "Is there anyone that does not know (τίς ἐστιν ἀνθρώπων ὃς οὐ γινώσκει) that the city of Ephesus is the temple warden of the great Artemis and of her image, which fell from heaven?" But one cannot miss that in this clash of the titans Demetrius recognizes that Artemis is losing.

In defense of Paul and his associates (Acts 19:37) the clerk says that the Christians have not "robbed the temple" (οὔτε ἱεροσύλους) nor "blasphemed the goddess" (οὔτε βλασφημοῦντας τὴν θεὸν ἡμῶν). Why does the clerk choose these phrases for their defense? The term "rob/plunder" (ἱεροσυλία)

---

99. See lines 86–87, LCL 10.160–61; line 977, LCL 10.254–255; lines 1384–85, LCL 10.300–301.

100. In this section, I continue to further my argument in light of the extensive inscriptional research of Immendörfer. See especially his 5.2.12 on Identity in *Ephesians and Artemis.*

101. Both Jews and Christians were in agreement that "gods made with hands are not gods" which may have brought the Jews into the conflict since the Ephesian gentiles likely did not distinguish between the two groups.

is also found in the Ephesus inscriptions and is a very serious term because to "rob" (ἱεροσυλία) the Artemision temple, known as the "bank of Asia," was also interpreted as "sacrilege" (ἱεροσυλία) against Artemis.[102] To "steal" (ἱεροσυλία) the savings of her citizens who were her representatives was the same thing as "sacrilege" (ἱεροσυλία) against her. A crime against them was a crime against her, the identity of her citizens and the goddess so woven together.[103] The decree of the *gerucia* of Ephesus (IEPH 26.22–23) during the reign of Commodus (161–192 CE) uses similar terms saying that everyone who opposes Artemis' festivals is guilty of "impiety and sacrilege" (ἀσεβεία καί ἱεροσυλία). The Salutaris Inscription (104 CE) records a similar ordinance that Artemis statues were to be placed inside the theatre at every gathering and whoever used them for a different purpose or damaged them is guilty of ἱεροσυλία καί ἀσεβεία (IEPH 27.217). These very serious offenses reveal little separation between the human and the divine in the minds of her citizens. They live as image-bearers of her kingdom authority even while under imperial rule.

Based on the above evidence, the city clerk argues on legal grounds that Paul and his associates have committed no prosecutable defense, dismissed the crowd, and saved their lives. The occasion of the riot itself reveals two important considerations relevant to the Ephesian letter: 1) The deep emotional connection that the crowd feels to the goddess makes clear that she is not some passing fancy who will be easily forgotten in the life of the new believer in Ephesus. Her memory and grip on her former representatives will linger as a problem that Paul must address in the Ephesian correspondence;[104] 2) and the Christian God is threatening to eclipse the primacy of the great goddess of Ephesus, which Paul will drive home in the Ephesian letter by comparing Christ's kingdom to hers. Luke's message in Acts 19 is that in the city of Ephesus, in Asia, and in the whole world the Christian God is challenging the sovereignty of Artemis. Luke sets up a contrast between the followers of Christ and Artemis to make clear that the God of whom Paul preaches is more powerful than the great goddess of

102. See Trebilco, "Asia, 354 (cf. Lampe, "Acts 19 im Spiegel der ephesischen Inschriften," 65).

103. See also Rogers, *Sacred Identity*; and Immendörfer, *Ephesians and Artemis*, 4.3.3.

104. One may find it difficult to imagine that by the time of the Ephesian letter Artemis still lurked in background of the gentile Ephesian believer's thoughts about the transforming *imago Dei* in them, but this really should come as no surprise when one considers the lengths that Paul went in his battles over circumcision (Acts 15; Rom 2:25–29; Gal 2; 5:11–12; 6:12–16) and dietary laws (Rom 14; 1 Cor 8) with Jewish Christians.

Ephesus. The fact that people have begun to stop spending money on silver replicas of Artemis affirms Paul's message that "gods made by human hands are no gods at all," while the Christian God is so strong that even a handkerchief touched by Paul can heal (19:10–11).[105] If Artemis is not a god, then the Ephesian citizen is nothing special, not an image-bearer of the great deity, just a person like everyone else. This is a frightening thought, making Paul's message of new identity as Christ's image-bearers in the Ephesian letter all the more significant. The silver statues made by human hands in Acts 19 are not the divine image of the goddess, but the newly created believers made by God's hands and inhabited by the Holy Spirit are. This message by Paul is reinforced in the Ephesian correspondence.

4.2.6 Image-Bearers for the God of the Universe

Paul wishes to make abundantly clear that while their "hometown goddess" has made a name for one city, Ephesus, the believers' "Father of glory" (Eph 1:17) has named every family in heaven and on earth (3:15).[106] This comparison of old identity to new, based on union with Christ (2:5–10), is highlighted in Ephesians more than any other NT letter.[107] Paul then compares the entitled position Israel previously enjoyed, with the alienated gentiles' failings as gentiles (2:11–12), to now unite Jew and gentile "into a new human" (ἕνα καινὸν ἄνθρωπον) bearing a new identity in Christ (2:13–18), in a new temple (2:19–22). That Paul begins 2:11 with "Therefore remember" (Διὸ μνημονεύετε) suggests that they are losing their sense of identity (2:11–18), may be under the influence of Artemis again, and require a reminder of who they were and are.[108] Paul continues to remind them who they are as a new humanity with a surprising number of "with/together" (συν) compounds. In 2:19 the readers are "fellow citizens with the saints" (συμπολῖται τῶν ἁγίων), and in 2:21 "fitted together" (συναρμολογουμένη) and 2:22

---

105. For more on Acts 19 see Brinks, "Great is Artemis of the Ephesians," 776–94.

106. Ephesians 1:17 and 3:15 are part of two longer prayers (1:15–23; 3:14–21) with similarities to Colossians 1:23—2:10. See Lincoln, *Ephesians*, 199–200, for a handful of these similarities. Yet neither "the Father of glory" (ὁ Πατὴρ τῆς δόξης) in 1:17 nor "family" (πατριὰ) in 3:15 occurs in the Colossian account, perhaps suggesting that the Ephesian writer is using such language as an allusion to Artemis.

107. Scholarship often sees identity formation as the main objective (or one of the main objectives) of the Ephesian letter. See, for example, Snodgrass, *Ephesians*, 23; O'Brien, *Ephesians*, 57; and Arnold, *Ephesians*, 58.

108. See Lincoln, *Ephesians*, 133; also, Campbell, "Unity and Diversity in the Church," 18.

"built together" (συνοικοδομεῖσθε) to build a holy temple. In 3:6 they are "joint-heirs" (συνκληρονόμα) of the "joint-body" (καὶ σύσσωμα) and "joint-partakers" of the promise (καὶ συμμέτοχα τῆς ἐπαγγελίας). The wording "fellow citizens with the saints" (συμπολῖται τῶν ἁγίων) is reminiscent of their former unity within the sacred community of Artemis. Standing in contrast to their former identity with the goddess, this message of the new creation is clearly one of reconciliation, unity, peace, and new relationships with unlikely candidates.[109]

In the old world as image-bearers for Artemis' reign they represented a united Ephesian city, but Paul wants them to know that as Christ's image-bearers in the new world they represent much more. They embody Christ who unites the universe (1:10) and reigns over it (1:20–22). Their superior state of existence is because of the Holy Spirit in them (1:13; 3:16, 20; 4:30) who enlightens them to the magnitude of this inheritance (1:17–18). God has recreated them to be holy like him (2:5; 4:23), to do good (2:10) as the temple where God lives (2:22). With Christ living in their hearts (3:17) they are children of light (5:9), filled with the Spirit (5:18) recreated in 4:24 "in righteousness and holiness" (ἐν δικαιοσύνῃ καὶ ὁσιότητι) as *theosis*[110] (4:22–24) because of the transforming *imago Dei* in them (2:7,10, 22; 4:13, 24; 5:1, 8).[111] Their heightened state of existence as God's image-bearers (5:1) is a spiritual iconography that Paul uses to replace the literal iconography of Artemis' statues prominently displayed through Ephesus.

This resonates with Paul's robust understanding of the restored *imago Dei* in his undisputed letters where believers in Christ are: predestined to be conformed to the image of his Son (Rom 8:29); bearing the image of Christ (1 Cor 15:49); a "new creation" (καινὴ κτίσις), who have been reconciled to God and given the ministry of reconciliation (2 Cor 2:17–18) as

---

109. See Strelan, *Paul, Artemis, and the Jews*, 192–99, where he comments on various special concessions to the Jews such as release from military service, being exempt from appearing in court on the sabbath, the right to their ancestral laws and customs, sending money to Jerusalem for the temple tax—all of which would have created tension with the gentiles.

110. Theosis (θέωσις) here defined as the transformative process with the aim of likeness to or union with God, not that of becoming God.

111. Ephesians 4:17–32 provides additional description of their former selves indicating that Artemis was not one to bring about the inward transformation wrought by the Holy Spirit. Contrast deceitful desires (4:22), falsehood (4:25), theft (4:28); corrupt talk (4:29); bitterness, wrath, anger, slander (4:31); with renewed mind (4:23), righteousness and holiness (4:24); truthfulness (4:25); honest work (4:28); encouragement and grace (4:29); kindness and forgiveness (4:32).

Christ's ambassadors for a new humanity (2:20), where their former way of judging people from a worldly perspective (2:16)[112] is contrasted with Christ's actively reconciling people to himself in forgiveness (2:18–20); and again in Galatians 6:12–16 where impressing people in the flesh (ἐν σαρκί) with circumcision, or uncircumcision, no longer matters when what counts is instead a "new creation" (ἀλλὰ καινὴ κτίσις). The word πρεσβεύω for "ambassador" (1 Cor 2:20) is used in the NT on only one other occasion, where Paul describes himself Ephesians 6:20 as "a prisoner in a chain" (πρεσβεύω ἐν ἁλύσει), making clear his evangelistic intent for which he has paid a hefty price, accompanied by his request that the Ephesians pray that as "an ambassador in chains" he can continue to evangelize (Eph 6:19–20). Of all the prayer requests that Paul could have uttered, his only ask in 6:19 is that he might continue to make known "the mystery of the gospel" (τὸ μυστήριον τοῦ εὐαγγελίου). Paul as the *imago Dei* is completely other centered in his attempt to unite humanity under Christ. By this point in the letter, one would hope that the Ephesians recognized their responsibility as the *imago Christi* to be the same.

By contrasting "the old self" (τὸν παλαιὸν ἄνθρωπον) in Ephesians 4:22 with "the new self" (τὸν καινὸν ἄνθρωπον) in 4:24 he highlights the transformation from who they were as image-bearers of Artemis to who they are as image-bearers of Christ.[113] As the "torch of Artemis" (depicted on coins, statues, and paintings) once illuminated the processional path for their induction into the cult as her image-bearers,[114] so "Christ will shine upon you" (ἐπιφαύσει σοι ὁ Χριστός) in 5:14 now lights the way of transformation into his image-bearers.[115] The transforming *imago Dei* in the life of the Ephesian believer is reiterated by the repetition of "in Christ" (ἐν Χριστῷ)

---

112. Literally "according to the flesh" (κατὰ σάρκα) which is a power that is opposed to the Holy Spirit, hostile to God, and leading to death (Rom 8:1–17).

113. See Arnold, *Ephesians*, 292–93.

114. For inscriptional example see IEPH 27.168. Also see Rogers, *Sacred Identity*, 115, 138 for more detail on the meaning of the torch. Most of the processions took place at night and were associated with the mysteries of Artemis.

115. See the detailed analysis of Eph 5:14 in 5.3.1 of Immendörfer, *Ephesians and Artemis*, 253–63.

standing against "in Artemis" (ἐν Ἀρτέμιδι)[116] with "in Christ" occurring double the Pauline average.[117]

Abundant Pauline scripture read alongside abundant epigraphical evidence clarifies that, when thinking of what the *imago Dei* looks like in people, Paul's interests did not lie with the Genesis 1 debate of which gender is most like God and who gets to rule, but with how to combat the very real influence of Artemis upon the identity of Ephesian believer. Artemis was their near frame of reference for what the *imago Dei* looked like in people, not Genesis 1. Further, if the dimension of rule is not central to Paul's thinking about the *imago Dei* in the Ephesian letter, then it will become clear that it is not central to his thinking in its marital *Haustafel*.[118]

4.3 SUMMARY

Chapter 4 began with two questions which I answered in two parts. Part One answered the question, "What did Paul think the *imago Dei* looked like in people intertextually?" I began with an intertextual investigation of what the image of God looked like in people from Paul's perspective, followed by an examination of the Genesis 1 debate over which gender is more like the image of God, thus giving them the right to rule. I concluded that the dimension of rule, which appears to be so important to modern scholarship, is insufficient to describe Paul's concept of the *imago Dei* in people and the transformation of the Ephesian believer into a new creation. More importantly, if a patriarchal reading of Genesis 1 is correct for the ancient world this does not mean it equates to a correct application of Paul's gospel to our modern world or to his modern world of first century Ephesus. Scholarship has overlooked the weight of inscriptional evidence showing that Paul's interests regarding the *imago Dei* for his audience lie not with the Genesis 1 gender debate of who's in charge but with their former lives as image-bearers for the goddess. And, if the notion of who's in charge is

---

116. See, Apollonius of Tyana (c. 3 BCE–c. 97 CE), *Let.* 65, LCL 458.60–61. where he writes "To the Ephesians in Artemis" (Ἐπεσίων τοῖς ἐν Ἀρτέμιδος). The phrase "in Christ" (ἐν Χριστῷ) or "in him" (ἐν αὐτῷ) or "in whom" (ἐν ᾧ) occurs in 1:1, 4, 7, 9, 10, 11, 12, 13, 20; 2:7, 10, 13, 15, 21; 3:6, 11, 12, 21; 4:21, 32. For a survey of the various forms that the phrase takes in Ephesians, see Hoehner, *Ephesians*, 173–74.

117. And more often than in Colossians. See Allan, "The 'in Christ' Formula in Ephesians," 54–55.

118. This will receive detailed discussion in ch. 6.

not the focus of Paul's thinking about the *imago Dei* in the Ephesian letter, then scholarship is mistaken to make the focus of Paul's marital *Haustafel*.

Part Two answered the question, "Did the Ephesians have the same frame of reference as Paul when they thought of the *imago Dei* in themselves?" Evidence was presented to support that the Ephesians believed themselves to be representatives of the goddess on earth, united with her as her image-bearers, making the Acts 19 riot plausible and relevant to the Ephesian letter. The occasion of the riot coheres with epigraphical evidence supporting that Artemis is not easily forgotten by the new believer. Paul is well aware of their frame of reference as not being in alignment with his. Their former lives as her image-bearers will linger as a problem which Paul, as Christ's ambassador, addresses by comparing Christ's universal kingdom to her rule over just one city. In this respect, being the *imago Christi* for the God of the universe far exceeds any notion the Ephesians may have had as the *imago Artemis*, although having viewed themselves as her representatives provides a bridge for Paul to teach them who they now are as the *imago Dei* on earth.

Transforming deficient human relationships into restored relationships as image-bearers for Christ who would evangelize the world is Paul's message in Ephesians, cohering with Paul's evangelistic success Acts 19. With the abundance of imperial busts of the deified Caesar carried in processionals right down the promenade along with Artemis for all Ephesians to see, the notion of a human transforming into the divine was no stranger to their thinking.[119] Paul's message of transforming from the fleshly sphere to the divine sphere of personal holiness as the *imago Dei* was an attractive one to the average male and female living in hierarchical Hellenism. Especially relevant to the marital *Haustafel*, how then might the idea "to put on the new self in the likeness of God" (Eph 4:24) be understood, or misunderstood, by former worshippers of Artemis whose new objective was to become like the God-man Christ, with whom they were united (2:5–6) as a new human (2:11–22)? Specific to the next chapter, what might this look like to the Ephesian believer in terms of gender, marriage, and celibacy as new creatures in an emerging new kingdom? This question will be answered in two parts.

---

119. The difference being that Paul's message aims at transforming the believer into the likeness of God through personal holiness, not that of becoming God. For additional discussion on the connection between Christianity and Roman religion see Howard-Johnston and Hayward, *The Cult of Saints in Late Antiquity and the Middle Ages*; Thacker, "Loca Sanctorum," 1–44.

5

The Image of God, Marriage, and Celibacy

THIS CHAPTER HAS TWO parts. Part One answers the question: what the *imago Dei* might look like in people to the Ephesian believer regarding gender, marriage, and celibacy, by suggesting that two traditions emerge for the Ephesian believer wishing to be like Christ. One tradition pursues holiness as the *imago Dei* in marital interdependence, and the second pursues holiness as the *imago Dei* in celibacy. Both traditions converge in desire to be the *imago Christi* but diverge in which is the best path to get there. The development of these two traditions is witnessed beginning with the negative reception history of Eve in Second Temple Jewish writings and early Christian writings, contrasted with the positive reception history of Artemis in inscription and literature, including popular novels. The portrayal of Eve as the dependent and weak wife of Adam makes her an unattractive candidate for the Ephesian matron wishing to be like Christ, while the independent and strong celibate Artemis makes her an attractive one. One may even wonder to what extent "Eve tradition" was known to gentile believers in Ephesus when compared to the wealth of "Artemis tradition" at their fingertips, pushing the virgin goddess, with no need for a male consort, to the front as a near reference for the Ephesian female as to what the image of god is supposed to look like in her.[1] Part One reviews stories

1. Dialogue regarding gender and the restored *imago Dei* among church fathers, scholastics, and reformers goes well into the fifteenth century. Attempting to keep a narrow chronological focus, I have limited the discussion to within a few hundred years of first century Ephesus out to the Cappadocians (330–395 CE), including them because

of female autonomy that were likely familiar to the Ephesian listener, contrasted with efforts to place restrictions on women, to support the idea of an emerging celibate tradition for believing women. Sharing the geography of Asia Minor with Ephesus, an examination of the actions and teachings of the Cappadocian mothers and fathers reveal the ongoing acceptance and development of both traditions for women, freeing them from the Hellenistic old-world order. Part Two supports Part One by demonstrating a trajectory of celibacy as observed 1) in Caesar's marriage laws intended to combat celibacy, 2) in the rise of Christian celibate communities, 3) and in the promotion of attitudes toward sexual intercourse as sinful by the early church fathers. The combination of these various elements in Parts One and Two suggest that Paul was at the least facing a church in first-century Ephesus where, based on their misunderstanding of what the *imago Dei* looked like in them, spouses were living independently of one another rather than interdependently. And this, combined with the rise of celibacy which produced more independence, posed a threat to his evangelistic mission in the conservative Mediterranean Ephesus and Asia Minor. Hence, in my chapter 6, Paul argues for one tradition over another to fulfill his mission.

5.1 PART ONE—THE IMAGE OF GOD AND THE RISE OF TWO TRADITIONS

The story of Eve as told by Second Temple Jewish writers and early Christian writers is a cautionary one—Eve the sinner, Eve the temptress, Eve the gullible who instigates the fall of humankind. Holly Morse observes that Eve with the snake with the forbidden tree (Gen 2:17; 3:1–5, 6–8, 12–13, 15–16) has well served the claim that women are more sinful than men and that Eve led to Adam's undoing.[2] She listens to the snake (3:1–5), she eats

---

of the direct line of sight they have to Origen (c. 184–253 CE) who instructed Bishop Gregory Thaumaturgus (c. 213–270), who discipled their grandmother, Macrina the Elder. Hence, the conversation remains close to the first-century Ephesian letter by way of second-century Origen.

2. Morse, *Encountering Eve's Afterlives*, remarks, "Pamela Milne, working with a structural perspective on the text, suggests . . . 'Since the creation of the woman follows the prohibition, the text is stressing that it is only the man's fate which is at stake: the woman and the snake are essential actors in the working out of the man's fate but the focus is on the man . . .' then it is possible to discern a narrative stimulus for an interpretation of Genesis 2–3 that lays blame for the demise of man directly on the actions of

of the tree (3:6), she entices her husband Adam (3:7). Eve, the covetous seductress, plunges us all into destruction to get what she cannot have. What Jewish literature may have been available to the Ephesian gentile believer that would influence their thinking about Eve, marriage, and celibacy? How much of Eve's negative typecast might have been experienced by them in a first-century mixed congregation with Jewish believers teaching from the LXX, making Eve an unlikely candidate for the Ephesian woman to consider when compared to Artemis, the nurturing mother of Ephesus?

5.1.1 Reception History of Eve

Ben Sirah (c. 200–175 BCE) makes Eve the author of sin and death (25:24): "From a woman sin had its beginning and because of her we all die."[3] And Eve is the primary sinner in the Life of Adam and Eve (cf. 18:1–2)[4] as well as in the Greek version Apocalypse of Moses (32:1–3).[5] Philo of Alexandria (c. 15 BCE–45 CE) deems her gender an easy target in Genesis 3:1, "But the judgment of woman is more feminine, and because of softness she easily gives way and is taken in by plausible falsehoods which resemble the

---

the woman before she has even been created," 13. See Milne, "The Patriarchal Stamp of Scripture," 146–72. See also Morse's contrast of the Hebrew account, where no seduction is implied, with Jerome's Vulgate where Eve's reputation as a temptress is based on silence (19–20), and the LXX which allows room for a sinful animal-human relationship (22), then leaving room for 3:16b to be interpreted as woman being controlled by her sexual desire and in need of domination by man (24–25). See her Gallery II, Parts I and II for a detailed discussion of the Hebrew and LXX texts.

3. Sirah (c. 200–175 BCE). To be fair, Morse, *Encountering Eve's Afterlives*, 28–29, observes that Levison and Ellis point out that the Hebrew text of *Sirah* 25.24 may not have been written as an interpretation of Eve, hence we should not uncritically take it as early evidence of a tradition focusing blame on her. Yet, one must agree that this text has certainly been understood by later readers to refer to her, thus is highly significant in the formation of the tradition of the woman as a source of sin. See Levison, "Is Eve to Blame?," 617–23 and Ellis, "Is Eve the 'Woman' in Sirach 25:24?," 723–42.

4. *Life of Adam and Eve Collection*, Kindle loc. 84, trans. SRI from Meyer, *Vita Adea et Evae*. The earliest Greek version (also known as *Apocalypse of Moses*) has a likely pre-140 BCE date (from when the Greeks ruled Judea between 330–140 BCE), while the source text for the Latin version (from which this quote is taken) indicates an early-Persian era of 525–330 BCE.

5. *Life of Adam and Eve Collection*, Kindle loc. 55, trans. SRI from Greek in Denis, *Concordance Grecque des Pseudepigraphes d'Ancien Testament*, 815–24. Note that Adam blames her as well at the opening of ch. 14.

truth."[6] She infects Adam's thoughts in Philo's, *On the Creation of the World*, "Pleasure does not venture to bring her wiles and deceptions to bear on the man, but on the woman, and by her means on him."[7] And if she engages in the public conflicts of the man's sphere will "unsex herself by a boldness beyond what nature permits."[8] Morse observes:

> In Philo's writings, not only is the woman a symbol of intellectual weakness, but she also functions as a facilitator of feminine carnal transgression. All of this serves to emphasize that Philo understood Eve, specifically as female, to be the vehicle of sin, and that he also closely aligned her both literally and allegorically, with weakness and lack of self-control.[9]

Men are warned against being seduced by her beauty,[10] that she is evil, that she will "bewitch by outward attractions and craft,"[11] that she is naturally inferior,[12] "a selfish creature, excessively jealous and adept at beguiling the morals of her husband,"[13] easily deceived,[14] and belonging to the lower domestic sphere.[15] The book of Proverbs usually blames the woman if there is a sexual transgression.[16] And Josephus writes (c. 93–94 CE) that female testimony in court cannot be trusted.[17] He adds that according to the law she is inferior to the man and must be submissive so that she may be directed

---

6. See I.33 *QG*, LCL 380.20-21. Morse comments, "Manipulating the biblical account, Philo develops an image of Eve alone speaking to the snake and immediately being tricked. He forgets that in the LXX the snake uses masculine plural verbs in his speech, and that the woman does initially attempt to correct the snake" (*Encountering Eve's Afterlives*, 34).

7. See line 165, LCL 226.130-31.

8. Philo, *Spec. Laws* 3.171, LCL 320.582-83.

9. Morse, *Encountering Eve's Afterlives*, 35.

10. *T. Jud.* 17.1 (109–106 BCE).

11. *T. Reu.* 5.1-2 (109–106 BCE). For more on women and the destabilizing power of sexual desire see Grossman's examination of the penal code of the Community Rule and the rules of exclusion in the War Scroll in "Postmodern Questions and Sexuality Studies," ch. 22 in *T&T Clark Companion to the Dead Sea Scrolls*.

12. Philo (c. 15 BCE-45 CE), *Spec. Laws* 2.124, LCL 320.380-81.

13. Philo, *Hypoth.* 11.14-17, LCL 363.442-43.

14. Philo, *QG* 1:33, LCL 380.20.

15. Philo, *Spec. Laws* 3.169-70, LCL 320.580-83; *QG* 1:26, LCL 380.15.

16 Proverbs 2:16-19; 5:2-11; 23:27-28; 30:20. See also Proverbs 5:15-18; 6:24-35; 7:5-27; 22:14; 11:22; 31:3; 11:16; 12:3; 19:13; 21:9, 19; 25:24; 27:15-16.

17. Josephus, *Ant.* IV.219, LCL 490:106-7.

by man to whom God has given authority.[18] He defines her as headstrong and subject to sudden changes of opinion since she is illogical.[19] Pseudepigraphal *Testament of Judah* (109–106 BCE) identifies her as seductive (17.1) while the *Testament of Reuben* (109–106 BCE) identifies her as evil and bewitching (5:1–2).[20] And the book of Proverbs usually blames the woman if there is a sexual transgression.[21]

A representative sampling of rabbinical quotes from the Mishnah and Talmud which go back hundreds of years provide insight regarding prevailing attitudes toward women.[22] Negative appraisals include renowned Hillel (c. 110 BCE–10 CE): "Many women, much witchcraft";[23] Rabbi Joshua (first cent. CE): "A woman would rather have a single measure (of food) with wantonness than nine measures with continence";[24] Rabbi Simon ben Jochai (c. 150 CE): "The most virtuous of women is a witch";[25] and "At the birth of a boy all are joyful . . . at the birth of a girl all are sorrowful."[26] Positive appraisals from Jewish literature are typically in relation to the man as a wife: "It was taught, he who has no wife dwells without good, without help,

---

18. Josephus, *Ag. Ap.* II.201, LCL 186.372–73.

19. *Let. Aris.* v. 250. Josephus (c. 37–100), who paraphrases two-fifths of the letter, ascribes it to Aristeas of Marmora and to have been written to his brother Philocrates. The letter's author claims to be a courtier of Ptolemy II Philadelphus (r. 281–246 BCE).

20. Perhaps the most widely known rabbinic saying from the early mishnaic period which describes her situation is the three-fold daily prayer, attributed to Rabbi Yehuda ben Ilai (mid-second cent. CE): "Praised be God that he has not created me a gentile. Praised be God that he has not created me a woman. Praised be God that he has not created me an ignoramus. Praised be God that he has not created me a gentile: "For all gentiles are as nothing before him," (Isa. 40:17). Praised that he has not created me a woman because the woman is not obliged to fulfil the commandments. Praised that he has not created me an ignoramus for the ignorant man does not avoid sin" (*Tos. Ber.* 6.18).

21. Proverbs 2:16–19; 5:2–11; 23:27–28; 30:20). See also Proverbs 5:15–18; 6:24–35; 7:5–27; 22:14; 11:22; 31:3; 11:16; 12:3; 19:13; 21:9, 19; 25:24; 27:15–16.

22. The Mishnah (codified 200 CE) and Talmud (Palestinian codified fourth cent. CE/Babylonian codified fifth cent. CE) contain a myriad of material, going back hundreds of years. Although not all quotes can be located in the first century world of Christ and Paul, these teachings of the rabbis reflect the influence of prior centuries on first century thought as well as the first century's influence on subsequent thought.

23. *Aboth* 2, 7.

24. *Sotah* 3, 4.

25. This saying is quoted in three different rabbinic collections, giving some clue to its popularity: *Terum* 15; *pKid.* 4, 66b, 32; *Soferim* 41a.

26. *bNid.* 31b.

without joy, without blessing, and without atonement";[27] from a series of sayings gathered together in the Talmud: "Rabbi Alexandri said, 'The world is darkened for him whose wife has died in his days . . . Rabbi Johanan also said: 'He whose first wife has died, (is grieved as much) as if the destruction of the Temple has taken place in his days . . .' Rabbi Samuel ben Nahman said: 'For him who divorces the first wife, the very alter sheds tears.'"[28]

To say that there exists a balanced tradition in Jewish literature of repudiation and affirmation of Eve and women in general would be an overreach of epic proportions. Rather, the tragedy and summary judgment of Eve pouring from Jewish pens is bound metonymically to all women across the centuries, leading up to, including, and following the first century. Of particular note are the first-century writings of Philo of Alexandria, the Hellenistic Jewish philosopher, and Josephus, the Roman-Jewish historian, both whose learning and life experience traversed Greco-Roman and Jewish cultures, and both whose assessment of women in general is abundantly negative.

The reception history of Eve fares no better among post-canonical Christian writers.[29] Justin Martyr (c. 100–165 CE) describing Eve in his *Dialogue with Trypho* writes, "For Eve, who was a virgin and undefiled, having conceived the word of the serpent, brought forth disobedience and death."[30] Irenaeus of Lyons (c. 130–202 CE) describes Eve as "having become disobedient, was made the cause of death, both to herself and to the entire human race," contrary to her true biblical title as mother of all living.[31] Tertullian (c. 155–220 CE) adds, "in fact she did give birth, to the devil, the murderer of his brother,"[32] and to women in general he writes, "You destroyed so easily God's image, man. On account of your desert—that is, death—even the Son of God had to die."[33]

Even so, woman is not without hope. Abdicating desire and sexual activity will set her soul on the path of heavenly ascent, its transformation

27. Gen. Rab. 18, 2.

28. bSan. 22a.

29. The following comments from Justin Martyr, Irenaeus, and Tertullian are part of a larger conversation as contrasting Eve's seduction with the Mary's obedient attention to the divine message, and Eve's link to death with Mary's link to life. For more on this contrast see Morse, *Encountering Eve's Afterlives*, 47–55, 69–70.

30. *Dial.* 100.

31. *Haer.* III.22.4.

32. *Carn. Chri.* XVII.5.

33. *Cult. Fem.* I.1.

to virginity, and attainment of divine wisdom. According to *The Gospel of Thomas* (c. 150 CE), all she needs do is become male: "Simon Peter said to them, let Mary Magdalene leave us, for women are not worthy of life. Jesus said, I myself shall lead her in order to make her male, so that she too may become a living spirit (cf. Gen 2:7) resembling you males. For every woman who makes herself male will enter the kingdom of heaven."[34]

Clement of Alexandria (c. 150–215 CE) is the first Christian author to make use of Ephesians 4:13, exhorting believers to become "male and perfect" (*Strom.* IV, 132.1). In *Stromata* VI, 100.3 he writes of the Christian gnostic wife who frees herself from the bondage of the flesh and reaches perfection in the same way as her husband: "Souls are neither male nor female when they no longer marry nor are given in marriage. And is not woman turned into a man, the woman who is no more female than he, the perfect, manly woman." Hence, God's image is incorporeal and is consequently a sexless quality linked to human virtue and intellect, making virtuous women into honorary men. Citing Luke 20:34–35 on the absence of marriage in the resurrection Clement argues that the female differs from the male only in this world.[35] By dominating inferior female bodily appetites, she can become an honorary man.[36]

Origen (c. 184–253 CE) in *Homily 1* from his *Homilies on Genesis*, describes the inner man as having both spirit and soul, aligning the first woman with the inferior human element of soul, and the man with the superior element of spirit.[37] Hence, if her female soul turns away from the male spirit the pursuit of pleasure will take over her mind.[38] On the other hand, Origen also sees men and women as distinguished according to differences of heart. "How many belong to the female sex who before God are strong men, and how many men must be counted weak and indolent

---

34. Log. 114. Hence the transformation of Mary Magdalene from woman to man as a condition of her assumption into the "reign of God" in which she becomes a "living spirit" resembling a man. See also Philo, *On the Cherubim* 50, LCL 227.38–39 and *On Rewards and Punishments* 159, LCL 341.414–15 for more on becoming male.

35. *Paed.* 1.4.

36. *Strom.* 4.8.

37. Writing on Genesis 1:26. By citing Philo in his writings, Hadas-Lebel, *Philo of Alexandria*, 208, concludes that Origen was a central link in the transmission of Philo's work. See also Rogers, "Origen in the Likeness of Philo," 1–13; Heine's introduction in *The Commentaries of Origen and Jerome on St. Paul's Epistle to the Ephesians*; and his "Recovering Origen's Commentary on Ephesians from Jerome," 478–514.

38. See Morse, 37, *Encountering Eve's Afterlives*, where she refers to Origen, *Hom. Gen.* 1.15.

women."³⁹ Hence, a regenerate woman may be turned into a man, while a man by being degenerate may become a woman.⁴⁰ Yet in his allegorical *Homily on the Song of Songs* he identifies the soul as neither male nor female in the figure of the bride and bridegroom which is instilled with the love of things divine and heavenly.⁴¹ Origen deeply influenced the Cappadocians (see 5.1.4), his commentary on the *Song of Songs* serving as an ascetic reorienting away from physical pleasure and toward God.⁴²

Is the suspicion of women exclusive to Second Temple Jewish writers and post-canonical Christian writers or might external influences be at play that the Ephesian gentile believer knows well? Morse persuasively argues that with the Hellenization of Western Asia, Hesiod's account of Pandora may have become a template for the story of Eve by Jewish and Christian writers who over centuries develop the motif that females bring human suffering.⁴³ Hesiod (c. 750–650 BCE) in his *Theogony* writes of Pandora, "For from her is the race of women and female kind: of her is the deadly race and tribe of women who live amongst mortal men to their great trouble, no helpmeets in hateful poverty, but only in wealth."⁴⁴ Beautiful Pandora brings with her a jar (also called a box)⁴⁵ containing countless plagues. Prometheus had warned his brother Epimetheus to accept no gifts from Zeus, but Epimetheus accepts Pandora anyway who then scatters the contents of her jar to fill the earth and sea with evils.⁴⁶ It is possible that the story of Eve may have been a different one was it not for Hesiod. Beyond this, Hesiod's Pandora supports a cross-cultural predisposition of distrust for women that the Ephesian believer would have been privy to, and perhaps

---

39. *Hom. Josh.* 9:9.

40. For more on the sex change metaphor, see Vogt, "'Becoming Male," 217–42.

41. Origen, *Hom. Song,* 41. For more, see Sunberg, *The Cappadocian Mothers,* 134–35.

42. See Cameron, "Sacred and Profane Love," 11. See also Harrison, "Allegory and Eroticism in Gregory of Nyssa," 113–30. Gregory allegorized the expression of conjugal love which he found in the Song of Songs, because it was "pastorally inapplicable in its literal sense."

43. Morse, *Encountering Eve's Afterlives,* 29–31. It is noteworthy that my argument regarding the influence of Artemis on the Ephesian believer bears similarity to Morse's argument regarding Hesiod's influence on the account of Eve.

44. Lines 590–93, LCL 57.50–51.

45. The mistranslation of "jar" (πίθος) into "box" or "vessel" (πυξίς) is attributed to Erasmus of Rotterdam (1466–1536) when he translated Hesiod's tale into Latin. See West, *Hesiod Theogony Works and Days,* xiv.

46. See his *Works and Days,* 60–105, LCL 57.90–95.

have adhered to as part of the Hellenistic honor and shame culture of Asia Minor.[47]

Beyond the availability of the LXX via Jews living in the Mediterranean one cannot say precisely what literature was available to the gentile Ephesian believers. But one can say that prevailing Second Temple Jewish attitudes toward Eve, and women in general, were unfavorable and that the Ephesian believers were likely aware of such attitudes among their Jewish contemporaries and perhaps shared in them. This negative disposition toward women continued to prevail through the pens of post-canonical Christian writers, cementing that such attitudes toward women were firmly entrenched in Jewish and gentile cultures, and that an alternative role of celibate honorary male might be far more attractive to the first-century Ephesian woman wishing to manifest the *imago Christi* than that of a wife under the control of her husband as the weaker sex. The influential near reference of the venerated hometown celibate goddess who roams the mountains with dogs, stags, bow and arrows, and no need for male protection is the picture of an honorary male. Powerful Artemis presents herself as an alluring alternative to that of associating oneself with the gender of Eve as the weak matron of Adam, responsible for the fall of humanity.

5.1.2 Reception History of Artemis

Multiple hymns revere Artemis as an honorary male. *Homeric Hymn 27* (c. seventh cent. BCE) esteems her as a strong, independent virgin who makes the mountains tremble and the earth shake (v. 10), an archer (v. 1, 5) who cheers on the hounds, the goddess with a bold heart who turns every way destroying the race of wild beasts (v. 10).[48] *Homeric Hymn 9* calls her a delighter in arrows (v.1) driving a golden chariot (v. 5), both hymns assigning her qualities for that time that are far more typical of a man than a woman.[49] Callimachus, *Hymn 3 to Artemis* (c. third cent. BCE) recounts her childhood request of her father, Zeus, that she may keep her virginity and have many titles so her brother Apollo will not rival her (vs. 5–7), her request equivalent to being that of an honorary male,[50] while *Orphic Hymn*

---

47. For more on Greek attitudes toward women see 3.1.
48. LCL 496.208–9.
49. LCL 496.190–91
50. LCL 129.234–35. See also *Hom. Hymn 5 to Aphrodite*, LCL 496.160–61, and *Orphic Hymn 36 to Artemis*. One might argue that Homer's Artemis and Ephesus' Artemis

2 to *Prothyraia* (c. third cent. BCE-second cent. CE) reveals her feminine side as compassionate, sympathetic, and powerful to young women that suffer the pains of childbirth.[51]

While the recorded reception history of Eve paints her as a destabilizing force upon humanity, the reception history of Artemis is the opposite. Titles venerating Artemis such as "our Sovereign Lady Artemis" (ἡ κυρία ἡμῶν Ἀρτέμιδος) told all she was special.[52] For example, in IEPH 1078 (vs. 1–17) priest Eutuches expresses thanks to Hestia and all the gods (εὐχαριστω Ἑστία Βουλαία καὶ τοις θεοις πασιν) and wishes "good fortune upon our Sovereign Lady Artemis" (ἀγαθη τύχη ἐπὶ πρυτάνεως της κυρίας ἡμον Ἀρτέμιδος). And in IEPH 3059 (v.13) priestess Aurelia names her "our Lady, goddess Artemis" (τη κυρία ἡμων θεα Ἀρτέμιδι). An altar dedicated to Artemis as Savior (Σώτειρα) in IEPH 1255, a decree by the Ephesian council of elders twice calls her Σώτειρα (IEPH 26.4, 18)[53] testify to their belief in her as Savior. An honorific inscription for Gaius Iulius Atticus identifies him as priest of Artemis Σώτειρα (IEPH 1265).[54] And *Neopoios* Marcus Aurelius Hortensius offers an inscription of thanksgiving to Artemis Σώτειρα (IEPH 2928).[55] She is abundantly referred to as "goddess" (ἡ Θεός/ἡ Θεά),[56]

---

are different goddesses separated by time and culture, that the first century many-breasted Artemis reflects the influence of Mediterranean Cybele or an Anatolian Mother Goddess, voiding memory of the seventh century BCE Greek huntress of Homer. But numismatic evidence would disagree. See Immendörfer, *Ephesians and Artemis*, 143; and Karwiese, "Ephesos: C Numismatischer Teil," col. 316, 337; also, Head, *On the Chronological Sequence of the Coins of Ephesus*. Additionally, both Greek and Ephesian versions of the goddess remained celibate and independent.

51. The relationship of the goddess Eileithyia of childbirth as an epithet of virginal huntress Artemis makes Artemis one who aids women in childbirth.

52. For more inscriptions where she is worshipped as Lady/Lord, see IEPH 27.110–12; 724; 892; 985; 1078. Κυρία is frequently deployed in a thanksgiving phrase IEPH 940; 943; 957; 958; 960; 961; 962; 963; 1578B; 1580; 1581; 1582A; 1582B; 1586A; 1588B; 1590A; 2928.

53. Occasioned by a donation given by Nikomedes (between 180 and 192 CE).

54. The inscription reads, "Gaius Iulius Atticus priest of our revered Savior Artemis" (Γάϊος Ἰούλιος Ἄττικος ἱερεὺς Ἀρτέμιδος Σοτείρας Σεβαστου γένους).

55. *Neopoios* literally refers to an "official in charge of constructing the temple" but could have other administrative and sacred functions. The inscription reads "*Neopoios* Marcus Aurelius Hortensius with my own accord thank lady Saviour Artemis" (Μαρκος Αὐραλιος Ὁρτασις νεοποιὸς αὐθαίρετος εὐχαριστω τη κυρία Ἀρτέμιδι Σοτείρια μετα).

56. See IEPH 2.1; 17.41, 57, 58, 66; 18B.4; 21.19, 40; 22.4, 22, 63; 24A.11; 24B.8, 22, 25, 32; 24C.9; 26.6, 9; 27.12, 68, 85, 118, 142, 148, 175, 215, 234, 249, 261, 267, 271, 275, 282, 310, 313, 353, 367, 396, 420, 456, 462, 494, 524, 535, 537, 539, 553, 556; 28.16; 46.4;

a title frequently combined with superlatives for "holy" (ἁγιωτάτη) and "splendid" (ἐπιφανεστάτη).[57]

Festivals venerating Artemis and regular processionals were abundant.[58] The Mysteries of Artemis (τὰ μυστήρια τῆς Ἀρτέμιδος)[59] which celebrated her birth was the largest and most important, followed by the Artemisia (Ἀρτεμίσια)[60] and the Daitis (Δαιτίς) festivals.[61] The Ἀρτεμίσια, her namesake festival, was a month-long celebration dedicated to her worship.[62] According to the Xenophon's tale of *Anthia and Habrocomes* young people sought a bride or bridegroom during the festival, revealing both religious and social components of the festival;[63] the annual Δαιτίς festival revealed a decorated and clothed Artemis figure carried in solemn procession from the temple to the sea where she was ritually bathed, then concluded with a holy banquet. As a nourishment festival people carried salt, celery, textiles, and jewelry, and were accompanied by a singer.[64]

Vows of chastity, undying love, trust in her discernment and fair judgment are found in novels venerating Artemis such as Xenophon's *Ephesian Tale* (second cent. CE) where the star-crossed lovers Anthia and Habrocomes promote the theme of reverence for the great goddess.[65] Albeit

---

127; 200; 203; 212; 213; 251; 274; 280B; 290; 293; 428; 449; 612; 618; 645; 660C; 666A; 669; 678; 690; 692; 704; 708; 710B; 710C; 725; 731; 742; 802; 803; 836; 852; 853; 859A; 987; 988; 992.

57. For example, ἐπιφανεστάτης καὶ μεγίστης θεᾶς Ἀρτέμιδος as "the most splendid and greatest goddess Artemis" (IEPH 27.344-45). See also IEPH 27.384-85.

58. See first century BCE inscription IEPH 14.19-23.

59. Celebrated on the 6th of Thargelion (May/June).

60. Celebrated in the spring of the month of Artemision (March/April).

61. See Arnold, "Festivals of Ephesus," 17-22, for some of the smaller festivals. Festivals were happy times in Ephesian life but failure to observe such holy days was considered "sacrilegious and impious" (IEPH 27.217).

62. See inscriptions IEPH 712B; IEPH 924A; IEPH 24C.4-5 bearing the title "Great Artemisia."

63. Xenophon of Ephesus, *Anthia and Habrocomes* (also known as *Ephesian Tale*) 1.2.1-4, LCL 69.214-17.

64. The ritual had started as a game between Clymene, daughter of a mythical king of Ephesus, and her female friends who had prepared a bed of celery and herbs and a meal of salt for Artemis, and offered it to her statue, which had already been carried to the coast. In turn Artemis asked that the celebration be repeated each year. For more see Evridiki, "Artemis of Ephesus (Statue)" in *Encyclopaedia of the Hellenic World*, entry 'Δαιτίς, 228-29; also, Romano, "Early Greek Cult Images and Cult Practices," 127-34.

65. For more on Xenophon's *Ephesiaca/Ephesian Tale* see Cueva, *The Myths of Fiction*, ch. 2; and Tagliabue, *Xenophon's Ephesiaca: A Paraliterary Love-Story*.

Xenophon's novel falls outside the timeframe of Ephesians, the work still contributes to the attitude of veneration for Artemis leading up to, during, and after first-century Ephesus. At the festival processional donning a fawn skin, carrying arrows, a javelin and accompanied by hunting dogs (2.6),[66] Anthia's luminescence is so breathtaking that onlookers believe that she is the goddess Artemis in person or has been made by the goddess in her divine image and worship Anthia as Artemis (2.7).[67] Anthia's physical appearance in imitation of Artemis the huntress confirms that the merger of two forms of Artemis, the Greek huntress with the Ephesian many-breasted goddess, had occurred by Xenophon's writing in the second century. This is in line with the syncretistic impulse of Hellenistic society.[68] Habrocomes cannot help but fall in love, "He kept gazing at the girl and though he tried he could not take his eyes off of her" (3.2),[69] and swears an oath of undying love to Anthia by invoking Artemis, as does she, "I swear to you by our ancestral goddess, the great goddess, Artemis" (11.5–6).[70] The unfortunate lovers are separated, endure misadventures, but are reunited in the end and return to Ephesus, immediately to the Artemision, where they offer prayers and sacrifices to thank the goddess who watched over them and brought them back together (15.2).[71]

In Achilles Tatius romance novel (also c. second cent.) *Leucippe and Clitophon*, faithful to her true love, Clitophon, the brave Leucippe rejects the sexual advances of adulterous Thersander, saying "What do I care about Thersander . . . I shall esteem Thersander when he stops forcing his attentions on other men's wives" (6.12)[72] and "have you no fear of your own patroness Artemis, that you would ravish a virgin in the virgin's city" (6.21).[73] Rebuffed Thersander seeks to exact vengeance by accusing her of not being a virgin (6.21), and thus violating Artemis by having entered the Artemision through a grotto that only slaves and virgins may access. Thersander's accusation puts Leucippe's claim of virginity to the test where "she is to be

---

66. LCL 69.216–17.

67. LCL 69.216–17.

68. For more see Frayer-Griggs, "The Beasts at Ephesus and the Cult of Artemis," 459–77.

69. LCL 69.216–17.

70. LCL 69.236–37

71. LCL 69.362–63.

72. LCL 45.328–29

73. LCL 45.344–45.

shut into the grotto of the panpipes" (8.11).[74] A special grotto behind the Artemision has magical panpipes given to Artemis by Pan which can avow or disavow the virginity of a maiden: she enters the grotto, and the doors are closed; if she is a virgin, lovely sounds emanate from the panpipes, and she is vindicated; if she is not a virgin the pipes let out a groan or remain silent. Upon Leucippe's entry "never has sweeter notes been heard from the grotto," vindicating her with the divine stamp of approval from Artemis as sufficient proof for all (8.13–14).[75]

5.1.3 Eve and Artemis Compared

Titles, Hymns, Inscriptions, and Novels reveals a 1000-year reception history of veneration for Artemis as the goddess. Sovereign Artemis, Savior Artemis, Lady Artemis, Holy Artemis, Huntress Artemis is the powerful virgin who shakes the mountains and exhibits behaviors common to men yet is compassionate and sympathetic to young mothers in distress and makes sure that star-crossed lovers who revere her wind up together in the end. Contrast her reception history with Eve and who becomes the more attractive candidate to revere in the mind of the Ephesian woman? One might argue that it is unfair to compare a goddess to a human and that the objective of the Ephesian letter is for believers in the *imago Dei* to emulate Christ, not Eve, and certainly not Artemis. But Christ being God took on human form whose *imago* serves as the example for Ephesian believers to emulate. Perhaps it is not so great a stretch for the Ephesian woman to envision a female candidate in the form of the goddess who on occasion manifests herself in human form like Anthia in Xenophon's *Ephesian Tale*. Artemis was no longer to be worshipped by the newly converted Ephesians, but that does not mean her memory no longer influenced their consciousness as they worked out what it meant to represent Christ as his new creation, and what the image of God was supposed to look like in them.

5.1.4 The Rise of Two Traditions

Alongside the contrasting reception histories of Eve and Artemis run stories of independence where women choose paths that run counter to

---

74. LCL 45.432–33.
75. LCL 45.438–41.

the predictive norms of immediate culture. Such stories may not appear in abundance but indeed exist, nonetheless. Coupled with the abundant negative reception history of Eve and positive of Artemis, the stories of women in Joseph and Aseneth, 1 Timothy, and the Acts of Paul and Thecla continue to build a case for the growth of female autonomy before God, despite efforts to reinforce her moral weakness and need of male supervision. Why take the time to examine such stories if they post-date the Ephesian letter? What influence could they possibly have upon a text that pre-dates them? While such stories may not have been written before or during the composition of the Ephesian letter, they are close enough to reflect social attitudes that were building at the time of its composition, in addition to the possibility of having existed in oral tradition before Ephesians.

Joseph and Aseneth (c. 100 BCE-200 CE) is a tale of the conversion of an Egyptian noblewoman to Judaism and her marriage to Joseph (cf. Gen 41:45).[76] She is assertive, rebuffing her father's attempt to marry her to Joseph:

> Why does my lord father speak words such as these to hand me over like a captive to a who is an alien and a fugitive and was sold as a slave? Is he not the shepherd's son from the land of Canaan, and he himself was caught in the act when he was sleeping with his mistress, and his master threw him into the prison of darkness, and Pharaoh brought him out of prison because he interpreted his dream just like the older women of the Egyptians interpret dreams? No, but I will be married to the kings first born son, because he is a king of the whole land of Egypt (4:9–11).

But upon meeting Joseph she is swept away by his handsomeness and royalty, and full of regret because "I, foolish and daring have despised him" (6:3). Joseph sees her as her own person with religious commitments and will only marry her when she worships the one true God (8:1–7). In individual rebellion against her family and Egyptian society she "took all her gods that were in her chamber, the ones of gold and silver who are without number, and ground them to pieces, and threw all the idols of the Egyptians through the window looking north" (10:11), converts to the God of Judaism (chs. 11–13), and receives special revelation from an angel (chs. 14–16) who declares her blessed and that he is, "giving you today to Joseph for a bride, and he himself will be your bridegroom forever and ever" (15:6). The angel instructs her to eat from a honeycomb of angelic food

---

76. Charlesworth, *Old Testament Pseudepigrapha* 2, 176–247.

that is full of the spirit of life and bestows immortality, announcing that, "Behold you have eaten bread of life, and drunken cup of immortality, and been anointed with ointment of incorruptibility.... And you shall be like a walled mother city of all who take refuge with the name of the Lord, the king of the ages" (16:16), a scene that appears to undo Eve's deception by the serpent. Aseneth becomes the new Eve, recipient of divine knowledge, sharer in eternal life, and privy to the revelations of Levi the prophet who sees letters written in heaven by the finger of God then passes them on to Aseneth in secret (22:13).

Aseneth's conversion affirms her individual standing before God as a woman. God gives her divine knowledge, immortality as the new Eve, and a husband who respects her. One might argue that the story is strictly for a Jewish audience, that the reader is supposed to know Genesis and the Joseph story to understand the scriptural allusions in Joseph and Aseneth. But one would do well to remember that the Egyptian diaspora, as with others, included proselytes and God-fearing sympathizers as depicted in the book of Acts. And the fact that Paul refers to the marriage account of Genesis 2:24 in Ephesians 5:31 indicates that he thought his gentile audience had knowledge of Genesis, which opens the door to the possibility of them having knowledge of the popular Jewish novel. Aseneth is clearly not in pursuit of a celibate life. But her assertive, independent thinking and casting off the religious traditions of her family in pursuit of the one true God can serve as the impetus for similar actions by first-century believing women.

In 1 Timothy the young widows of Ephesus, embracing celibate ascetic life and moving freely between houses (1 Tim 5:13), manifest independence exceptional to Hellenistic values.[77] Paul reacts by stressing a woman's place in the private domain of the home (5:14) with instruction to manage the household, bear children, and in so doing avoid slander from the outsider. His admonition for women to learn in quietness and submission (2:11), including prohibition from teaching or exercising authority over a man, he supports with Adam's priority in birth before Eve (2:13) and Eve's susceptibility to deception (2:14). Perhaps his reasons are an attempt to

---

77. The composition date for 1 Timothy is debated, scholarship generally placing it in late first/early second century. For an overview of the debate see Towner, *The Letters to Timothy and Titus*, 2–7; Guthrie, *The Pastoral Epistles*, 17–62 (cf. 57–58); and Wallace, https://bible.org/seriespage/15-1-timothy-introduction-argument-outline (accessed 3 May 2023). The precise composition date for the pastoral letter does not influence the outcome of my argument.

balance the scales against Ephesian women teachers claiming authority over men based on the priority of Artemis in creation as firstborn before Apollo, and their claim to procreative authority as the gateway to life based on the procreative authority of the Anatolian mother goddess who gave birth to the other gods, the first humans, and whom they have conflated with Artemis.[78] Much of 1 Timothy concerns itself with combatting false teaching (1:3–7, 18–20; 4:1–15) which may have been syncretistic and carried from house to house by these independent women whom Paul believes to be deceived like Eve, hence, Paul calls them to return to traditional female roles of childbearing (5:14) since they are unqualified teachers. Placed in this context, the purpose of the author's message would not have been to restrict women everywhere indefinitely or to demonstrate women's inferiority but to challenge their notion of superiority and to address the specific syncretistic situation in second-century Ephesus.[79] Whatever the exact reasons behind his admonition, women are acting in an independent manner in Ephesus some years after the Ephesian epistle, indicating that the seeds of independence are likely present at the time of Ephesian epistle.

The Acts of Paul and Thecla (c. 180 CE) suggest that segments of the Pauline movement were determined to protect a celibate way of life.[80] Set during Paul's first missionary journey, Paul travels to Iconium, promoting abstinence.[81] At the house of Onesiphorus, Thecla, a young noble virgin listens to Paul from her window in an adjacent house and watches "many women and virgins going in to see Paul." Her fiancé and mother worry that she will heed Paul's message that one must remain a virgin, so they form a mob to drag Paul before the governor, who imprisons Paul. Thecla bribes a guard to gain entrance and sits at Paul's feet all night listening to

---

78. For more on the authority of motherhood and reverence of the mother goddess, see Anadolu-Okur, *From Cybele to Artemis*, 197–221.

79. A definitive understanding of exactly which false teachings are being referenced in 1 Timothy is another project that goes beyond the scope of my objectives here. See also, MacDonald, *Early Christian Women*, 154–82; and Glahn's treatment of "saved through childbearing" in *Nobody's Mother*, chapter 6 for more.

80. For more on the points of contact between 1 Timothy and the Acts of Paul and Thecla, see Dennis McDonald, *The Legend and the Apostle*, 54–77, where he identifies second-century Asia minor as the setting. Margaret McDonald adds that even if the current form of the Acts of Paul and Thecla come from a generation later than 1 Timothy, the stories would have been in oral circulation earlier. See also Kraemer, *Her Share of the Blessings*, 151–54; and Margaret MacDonald, *Pauline Churches*, 181–87.

81. A debt of gratitude to Margaret MacDonald her for the detailed description of Thecla juxtaposed with 1 Timothy 5:3–16 in *Early Christian Women*, 165–82.

his teaching. Her family brings both she and Paul before the governor who sentences Paul to scourging and Thecla to be burned at the stake. God saves her by sending a storm to douse the flames. She then goes to Antioch with Paul where the nobleman, Alexander, desires Thecla and tries to take her by force. She tears his cloak and knocks the crown off his head. Embarrassed, Alexander drags her before the governor on the charge of assaulting a nobleman. She is sentenced to be eaten by wild beasts in the arena but is defended by a lioness who fights off the other beasts. Thecla then, to the lament of the multitude of women in the crowd, casts herself into a large pit full of water and deadly seals. In that moment a flash of lightening kills the seals but saves her, followed by a ring of fire that surrounds and protects her. She then rests in the house of the wealthy widow Tryphaena, instructing her and her maidservants in the word of the Lord. Hearing that Paul is in Myra she travels with a band of maidservants and young men to see him. Leaving her worldly possessions with Paul to care for the poor she retires to a cave in Seleucia as a hermit and healer for seventy-two years. Local doctors, fearing loss of income due to her healings, solicit a group of young men to rape her. As they are about take hold of her a passage miraculously opens in the cave then closes behind her. Thecla then leaves for Rome to see Paul who is executed before she arrives, the story ending with her laying down beside his tomb.[82]

The story violates acceptable Hellenistic female behavior on multiple levels: women and virgins move freely from house to house to meet Paul (v. 7); as the teacher of Tryphaena and her maidservants (v. 39) Thecla crosses the line into the forbidden public male sphere (v. 41);[83] standing in contrast to the role that 1 Timothy wishes to encourage (1 Tim 5:9–16) she refuses to marry and instead ventures outside her home (vs. 10, 18–20), rejecting the Hellenistic values of being a wife, mother, and mistress over maidservants; she defends herself against Alexander's advances (v. 26); rather than a man, it is the wealthy widow Tryphaena who shelters Thecla (vs. 27–29) and preserves her purity (vs. 27, 31). In common with Artemis, she remains a virgin with no need of protection from a man.

---

82. See Elliott, *The Apocryphal New Testament*, 372–74.
83. See MacDonald, *Early Christian Women*, 171–72.

By the third-fourth century she is a legend,[84] a shrine to her having been erected in Seleucia to honor her ministry and celibacy.[85] When Emmelia (d. 375 CE), the Cappadocian mother of Basil the Great and Gregory of Nyssa, was told in a dream that her daughter, Macrina the Younger (324–379 CE), was to bear the secret name Thecla, the implications of these legendary stories upon Macrina's future would not have been missed by Emmelia.[86] Nyssen would establish Macrina as the new Thecla, continuing the legend of the past while providing a new model for ascetic virginity in complete devotion to God, leading to transformation and union with Christ as his bride. The naming of Macrina as Thecla also provides a direct line of sight from two hundred years prior, endorsing the continued celibate influence of the Acts of Paul and Thecla (c. 150 CE) all the way to the Cappadocians (mid fourth cent. CE) who then provide a model for a female restored in the *imago Dei* whether virgin or married, based on their relationship to Origen (c. 185–c. 253 CE), who discipled Thaumaturgus (c. 213–270 CE), who discipled their grandmother, who discipled them.[87]

Carla Sunberg writes that the Cappadocian fathers, Basil the Great (330–379 CE), his brother Gregory of Nyssa (335–395 CE), and Nyssan's friend, Gregory of Nazianzus (329–389 CE),[88] "building upon the work of Origen, extolled the goal of personal holiness for Christian women and men, married or celibate, by being transformed into the image of God through a virtuous life of imitating Christ. This was their notion of *theosis*."[89]

---

84. Mary, the mother of Jesus, does not gain much traction as a figure until the theological arguments in which she becomes *Theotokos*, or the "Bearer of God" in 431 CE at the Council of Ephesus.

85. Davis, *The Cult of St. Thecla*, 36–48.

86. See Nyssa, *The Life of Saint Macrina*, trans. Corrigan, 21–54; also, Nazanzius *Ep.* 163, LCL 68.470–71. The Cappadocian mothers were the mothers and sisters of Cappadocian fathers, Basil, Gregory, and Gregory.

87. My intent has been to remain close to the first century in describing the emergence of two traditions to represent the *imago Dei*. Basil and Nyssen are fourth century, but there is a clear line of sight from them to Origen (c. 184–c. 253) via their grandmother Macrina the Elder (c. 260–c. 340 CE) who studied under Gregory Thaumaturgus (c. 213–270 CE) who studied under Origen from 231–239. These dates bear further investigation since from the above it appears Macrina would have only been age ten at the time of Gregory's death.

88. Traditionally known as The Three Cappadocians, Basil the Great was bishop of Caesarea; Basil's younger brother Gregory of Nyssa was bishop of Nyssa; and Nyssen's close friend, Gregory of Nazianzus was patriarch of Constantinople. The Three Cappadocians played a key role in shaping the final form of the Nicene Creed.

89. See Sunberg, *Cappadocian Mothers*, Kindle loc. 117. For more on the notion of the

THE IMAGE OF GOD, MARRIAGE, AND CELIBACY

Their theology of holiness is best understood by way of the influence of Origin mediated via the influence Thaumaturgus, who as a young man travelled to Palestine to study under Origen. We learn of him from Basil in *Epistles* 28, 204, and 207 of *To the Church of Neocaesarea*.[90] During the persecutions under Emperor Diocletian, Macrina the Elder, maternal grandmother of Basil and Nyssen fled to Neocaesarea where Thaumaturgus served as bishop. Basil writes:

> And what indeed could be a clearer proof of our faith than that we were brought up by our grandmother, a blessed woman who came from amongst you? I mean the illustrious Macrina, by whom we were taught the sayings of the most blessed Gregory (as many as she herself retained, preserved to her time in unbroken memory), and who molded and formed us while still young in the doctrines of piety....[91]

Blessed Gregory, discipled by his teacher, Origen, in turn discipled Macrina the Elder, who then passed on Origen's teaching on to the generations that followed. Basil and Nyssen's theological understanding was defined considering Origen, whether in agreement or making correction. While they did not physically sit at the knee of Origen, they were disciples of his teachings via Macrina, teachings that they refined into the *theosis* of women as women.[92]

Basil argued that the *imago Dei* was both male and female. In his *On the Human Condition*, Basil creates a conversation with a woman in which they discuss whether the image of God might be present in a woman:

Christianizing of the Greek concept of deification see Norris, "Deification: Consensual and Cogent" 411–28, and Sunberg, *Cappadocian Mothers*, ch. 2, "The Christianization of Deification." Their presentation of this notion is a general attribution to the pagan Greek concept of the gods' deifying animals, when perhaps the deification of the human Caesar might provide a nearer reference. Noteworthy is Juvenal's comment, "Is there anyone who doesn't know the kind of monsters that crazy Egypt worships.... Entire towns worship cats in one place, in another fish, in another river fish, in another a dog—but no one worships Diana," *Sat.* 15.1–13, LCL 91.489.

90. Basil, *Let.* 28, LCL 190.158–71; *Let.* 204, LCL 243.154–75; and *Let.* 207, LCL 243.180–93. See Sunberg, *Cappadocian Mothers*, 30–31; 179–81.

91. Basil, *Let.* 204, LCL 243.154–175.

92. See Clarke, *St. Basil the Great*, 28; Russell, *The Doctrine of Deification in the Greek Patristic Tradition*, 123; Wilkin, *Spirit of Early Christian Thought*, 138–39; Rousseau, *Basil of Caesarea*, 3.

> The woman is equal with the man and has the honor to be created in the image of God. The creation of each is equal, equal in good deeds, equal in honor, and identical in reward. May [the woman] not say, "I am weak." Weakness comes from the flesh, but strength is in the spirit (soul). Since the image of God is identical in each of them, may there be equal honor and equal good works done by both.[93]

The attitude of women being equal to men in *imago*, honor, good deeds, and so on, spread beyond gender toward slavery, and class distinctions. The outworking of this theology led to transformed daily relationships. When Macrina and Emmelia, moved to the family estate at Annesi, they took their servants with them who then lived as equals in a new community, a Cappadocian household where there was "neither slave nor free" (Gal 3:28).[94]

Basil's brother, Nyssen, enlarged Basil's conclusions related to the *imago Dei* and made plain that all of humanity is included in the first creation, and the *imago* is for the whole human:

> For the image is not in part of our nature, nor is the grace in any one of the things found in that nature, but this power extends equally to all the race: and a sign of this is that mind is implanted alike in all: for all have the power of understanding and deliberating, and of all else whereby the Divine nature finds its image in that which was made according to it: the man that was manifested at the first creation of the world, and he that shall be after the consummation of all, are alike: they equally bear in themselves the Divine image.[95]

Contrary to Origen's concept of the pre-existence of the soul,[96] Nyssen thought the human soul and body were joined into one. So, the life in the flesh affects the soul, and the soul in turn affects the flesh. Pursuit of union with God leads humanity toward perfection which proceeds to renew the

---

93. Basil, *Hom.* 10 & 11 or *Or. 1, Hum. Cond.*, a source that was considered controversial until the SC 160 (1970) declared it an authentic work from Basil; see Sunberg, *Cappadocian Mothers*, 73, fn. 364.

94. Sunberg, *Cappadocian Mothers*, 158. A debt of gratitude to Dr Sunberg for her work which has informed much of my research in 7.5.

95. Nyssen, *Making of Man*, Schaff and Wace, *Nicene and Post Nicene Fathers*, 2.5.406.

96. See Schaff, *History of the Christian Church*, 3.831 where he writes, "Origen himself allowed that the Bible does not directly teach the pre-existence of the soul, but maintained that several passages, such as the strife between Esau and Jacob in the womb, and the leaping of John the Baptist in the womb of Elizabeth at the salutation of Mary, imply it." For examples see Origen, *De Prin.* II.IX.7 and II.III.5 in Schaff, *Ante-Nicene Fathers* 4, Kindle loc. 16981–93 and 19394.

imago Dei in the believer.⁹⁷ Using Origen's metaphor of the bride and the bridegroom, believing humanity takes on femaleness as the bride of Christ in the eschaton, making all men and women brides.⁹⁸ This is quite the opposite of Clement's teaching that women needed to become honorary men.

Nyssen's writing of *De Vita Macrinae* in honor of his sister extols Macrina as the living model of *theosis*. Her life of virginity, separation from social responsibilities, separation from the desires of the flesh, and nurturing of her soul makes her the physical embodiment of being transformed into the image of God. Macrina the Younger becomes the ideal of ascetic piety, and she achieves this as female, as a virgin. Hence, the message is clear to young women that, like Macrina, they could leave the world of the household matron for a life of virginity as the bride of Christ.⁹⁹

In his *Oration on Holy Baptism*, Gregory of Nasianzus spoke to both the married and single catechumens, affirming that both the married and unmarried were acceptable: "Are you not yet wedded to flesh? . . . You are pure even after marriage. I will take the risk of that. I will join you in wedlock. I will dress the bride. We do not dishonor marriage because we give a higher honor to virginity. . . . Only let marriage be pure and unmingled with filthy lusts."¹⁰⁰

While Nyssan extols his sister Macrina the Younger for her virginity as a path to *theosis*, in *Oration 8* Nazianzen extols both his mother Nonna and his sister Gorgonia for their commitment in marriage as a path to the same goal of union with God. When Nonna married, her husband, Gregory, was not a Christian, but he eventually converted to Christianity, won over by her devotion to Christ and her virtuous prayers.¹⁰¹ As Nazianzen reflected on his parents' lives, he saw their companionship as a model of prelapsarian marriage. Nazianzen's believed that the restoring image of God, which transcended gender, led to the partnering of equals he saw between his parents: "For the best in men and women was so united so that their marriage

---

97. See Nyssen, *Making of Man*, Schaff and Wace, *Nicene and Post Nicene Fathers*, 2.5.419–20, 426–27.

98. See Sunberg, *Cappadocian Mothers*, 135.

99. Nyssen, *Virg.*, Schaff and Wace, *Nicene and Post Nicene Fathers*, 2.5.343–71.

100. Nazianzen, *Or.* 40.18 Wace and Schaff, *Nicene and Post Nicene Fathers*, 2.7.365. To be fair, Nyssen also clarifies his stance: "Let no one think that, for these reasons, we are disregarding the institution of marriage. We are not ignorant of the fact that this also is not deprived of God's blessing." Nyssen, *Virg.* 8, Schaff and Wace, *Nicene and Post Nicene Fathers*, 2.5.352.

101. Nazianzen, *Or.* 18.4, Wace and Schaff, *Nicene and Post Nicene Fathers*, 2.7.255–56.

was more of a union of virtue than of bodies. Although they surpassed all others, they themselves were so evenly matched in virtue that they could not surpass each other."[102] Focusing on transformation into the *imago Dei* was the goal for Nonna and Gregory which translated into a reflection of the restored marriage relationship. Gorgonia followed the example of her mother in bringing her husband to Christ and "gained for herself a virtuous fellow servant, rather than a virtual tyrant."[103]

> For when she was joined to the flesh, she was not, by that same action, separated from the spirit; nor, because she looked on her husband as her head, did she disregard our chief head. Rather, after paying service for a little while to the world and to nature, as far as the law of flesh—or rather, as far as the one who gave flesh its laws—demanded, she then consecrated herself entirely to God.[104]

Sunberg writes, "By utilizing his mother and sister as the examples of restoration, Nazianzen was providing hope for all of humanity, male and female, and endorsing marriage as a path to *theosis*."[105]

The Cappadocian women became models for an inaugurated eschatology, their lives a theological message of transformation to *theosis*. This grew into a theology amongst the Cappadocian fathers where the *imago Dei* was located in humans before gender differentiation, resulting in both men and women being considered of equal value, and marriage to Christ being the ultimate goal of their union. The result is a message that provides a road map for deification of women as women leading all the way back to the teachings of Origen and bringing us closer to the first-century *Sitz im Leben*. Nyssen appears to favor virginity as the path to transform into the *imago Dei*[106] while his friend, Nazianzen, praised his mother, Nonna, and sister, Gorgonia as transforming into the image of God as wives and mothers,[107] but this does not mean that one is exclusive of the other. Married and virgin, Macrina the Elder, Emmelia, Nonna, Gorgonia, and Macrina the Younger, exemplified deification for the Cappadocian fathers and provided a model for a female restored in the *imago Dei*, whether virgin or married. While the Cappadocians affirm the development of both traditions

---

102. Nazianzen, *Or.* 18.7, Wace and Schaff, *Nicene and Post Nicene Fathers*, 2.7.256
103. Nazianzen, *Or.* 8.8, Wace and Schaff, *Nicene and Post Nicene Fathers*, 2.7.240.
104. Nazianzen, *Or.* 8.8, Wace and Schaff, *Nicene and Post Nicene Fathers*, 2.7.240.
105. Sunberg, *Cappadocian Mothers*, 113.
106. Schaff and Wace, *Nicene and Post Nicene Fathers*, 2.5.343–71.
107. Nazianzen, *Or.* 8, Wace and Schaff, *Nicene and Post Nicene Fathers*, 2.7.238–45.

fomenting in the deification of women as women, a clear trajectory specific to the appeal of celibacy as the path to becoming the restored *imago Dei* is observable and significant.

5.2 PART TWO—THE IMAGE OF GOD AND A TRAJECTORY OF CELIBACY

Unlike Paul's correspondence in 1 Corinthians 7 and 1 Timothy 5, nothing is written of celibacy as an alternate lifestyle in Ephesians.[108] Rather, Christian marriage is celebrated as the mysterious relationship between Christ and the church (Eph 5:32). The female body in matrimony "without stain, or wrinkle, or any other blemish" becomes a symbol of the church as "holy and blameless" that marks a clear boundary between the believing Ephesians and the immoral outside (Eph 5:26–27). Celibacy goes unmentioned. Multiple reasons are possible for this omission: 1) Paul may not be interested in issues surrounding the celibate at this time; 2) he may only wish to address an area of marital tension in the Christian home; 3) or he may not wish to shine a spotlight on celibacy thereby promoting it as an alternate way of living. Another possibility, which I offer up here, is that there exists a history and trajectory of celibacy, visible before, during, and after the first century that Paul wishes to resist in an unspoken manner through his lengthy Ephesian *Haustafel* extolling marriage. Paul hints at combatting a trajectory of celibacy in the Ephesian church by encouraging a culture of marriage and family to best promote his evangelistic intentions in the Hellenistic Mediterranean.[109] An examination of Caesar's marriage laws, the rise of celibate communities, and the perceived sinfulness of sex will illumine this possibility.

In 18/17 BCE Emperor Augustus (r. 27 BCE–14 CE) enacted the Julian Marriage Laws in response to widespread extravagance, population decline, and adultery among Rome's elite. Marriage was becoming less frequent in the upper classes and many marriages did not produce offspring. Hence, he enacted laws to encourage marriage and having children and making adultery a crime.[110] Under the Lex Julia there was no time limit for the period of

---

108. For more on celibacy and 1 Corinthians 7, see Wenham's discussion in *Paul: Follower of Jesus or Founder of Christianity?,*" Kindle loc. 2704. For more on 1 Timothy 5 see MacDonald, *Early Christian Women*, 154–78.

109. Socially conservative when compared to the more liberal Roman upper classes.

110. Lex Julia de Maritandis Ordinibus and Lex Julia de Adulteriis Coercendis. For a

engagement, so bachelors used this loophole to get engaged to young girls to put off marriage and extend singleness. In 9 CE Augustus amended the Lex Julia with the Lex Papia laws which limited the engagement period to two years and forbade betrothal with girls under the age of ten, with the age of twelve being the time when they could marry. Lex Papia penalized unmarried men from the ages twenty-five to sixty and unmarried women from ages twenty to fifty who did not have children and did not marry if they were divorced or widowed,[111] and incentivized married couples to have children.[112] Although Augustus' initial intended target for the laws may have been Rome's senatorial and equestrian classes, the laws were still applied throughout the empire in a manner that rewarded Mediterranean Hellenistic culture's emphasis on marriage and propagation with elevated financial and social status. Rewards were made to encourage a "freedman" to produce children.[113] If he had four children, he could exclude his patron from any claim on his estate.[114] Similar laws applied to "freedwomen." Celibate communities in pursuit of personal piety were not the impetus behind Caesar's laws, but the licentious living of Rome's wealthy coupled with ascetic celibate communities yielded the same net sum of no children.

Celibate communities were not a phenomenon originating with first-century believers. A Jewish monastic community, the Therapeutae, described in Philo's, *The Contemplative Life* (c. 30 CE), was made up of both males and females who were largely elderly virgins, with groups distributed throughout Egypt and Greece. Similarly, the Essenes (second cent. BCE–first cent. CE) are described by Pliny the Elder (d. 79 CE) in *Natural History* as existing for "thousands of ages," possessing no money, with no women among them, and populated by strangers who come to them.[115] Philo numbers them as more than four thousand in Palestine and Syria, extols their piety, study of scripture, avoidance of lawless cities, and devotion to arts which result in peace. He describes them as poor in material goods but rich in truth.[116] Albeit not sharing

---

detailed description of the laws including primary sources, see Field, Jr., "The Purpose of the Lex Iulia et Papia Poppaea," 398–416.

111. *Inst. Gaius* II.111, 286; *Ulp. Frag.* XVII; Suetonius, *Claud.* 23, LCL 38.44–45.

112. Lex Julia et Papia. Tacitus, *Ann.* XV.19, LCL 322.244–45; Pliny *Ep.* VII.16, LCL 55.514–17.

113. *Justinian Law* 38.1.37, Work of Freedmen.

114. *Ulp. Frag.* 29.3, Good Liberators.

115. *Contempl. Life* 3.1–3, LCL 363.112–15; 3.21–29, LCL 363.124–29; *Nat. Hist.* 5.25, LCL 352.276–77.

116. *Every Good Man is Free* 12.75–77, LCL 363.52–55.

the same faith in Christ, the pursuit of personal holiness in celibate communities would not have been a novel idea for the emerging church.

Arriving at 1 Timothy, Paul writes to the young pastor in Ephesus where it appears the number of celibate women has grown sufficiently to require a formal "office of widows" (5:11–15), the young ones of whom Paul is entreating to marry and have children (2:15; 5:14).[117] Yet, this does not mean that these widows agreed with or chose to adhere to Paul's exhortations for married life. Rather, by the early second century there are multiple groups of celibates. Ignatius greets a group of virgins who are called "widows" at Smyrna along with the "houses of the brothers with their wives and children."[118] Justin writes of men and women who are celibate into advanced years.[119] Minuscius Felix endorses perpetual virginity as an option for believers.[120] By the third century celibate groups are thriving. Cyprian encourages the virgins of Carthage to live the angelic life while on earth (cf. Matt 22:30/Mark 12:25), "That which we shall be, you have already begun to be. . . . You already possess the glory of the resurrection. . . . You pass through the world without pollution, equal to the angels of God."[121] The Genesis command to increase and multiply has been exchanged for the exhortation to remain abstinent. Emancipated from reproductive womanhood, celibate women could be free from the structure of socialized gender, ideally no longer the objects of male desire, but rather as equal to men or even as honorary men.[122]

A trajectory of celibacy continues its journey, reinforced by negative attitudes regarding sex as sinful. The Genesis 3 account with the expulsion of Adam and Eve from the garden, and Psalm 51:5, "Surely I was sinful at birth, sinful from the time my mother conceived me" are commonly used as the biblical grounds for the transmission of original sin. Paul carries

---

117. For more see MacDonald, *Early Christian Women*, 157–65.

118. Ignatius *Smyrn.* 13.1 (c. 110 CE); LCL 24.308–9.

119. Justin Martyr, *Apol.* 1.15 (c. 155–157 CE), Roberts and Donaldson, *Anti-Nicene Christian Library*, 2.18.

120. Minucius Felix, *Oct.* 31.5 (197 CE); LCL 250.408–9.

121. Cyprian, *Dress of Virg.* 22–23 (c. 248 CE), Deferrari and Keenan, *The Fathers of the Church*, 50.

122. For example, Pallidus (early fifth cent.), in his *Lausiac History* 41.1, speaks of heroic monastic men and of heroic masculine women to whom God grants trials equal to those of men; see Clarke, *The Lausiac History of Palladius*, 35–180. See also Clark, "Ideology, History, and the Construction of Woman in Late Ancient History," 154–84; and Aspegren, *The Male Woman: A Feminine Ideal in the Early Church*.

the notion forward to all the world in Romans 5:12–21 (cf. 5:15a), "For if the many died by the trespass of the one man . . ." making Adam's experience representative for everyone[123] and adding that all individuals are responsible for their own sin (5:12). In 2 Corinthians 11:3 he identifies Eve as deceived by the serpent, which some may take as the beginning of sin. As mentioned earlier, Ben Sirah (25.24) makes Eve the author of sin and death; as does the Life of Adam and Eve (18:1–2) and its Greek version, the Apocalypse of Moses (32:1–3).[124] Yet, Genesis 3 makes no association between sex and the disobedience of Adam and Eve, nor is the serpent associated with Satan, nor are the words sin, transgression, rebellion, or guilt mentioned. While the speaker in Psalm 51:1 traces his own sinfulness to the moment of conception, there is little to support the idea that it was applicable to all humanity.

Even so, the belief in "original sin" was in full bloom by the time of Augustine (354–430 CE), who identified male semen as the way original sin was passed down from Adam through intercourse, leaving Christ, conceived without semen, free from sin.[125] Prior to Augustine there appears a history of development indicating that sex "post fall" left the realm of controlled rational procreation to become unrestrained impassioned intercourse which overwhelmed one's mind, taking one's thoughts off of God while conceiving children in lust. Clement of Alexandria (c. 150–218 CE) counselled that the male should try to conceive without passion, but instead "with a chaste and controlled will."[126] Put bluntly: Jerome (c. 342–420 CE) writes, "Do you imagine that we approve of any sexual intercourse except

---

123. See also 2 Esdras 3:21–27 (c. 70–218 CE) for similar language to Paul.

124. Although copies of Life of Adam and Eve and Apocalypse of Moses are composed third to fifth century CE, there is general agreement the originals were composed in the first century or earlier.

125. *City of God* XXI.12, LCL 417:74–77; Also, his *Conf.* I.2, LCL 26.60–61; 19, LCL 26:54–57; VIII.2, LCL 26.358–61. Augustine was the first to use the phrase *peccatum originale* to describe the human condition. For more see Clark, *Saint Augustine on Marriage and Sexuality*. There are multiple responses to Augustine's line of thought about the transmission of original sin: 1) Mary already had the genetic material of Adam in her since she had a father; 2) Original sin and sin nature are not in scripture. Sin nature is a proclivity toward sin, which Jesus avoided; 3) Original sin can be passed along spiritually and does not require genetics to do so; 4) Scripture does not directly connect the virgin birth to sin or sin nature. Rather the virgin birth is a miraculous entrance into the world by fulfilling prophecies of Genesis 3:15 and Isaiah 7:14; 5) Augustine mistakenly accepted Aristotle's notion that male ejaculate was a complete human while the female womb was only a receptacle.

126. Clement of Alexandria, *Strom.* III.7.58.

THE IMAGE OF GOD, MARRIAGE, AND CELIBACY

for the procreation of children? ... He who is too ardent a lover of his own wife is an adulterer";[127] and Justin Martyr (c. 100–165 CE) "If we marry it is only so that we may bring up children."[128] The theme of sexual congress as equated with sin, loss of self-control, and taking one's eyes from God appears as an ever-present adversary.[129] Perhaps even Paul makes a veiled reference to sex as inherently sinful in Ephesians 2:1–3 when he claims that:

> You were dead through the trespasses and sins in which you once walked, following the course of this world, following the ruler of the power of the air, the spirit that is now at work among those who are disobedient. All of us once lived among them in the passions of our flesh, doing the will of flesh and senses, and we were by nature children of wrath, like everyone else. (NRSV)

The notion of associating sex with sin and impurity was not exclusive to Judaism or Christianity. Religions in antiquity had rules against sexual impurity and service to the gods. Rome's priestly vestal virgins vowed to serve goddess Vesta for thirty years while maintaining chastity throughout.[130] Eunuch priests, called Megabyzi, and virgin priestesses served Artemis.[131] The priests of Cybele, called Galli, castrated themselves in devotion to her service.[132] Scripture has such rules, albeit with less severe consequences: a menstruating woman could not enter the women's court of the temple until seven days following her period and she had bathed (Lev 15:19); and a man with a seminal emission had to bathe and remained unclean until evening (Lev 15:16).[133] The Gospel writers come close to the Therapeutae and Essene view that sex made one morally impure, where Jesus identifies eunuchs who have made themselves so for the kingdom of heaven (Matt 19:11) and alludes that there is no intercourse in heaven (Matt 22:31; Mark 12:25). The theme of sexual intercourse as equated with sin, loss of self-control, and distraction from God is common to religion in antiquity, with suggested remedies for control being virginity, celibacy, or

---

127. *Against Jovinianus*, 1.20.40.

128. *First Apology*, Roberts, *The Ante-Nicene Fathers*, 1.172.

129. Hunter, *Marriage and Sexuality in Early Christianity*, 18. See Hunter for a survey and sources of attitudes towards marriage and sex among the early Christians.

130. See Beard, "The Sexual Status of Vestal Virgins," 12–27.

131. Strabo, *Geogr.* 14.1.23, LCL 223.228–29; Also, Plutarch, *Whether an Old Man Should Engage in Public Affairs*, 795e, LCL 321.140–41.

132. See Vermaseren, *Cybele and Attis*, 115.

133. For more see all of Leviticus 15; Josephus, *JW* 5.227 and *Ant.* 17.166.

even castration. Eusebius of Caesarea (c. 260–339 CE) writes that, early in his career, Origen, (185–254 CE) castrated himself and that Origen's bishop approved.[134]

In the words of Irenaeus (c. 130–c. 202 CE), salvation comes through the virgin: "And thus, as the human race fell into bondage to death by means of a virgin, so is it rescued by a virgin; virginal disobedience having been balanced in the opposite scale by virginal obedience."[135] The tradition of the perpetual virginity of Mary[136] appears for the first time as early as the Protoevangelium of James[137] (second cent.) and is endorsed as orthodox in the Council of Ephesus (431 CE) and again in the second Council of Constantinople (553 CE).[138] Regardless of challenges to its historical accuracy, if the Protoevangelium of James was in circulation c. 150 CE, the notion of the perpetual virginity of Mary would correspond with the timing of the Acts Paul and Thecla, further supporting an influential trajectory of celibacy in the early church.[139] Hence, aspiring to virginal obedience presents an attractive option to the devout early Christian. Although Mary could serve as a candidate for the Ephesian believing woman to emulate if an oral tradition of Mary is in circulation prior to the writing of James' gospel, the weight of the evidence and timing continue to point to Artemis. The disobedient former virgin, Eve, may not have served as the ideal candidate for emulation, but the obedient virgin, Mary, could; and the independent virgin goddess of Ephesus likely was.

---

134. Some question whether Eusebius is relying on hearsay, since Origen deprecated castration in his *Commentary on Matthew* 15.1–4. See Hanson, "A Note on Origen's Self-Mutilation," 81.

135. *Haer.* 5.19.1.

136. In Western Christianity, the Catholic Church adheres to this, as do some Lutherans, Anglicans, and Reformed. Most Protestants reject the doctrine.

137. Also known as the Gospel of James, the author claims to be the half-brother of Jesus by an earlier marriage of Joseph. Origen, in his *Commentary on Matthew*, mentions the book, identifying the "brethren of the Lord" as sons of Joseph by an earlier wife. This would likely place the Gospel in mid-second century.

138. The doctrine has been challenged based on the following: the NT explicitly affirms Mary's virginity until the birth of Jesus (Matt 1:25); the NT identifies the siblings of Jesus (Mark 15:40); Matthew and Luke concur on Mary's pre-birth virginity but there is no biblical basis for her perpetual virginity; Luke 2:7 and Matthew 1:25 call Jesus the "first born" son of Mary.

139. Jesus requests for John to care for her as an adopted mother (John 19:25–29). Story has it that John brings Mary to Ephesus where she lived out her later years, where her legend is strengthened, and where the Church of St. Mary is erected.

5.3 SUMMARY

What did the gentile Ephesian believer think the *imago Dei* looked like in people regarding gender, marriage, and celibacy? Part One suggested that the weight of inscriptional and literary evidence led to the rise of two diverging traditions in the pursuit of holiness: marriage and celibacy, with Paul's *Haustafel* in favor of the former. A prominent reason for these diverging traditions among Ephesian believers is that the reception history of Eve as the disobedient wife of Adam makes her an unattractive candidate for the gentile Ephesian woman to emulate, while the reception history of the celibate goddess, Artemis, is quite attractive. Coupled with prevailing attitudes that the path to divinity is to become less female, as witnessed in post-canonical Christian authors, Artemis as an honorary male appears even more inviting. One might question the extent of "Eve tradition" known to the Ephesian believer, but Paul's reference to Genesis 2:24 (cf. Eph 5:31) indicates that some knowledge was present.

Part Two supported Part One with the notion that a female celibate tradition in the *imago Dei* was emerging in Ephesus. This is observed in the restrictions placed on believing women by 1 Timothy, the stories of Joseph and Aseneth as well as Paul and Thecla, and the lives of the Cappadocian mothers (who all share the geography of Asia Minor with Ephesus). That Paul may hint in the Ephesian letter at resisting a trajectory of celibacy is supported by Caesar's marriage laws, rising celibate communities, and promotion of the idea that sex is sinful. Albeit contextually enlightening, the rise of a celibate tradition in the *imago Dei* is not Paul's primary concern in his marital code. Paul's primary concern is that his evangelistic intentions for Ephesus will be derailed by the adverse influence of Artemis upon believing spouses who mistake being the *imago Dei* as independence from each other. Hence, he argues for marital unity as their way to be an image-bearer for the God of the universe. For the married Ephesian believer contemplating independence over interdependence as the path to personal holiness, Paul extols the holy and blameless Ephesian matron, and the nurturing, self-sacrificial devotion of the Ephesian husband, as the road to personal holiness. Intent on evangelizing the unbeliever, Paul appeals to spouses to love one another in a manner that represents what restored relationships in Christ can become—the subject of next chapter.

6

An Evangelistic Marriage Code

How does one best deploy the power to change the world? Relationships. Trusting, loving, self-sacrificing relationships change the world. Paul is counting on it. Paul is explicit in his evangelistic intent "to preach to the gentiles the boundless riches of Christ" and that "now the wisdom of God should be made known" (Eph 3:9–10). Even while an ambassador in chains his only prayer request for himself is that he may continue to evangelize (6:19–20). In Colossians he is equally explicit, "that God may open a door for our message, so that we may proclaim the mystery of Christ" (4:3) and "be wise in the way you act toward outsiders; make the most of every opportunity" (4:5).[1] The expansion of Christ's kingdom will come through attractive relationships.

Peter is also explicit that scattered Christians in Asia Minor should "live such good lives among the pagans that, though they accuse you of doing wrong, they may see your good deeds and glorify God" (1 Pet 2:11)[2] and "that by doing good you should silence the ignorant talk of foolish people" (2:15). Peter continues with explicit instructions to wives that they should "be submissive" (ὑποτασσόμεναι) so that unbelieving husbands will "be won over without words" (3:1–2). Trusting, loving, self-sacrificing relationships expand Christ's kingdom and change the world. Paul and Peter are in agreement.

Given that all three letters to churches in Asia Minor express their evangelizing intent, with Peter doubly explicit in his marital code, is it

---

1. See the discussion in 2.6 of similarities in the letters.
2. I use the name "Peter" with full knowledge that Petrine authorship is contested.

possible to argue that Paul sees the marital codes of Ephesians and Colossians as implicitly part of carrying out the evangelistic *missio Dei* as well?[3] The evidence available in answer to this question is not straightforward but the cumulative of the various strands make for a very plausible conclusion. Evangelistic intent in the letters resonates with Luke's picture of Paul's evangelistic success in Acts 19 and throughout Asia Minor in turning away many from Artemis (19:26–27). In light of the evidence already adduced it is equally plausible that Paul continues his confrontation of the goddess in the Ephesian letter via his inscriptional and allegorical references to the superiority of Christ over Artemis, including a *Haustafel* designed to attract unbelievers to a superior married life infused with new creation ideology as a slice of what relationships can be in Christ's new kingdom.

6.1 EVANGELISM IN THE FACE OF PERSECUTION

Paul and the other NT writers know that the intent to convert outsiders to a movement that would ultimately transform the established social order was not without peril. Enlarging family honor and avoiding shame were the prime influencers of behavior, especially women's behaviors as depicted by men.[4] Daughters played an important part in advancing family honor with a good marriage or bringing shame upon their family with what might be depicted as unchaste behavior. Thus, notions of individual choice for women would be treated with suspicion as disruptive to the fabric of ordered society. This is reflected in the amount of attention that is given to household relations in Ephesians 5:21—6:1, 1 Tim 2:11–15 and 5:3–10, 1 Peter 3:1–6, Titus 2:3–5, Colossians 3:18—4:1, all in Asia Minor. First Peter 3:1–6 spells out how a believer should behave in a house with a non-believing head.[5] Even a household with just one Christian meant there was hope for evangelistic expansion. While Ephesians 5:21—6:9 is concerned with the

---

3. MacDonald makes a brief allusion to evangelism, "The strong recommendations for believers to be subordinate to the pagan paterfamilias seem to have been made for two main reasons: a desire to limit the potentially controversial visibility of these members and a recognition of their strategic opportunities to evangelize nonbelievers within the home" (*Sacra Pagina: Colossians and Ephesians,* Kindle Loc. 4173–75). See also Henderson regarding Colossians in "Taking Liberties with the Text," 420–32 (cf. 429).

4. For more, see MacDonald, *Early Christian Women,* 27–41, 144–54; also, Osiek and Balch, *Families in the New Testament World,* 38–43.

5. For more on 1 Peter, see Khobnya, "So That They May Be Won Over without a Word," 7–16.

inner workings of the household of believers, in 2:19 the letter also identifies them as part of the much larger household of God that far exceeds the size of any house, city, region, or empire, and whose mission is to evangelize the whole world (2:10) thereby transforming society.

Speaking to believers in Asia Minor, Peter writes to the believers scattered throughout Pontus, Galatia, Cappadocia, Asia, and Bithynia (1:1), an area approximately 400 miles North to South and 500 miles East to West. The recipients of this letter are referred to as "exiles of the Dispersion" (1:1) who are maligned (2:12; 3:16) and reviled (4:14), who also are to be mindful that "your brothers and sisters in all the world are undergoing the same kinds of suffering" (5:9). To assume that the church of Ephesus would be exempt from the suffering of the other Roman provinces in Asia Minor is a bridge too far.

First Peter is clearly a circular letter, but what of the Ephesian letter? The description of the Ephesian recipients is general.[6] They are called holy (1:1, 15, 18; 3:18; 5:3; 6:18), and faithful (1:1, 13, 15; 2:18; 3:12), who love our Lord Jesus Christ" (6:24), experiencing his grace (1:6, 8; 2:5, 8) and love (2:4; 5:2, 25). Paul does not appear to personally know them, nor they him (1:15; 3:2).[7] If the message of Ephesians is for Asia Minor as well, then concerns such as that of the suspicious onlooker or the notion of an evangelistic strategy in Asia Minor is a shared one between the Pauline and Petrine letters. If persecution was a threat to the readers of Peter's letter, then it is likely to be a threat to the readers of Ephesians as well.[8]

Paul is aware of such threats. On the heels of instruction to wives and husbands (5:21–33), children and parents (6:1–4), slaves and masters

---

6. See 1.2 for detail regarding circular letter versus targeted letter, concluding that the letter was initially to Ephesus with the intent to circulate from there.

7. If Paul is the author of the letter, this would indicate that the audience is wider than Ephesus since Paul lived in Ephesus (Acts 18–19). If a Paulinist is the author then: 1) he has not been to Ephesus to meet the believers or, 2) the audience is wider than Ephesus.

8. As governor of Pontus-Bythinia (111–113 CE) Pliny the Younger, in a letter to Emperor Trajan, reveals that he has tortured two female slaves (*ancilla*) who are known as deacons (*ministra*) for information about the supposedly secretive early church. Pliny writes (cf. *Let.* 10.96, LCL 59.284–91), "This convinced me that it was all the more necessary to find out what the truth was by the torture of two female slaves who were called deaconesses . . . ." Social reforms regarding gender, celibacy, and slavery might very well have brought unwanted attention to the churches of Asia Minor, including Ephesus. By promoting loyalty to just one God who was worshipped in the privacy of the home, the church burned the bridge between religion and public matters of the imperial state. From Pliny's point of view, the church was dangerously private, private enough and perhaps threatening enough to torture female leadership for information.

(6:5–10) comes admonition to be strong (6:10), put on God's armor to stand against spiritual adversaries (6:11–17), to pray for the Lord's people and for Paul himself as an ambassador "in a chain" (ἐν ἁλύσει) for declaring the gospel (6:20).[9] The persecution the Ephesian believers face may be that of spiritual adversaries but the execution of such persecution is manifest physically as observed in Paul's suffering (3:13). Peter and Paul are not in the business of deliberately inviting persecution for the first-century church. Hence, the Petrine and Pauline marital *Haustafeln* in Asia Minor may appear on the surface to support Hellenistic social structures a means to not arouse suspicion and to avoid persecution, but a close reading reveals their true intent to transform such structures in the inaugural kingdom. Paul's *Haustafeln* was made to attract unbelievers to a married life permeated with love, trust, and sacrificial living across social constructs as a taste of what the new world order under Christ's reign can be. Paul thinks such relationships change the world. What might Paul want these relationships to look like?

6.2 EVANGELISTIC RELATIONSHIPS IN A SACRED COMMUNITY

Paul's message of an interdependent community being "fitted together" (συναρμολογουμένη) and "built together" (συνοικοδομεῖσθε) in united identity and rising to become a holy temple where the God of the universe dwells by his Spirit (Eph 2:21–22) is to be a superior marvel to the Artemision. Paul's use of temple metaphor in Ephesus (sect. 3.4) is among the multiple metaphors he deploys for the Corinthian believers: household (3:1–4; 4:1–2, 14–21), field (3:5–9), building (3:9–15), and temple (3:16–17): "Do you not know that you are God's temple and God's spirit dwells in you?" and "Do you not know that your body is a temple of the Holy Spirit within you, which you have from God, and that you are not your own?" (6:19). Paul defines a temple in terms common to any: a building (3:9–15); that is holy (3:17; 6:19); that is off limits to certain people (6:12–17); that maintains purity (6:18); and is indwelt by the spirit of the temple keeping it holy (6:19–20). Paul uses his metaphor of the body as a temple to admonish against joining bodies with an unbelieving prostitute (6:15–16)[10] and en-

---

9. Compare with "I have been bound" (δέδεμαι) as a similar phrase found in Colossians 4:3, Colossae another Asia Minor city.

10. The use of "the two will become one flesh" (Gen 2:24) which appears both with

courage joining bodies and spirit with one's believing spouse (6:17; 7:3–5) in sexual interdependence since both are members of Christ (6:15).[11] Paul uses the metaphors of body, temple, and spirit to structure how Corinth is to think about relational individuality verses unity.[12] He does the same in Ephesians.

Ephesians' message of interdependence in the "church" (ἐκκλησία) where God lives is repeated nine times, with six of the nine occurrences of ἐκκλησία occurring in the 5:21–33 pericope about marriage. Paul's marital code of unity in sacrificial living becomes a microcosm for how the entire believing household of God (2:19) is to live as part of an eschatological new humanity.[13] The imbalance of the instructions between parents and children (four verses), slaves and masters (two verses) and husbands and wives (thirteen verses) indicate that his marital *Haustafel* is not just another part of the household code. Rather, Paul is arguing for something in the elaboration of the husband-wife relationship that he does not argue for in children and slave relationships. What might have gone so wrong that Paul felt compelled to pen the longest marriage code in the NT?

6.3 MISTAKEN IDENTITIES IN A SACRED COMMUNITY

By the time the Ephesian letter is written, the Ephesian matron is already casting off notions of submission. There is no need for Paul to ask her to submit to (5:22, 24), to submit mutually (5:21), or respect her husband (5:33) if she is already doing so. Her understanding of what the *imago Dei* looks like in her has been polluted by the notion of the independent goddess Artemis. She has misread the pursuit of godlike holiness to be a solitary endeavor, independent from her believing husband.[14] And for unspecified

---

the prostitute (1 Cor 6:15–16) and spouse (Eph 5:31) will receive further discussion in 6.6.

11. It is noteworthy that Paul goes on: "I say this as a concession, not as a command. I wish that all of you were as I am. But each of you has your own gift from God; one has this gift, another has that (7:6–7).

12. For more see Marshall, "Community is a Body," 833-47.

13. For more see Gombis, "A Radically New Humanity," 317–30.

14. See 5.1.2 and 5.1.3. Although there are no recorded instances of Artemis worshippers aspiring to become the goddess, in a case of mistaken identity the onlookers at the festival processional believe that Anthia is Artemis or has been made by Artemis in her divine image, which I argue sows the seed for Artemis worshippers to consider the possibility of personal transformation into the divine. In another case of mistaken identity,

reasons, her husband has stopped loving her, or never loved her, given that first-century marriages were generally not for love but arranged to produce legitimate heirs.[15] There is no reason for Paul to call on the husband to love her if he is already doing so. Their understanding of what the image of God looks like in them is misconstrued as independence rather than *interde*pendence. Paul's evangelistic mission has been compromised because the onlooker observes an unsavory marriage of separation rather than unity. For this reason, Paul writes the lengthy marital pericope speaking to both husband and wife.

The 5:21–33 pericope asking the husband to follow Christ's loving sacrifice for the church (5:25)[16] contains far more instruction to him than her. The verb for love (ἀγαπᾶτε) is in the present imperative meaning that the husband's love is to be a constant, unconditional feature of his conduct toward her. The transcendent message of 5:21, "Submitting yourselves to one another in reverence of Christ" (Ὑποτασσόμενοι ἀλλήλοις ἐν φόβῳ Χριστοῦ) within temporal Hellenistic social structures will evangelize non-believers to a notion of marriage in a community of relationships that is far superior to their present experience.[17] Because they are the *imago Dei* empowered by the Holy Spirit Paul calls both genders to actions that transcend the first-century values of Asia Minor. Ostensibly compliant to Hellenistic social structures, the idea of mutual submission is subversive and evangelistic, calling the believer to live now as if they were physically in the heavenly realms (1:3) under the reign of Christ (1:10) with relationships built on trust and self-giving as a microcosm of the household of God (1:20–23).

Ephesian believing spouses have confused being "godlike" as Christ's image-bearers with being "Artemis-like" which Paul seeks to correct in the text. The abundance of epigraphical, allegorical, and literary references to the goddess (see sect. 3.4-5) throughout the Ephesian letter makes for a compelling argument that the marriage code as well is Paul's continued attempt to combat her influence.

15. Demosthenes, *Neaer.* 59.122, LCL 351.446–47 (c. 343–340 BCE). Also, Osiek and Balch, *Families in the New Testament World*, 40–43, 60–64.

16. The husband's love for his wife in 5:28 corresponds to the comparative adverbial conjunction in 5:25b (καθώς ... οὕτως): "Just as Christ loved the church ... so, husbands ought [also] to love their [own] wives." The pattern is similar to the use of the adverbial conjunction (οὕτως) in 5:24b, which corresponds to the comparative conjunction of 5:22b (ὡς ... οὕτως): "as [wives] submit to the Lord ... so should wives submit to their husbands."

17. This is not to say that true love did not exist between married couples in hierarchical social structures of the first century. But given her transformed status as his now equal, the exercise of his love for her while adjusting to her elevated position in new kingdom reality is beyond that of ordinary first century husband/wife love.

Taken together, the phrases "submitting yourselves to one another" (ὑποτασσόμενοι ἀλλήλοις) in 5:21, "speaking to each other" (λαλοῦντες ἑαυτοῖς) in 5:19, "singing and making melody" (ᾄδοντες καὶ ψάλλοντες) in 5:19, and "giving thanks" (εὐχαριστοῦντες) in 5:20 cohere with Paul's exhortation to "Take heed therefore carefully how you walk" (Βλέπετε οὖν ἀκριβῶς πῶς περιπατεῖτε) in 5:15 and to "be filled with the Spirit" (πληροῦσθε ἐν Πνεύματι) in 5:18. Hence, "Submitting yourselves to one another in reverence of Christ" (Ὑποτασσόμενοι ἀλλήλοις ἐν φόβῳ Χριστοῦ) in 5:21 is by the filling of the Holy Spirit rather than acquiescence to Hellenistic social structures. It is a supernatural endowment that enables the believer to live above the old-world order while living in it. Wives are admonished to mutually submit to (5:21–22) and respect (5:33) their husbands "as to the Lord" (ὡς τῷ Κυρίῳ). Husbands are to sacrifice themselves (5:25) and love their wives as they love themselves (5:28). Slaves are called to respect their masters "as servants of Christ" (ὡς δοῦλοι Χριστοῦ), not people (6:5). Masters are admonished to treat their slaves with respect (6:9) knowing that the Master of both slaves and masters is in the heavens. Their ability to carry out such supernatural actions affirm that indeed, as the *imago Dei*, each can live beyond earthly hierarchy. Their household, a small part of the universal household of God, begins to spread a new movement intent on evangelizing the non-believer by turning the question of "who gets to be in charge" on its head.

If earthly hierarchical structures have been turned on their heads in the new kingdom, what does one do with "the husband is 'head' (κεφαλὴ) of the wife, as Christ is κεφαλὴ of the church" (5:23) and "as the 'church submits' (ἐκκλησία ὑποτάσσεται) to Christ, so also are wives to their husbands (5:24) 'in everything' (ἐν παντί)"? If the dimension of rule from Genesis 1 is not central to Paul's thinking about the *imago Dei* in the Ephesian letter, nor in his marital *Haustafel* (see 4.1.2 and 4.2.6) why might he pen these verses?

Complementarians (favoring male leadership) and egalitarians (favoring equal leadership) agree that the "Submitting yourselves to one another in reverence of Christ" (5:21) is clearly "as to the Lord" (5:22) but then take well documented diverging paths. In the egalitarian home the husband or wife can function as the leader based on individual giftedness, one submitting to the other mutually as ontological and functional equals in Christ's new kingdom where Christ is κεφαλή. In the complementarian home the husband functions as leader while the wife exercises her gifts under his loving direction; she, an ontological equal who submits to him as her functional κεφαλή in Christ's new kingdom where Christ is κεφαλή of them both (sect. 1.1).[18] The intent of the egalitarian path leads to Ephesian spouses transforming society by treating each other as equals despite hierarchical social constructs, while the intent of the complementarian path leads to Ephesian spouses transforming society while adhering to hierarchical social constructs.

In this context much debate has occurred as to whether κεφαλή means authority, or source, or prominence, or pre-eminence; in tandem with debates over who is most like God in the Genesis 1 and 2 creation accounts so to decide which gender gets to rule. But if Paul's primary frame of reference for what the *imago Dei* looks like in people to the Ephesian believer is not the Genesis accounts, but Artemis, then what might this mean for how he wants them to understand κεφαλή in his marital *Haustafel*? The focus of the 5:21–33 pericope appears to have little to do with κεφαλή conjuring up notions of source, pre-eminence, prominence, or authority. However, the pericope goes into detail as to what it means to lead. If Christ is κεφαλή of the church, in what sense is Christ leading here? He leads in self-sacrificial love as if he were taking care of his own body (5:25–29), a body to which both husbands and wives belong (5:30). Hence, in the context of their mutual submission (5:21) to the Lord (5:22), if the wife is to submit to her husband (5:22) as her κεφαλή in this instance (5:23), and submit to his leadership in everything (5:24), to what exactly does Paul wish her to submit? In the next verse (5:25) Paul defines this when he calls on the husband to lead in self-sacrificing love for her just as Christ has for the church, a love which Paul describes in detail (5:25–29). In this instance leading in self-sacrificing love is the meaning of κεφαλή.

Though it is obvious to all from the letter that Christ is in charge, the marital code is not about which gender is in charge. Paul painstakingly spells out to the husband what love looks like in new kingdom relationships, precisely because this is not typical behavior for husbands in Hellenism; and tells the wife in this instance she should follow his lead "in everything" (ἐν παντί) to do with loving sacrificially (5:24) rather than continue with independent behaviors that work against Paul's evangelistic

---

18. See 1.1, fns. 5–7 for a list of scholars. See Westfall, 3.5.6.2, "Woman and Man as her Head in Ephesians 5:21-33" in *Paul and Gender*, and Lee-Barnewall, *Neither Complementarian, ch.* 8; also, Thielman, *Ephesians*, 376–79; Arnold, *Ephesians*, 536–38; Hoehner, *Ephesians*, 670–74.

intent for marriage. Paul is not concerned with laying down the nature of gender relations for all of time. He is addressing a specific problem in Ephesian marriage.

6.4 THE HOLY AND BLAMELESS EPHESIAN MATRON

To correct their notion of mistaken identity, Paul presents the reader with an analogy of marriage that elevates the status of the believing matron. Ephesians 5:26, "so that he might sanctify (ἁγιάσῃ) her having cleansed (καθαρίσας) her by the washing of water by the word,"[19] resonates with the Salutaris Inscription's[20] use of καθαρίζω to describe the purification of Artemis statues at processions, where the statue of Artemis was bathed, anointed, and adorned with a wreath (Sect. 4.4).[21] Strelan observes that these actions were performed "to renew the life and power of the image" and served as a reminder that "they carried the power of the being they represented"[22] giving them access to the power of the goddess through her image. He supports this with an example from Claudius Aelianus "Aelian" (c. 170–235 CE) where a boy carries away a golden leaf (lit. plate of gold) which has fallen from the crown of Artemis, is then charged with sacrilege and executed;[23] and a second example from Dionysius of Halicarnassus implying that power resided in the crowns worn by Greeks which had previously adorned images of Artemis.[24] Beyond the implication that by the husband bathing the wife Paul assigns to the matron the value of a goddess, he makes a point of her shared status with the church as the sanctified, cleansed, holy, and blameless bride of Christ who sacrificed himself for her (5:26–27). One might argue that this is precisely what females

---

19. Similar verses exist (Acts 20:32; 26:18; 1 Cor 1:2; 6:11; 1 Thess 5:23; Heb 2:11; 10:10, 14; 13:12) but the flow of thought and marital context in 5:26 is unique.

20. The Salutaris inscription is very large, in five square blocks, across six columns, with 568 lines.

21. IEPH 27.281 (104 CE) directs that cleaned the statues before they were returned to the vestibule of the Artemision should be paid 30 denarii each.

22. *Paul, Artemis, and the Jews in Ephesus*, 74.

23. See Aelian, *Var. Hist.* 5.16, LCL 486.224–25. It is noteworthy that the boy was not charged with theft, but sacrilege.

24. Dionysius of Halicarnassus, *Rom. Ant.* 2.22.2, LCL 319:370–73. This reference requires further investigation since it does not directly say that the teachers who wore the crowns from the images of Artemis and re-enacted the actions of the original *curetes* received power from the crowns.

were pursuing as celibate brides of Christ sans earthly husbands, but Paul equates their restored state within the context of shared identity with her loving husband in marriage (5:28). She need not pursue a path of ascetic celibacy for individual holiness when she already possesses it as a matron and the bride of Christ.

Paul continues his argument for united identity in that Christ has prepared for himself a glorious (ἔνδοξος) bride depicted as the church (5:27). Ἔνδοξος is common to the Ephesus inscriptions where the Ephesians express great pride in their glorious city and glorious goddess[25] but it is rare in the NT, occurring only in three other places besides 5:27. Luke 7:25 uses it to describe fine clothes worn at the royal court. Luke 13:17 speaks of the glorious things that Jesus did. First Corinthians 4:10 uses ἔνδοξος to emphasize the glorious opinion the Corinthians had of themselves. None of these occurrences of ἔνδοξος align with the way the Paul uses the word. But he has been consistently intentional throughout the epistle in choosing words relevant to the Ephesian inscriptions, so once again he chooses a word which the Ephesians understand intimately. He chooses ἔνδοξος.[26]

Ephesus is "glorious" (ἔνδοξος), the church is ἔνδοξος, and the Ephesian matron is identified as ἔνδοξος. Paul continues in 5:25–30 to say that in Christ's new kingdom her status has changed on a fundamental level. She is to be nourished and cherished on the same level that a man nourishes and cherishes (ἐκτρέφει καὶ θάλπει) himself (5:29), not because she is weak, but because she is the same as him. Both she and her husband are conjoint members of Christ's body, flesh, and bones (5:30).[27] She is the glorious

---

25. IEPH 7IB.12; 22.30; 24B.10, 33; 624; 647; 668; 686; 689; 724; 740; 743; 785; 792; 847; 875; 889; 936; 1095; 1107; 1111; 1112; 1113; 1333; 1353; 1575; 1822; 2063; 2073; 2109; 2940; 3014; 3016; 3017; 3030; 3058; 3063; 3071; 3073; 3221; 3239; 3263; 3810; 3812A; 4133; 4135; 4343. The IEPH 24B inscription alone twice underlines that Artemis, because of her godly nature and beneficence, made Ephesus a glorious city.

26. See 3.4 for more on the intentional word choices of the author. See also Immendörfer, *Ephesians and Artemis*, 243–45 where he provides analysis of the two closest textual parallels—2 Corinthians 11:2 and Colossians 1:22—and concludes that ἔνδοξος in 5:27, which does not occur in Colossians 1:22 and 2 Corinthians 11:2 supports a dissimilarity in 5:27 to the rest of the Pauline corpus. This suggests the deliberate use of ἔνδοξος to convey a message that was easy for the Ephesian readers to understand.

27. Some ancient texts contain the additional clause, "of his flesh and of his bones" (ἐκ τῆς σαρκὸς αὐτοῦ καὶ ἐκ τῶν ὀστέων αὐτοῦ). Evidence for the shorter reading includes P 46, ℵ*, A and B, while the longer reading includes ²ℵ, D, Peshitta and Irenaeus, among others. This longer reading is considered connected to the citation of Genesis 2:24 by Ephesians 5:31. See Matthews, "Fleshly Resurrection, Wifely Submission, and the Myth of the Primal Androgyne," 101.

imago Dei in her restored present state. Being a man will not make her any more so. Being a woman will not make her any less.[28]

How does Paul want the Ephesian believing wife to think of herself now? While the Artemision is indwelt by the goddess, the believing Ephesian woman herself is in fact the temple of God who is indwelt by God (Eph 2:20–22).[29] While the Artemision temple is the fabulously wealthy bank of Asia[30] the believing female is now rich in God's gracious forgiveness and kindness (1:7; 2:7), rich in God's glory (1:18), rich in the unfathomable riches of Christ (3:8), and rich in God's power (3:16) because she is image-bearer for God. Once married, the Ephesian woman may have lost status in the temple of the virgin goddess (Sect. 4.2.1, fn. 43) but as the transformed former image-bearer of Artemis, she now replaces it (2:22). She need not pursue the independent life of an honorary male, such as Artemis, since as a glorious wife she already possesses all that makes her equal to her husband.

6.5 THE NURTURING AND BLESSED EPHESIAN HUSBAND

Ephesus was the divinely appointed "Temple Warden" (νεωκόρος) of the cult of the goddess (4.2.4 and 4.2.5), her citizens determined to represent her glory to the world. This becomes the role of the Ephesian believing husband: to represent the glory of his wife to the world by the way he treats her. As married image-bearers, their identity is not one of independence from each other, rather it is one of interdependence with each other. The Ephesian thirteen verse marriage *Haustafel* is not only directed to the wife's actions of independence. Paul speaks also to the husband's independence with language he understands, language relatable to their community life

---

28. Oster comments on this parallel of IEPH 24B to the Ephesian letter, "Ephesians 5:27 depicts a church made ἔνδοξος through the benefaction of Christ, while this inscription depicts the city of Ephesos made ἐνδοξοτέρα [more glorious] through the benefaction and divinity of the Ephesian Artemis" in *A Bibliography of Ancient Ephesus*, 78. If the reign of Artemis made Ephesus a more glorious city on account of her godly nature, how much even greater glory will the church have because of Christ's godly nature and reign over the whole universe.

29. It is noteworthy that the subject of the temple is not addressed in Colossians, highlighting another difference between the two letters. One must assume that there were many temples in Colossae during the first century, yet there is not a single mention of one.

30. See Dio Chrysostom, *Disc.* 31.54, LCL 358.58–59; Strabo, *Geogr.* 14.1.22, LCL 90.400–401; Xenophon, *Anab.* 5.3.4–6, LCL 223.224–27.

of caring for the goddess. Ephesus used the term νεωκόρος to describe their divinely appointed union as keeper and protector of the goddess in "the city of Artemis" (τῆς πόλεως Ἀρτέμιδι)[31] and recipient of her many blessings (4.2.4).[32] It was no secret that the Ephesians wanted to make an impression everywhere (cf. Acts 19:35) as "the first and greatest metropolis of Asia" (τῇ πρώτῃ καὶ μεγίστῃ μητροπόλει τῆς Ἀσίας)[33] and in their minds the fame of the city was intimately linked to the fame of the goddess. It cannot be overstated just how important the reciprocal relationship of nurturing and return blessing was to them. A riot started over it in Acts 19. Aware of this, Paul deploys the verbs ἐκτρέφω and θάλπω to describe Christ's actions toward the church (see sect. 3.4).[34] Ἐκτρέφω "to nurture" occurs in the NT only here and in 6:4 where ἐκτρέφω speaks to how fathers should raise their children. But in 5:29 Paul ads emphasis to ἐκτρέφω by combining it with the verb θάλπω "to care."[35] Christ nurtures plus cares for his church. This coheres with how Artemis as "child nurturer" (κουροτρόφος) cared for her followers.[36] Just as it is normal for man to nurture his body, so it is normal for Christ to nurture his church, which is his body (5:28-29), so it is normal for a husband to nurture his wife. Paul defines the nature of normal relationships in the new kingdom as vastly different from normal relationships in Hellenism. He shines a spotlight on the importance of the spousal relationship in the inaugural kingdom by comparing it to the close relationship between Christ and the church.[37] Caring for Arte-

---

31. IEPH 1398.3, 14.

32. IEPH 24B.32-34.

33. IEPH 467.

34. For more see Immendörfer, *Ephesians and Artemis*, 245-47.

35. The greatest linguistic similarity in the NT is in 1 Thess 2:7 τροφὸς θάλπῃ, although its content does not refer to Christ but to the caring nature of Paul's apostolic ministry. Ἐκτρέφω occurs twenty-seven times in the Septuagint, mostly in the sense of "to grow up" or "to bring up children," while θάλπω occurs four times.

36. See Immendörfer, *Ephesians and Artemis*, 158; Strelan, *Paul, Artemis, and the Jews in Ephesus* 48-50, 83-84; LiDonnici, "The Images of Artemis," 404-5. See my discussions regarding her care of Anthia and Habrocomes as well as Leucippe and Clitophon (5.1.2; 4.2.2, fn. 47). See also my comments regarding maidens sacrificing to Artemis in thanks for the protection the goddess offered them in childhood, and virgins about to have sex dedicating their virginal undergarments to her (4.2.1).

37. Paul here switches from the word "body" (σῶμα; see 5:28a) to the word "flesh" (σάρξ; see 5:29a). Paul tends to use these words interchangeably (1 Cor 6:16; 15:39-40; 2 Cor 4:10-11), and he does so here, perhaps brought about in anticipation of his citing Genesis 2:24 in Ephesians 5:31, which uses the word "flesh" (σάρξ).

mis brought them blessing as citizens of her city. Paul wants the believing husband to know that, in Christ's universe, the husband's care for his wife in self-sacrificial love will result in the blessings for him. Such actions, considering Demosthenes, *Against Neaera* (c. 343–340 BCE) description of the social roles available for women: "Mistresses we keep for the sake of pleasure, concubines for the daily care of our persons, but wives to bear us legitimate children and to be faithful guardians of our households," would have been earth shaking for her.[38] Paul intends for the quality of their caring relationships, based on esteeming each other as the *imago Dei*, to send an evangelistic message to the non-believer that marriages in the new kingdom of Christ can be better than what they know now.

6.6 THE RESURRECTION OF EVE

Up to this point in the pericope Artemis has been a useful tool for Paul to reach the minds of the Ephesian believers with a near, albeit imperfect, reference to the grandeur of their new identity. But the virgin Artemis falls short in describing who the restored husband and wife are in relation to one another. For this Paul resurrects the story of the first couple, with a twist. With his citation of Genesis 2:24 in Ephesians 5:31, "for this reason a man shall leave his father and mother and be joined to his wife and the two shall become one flesh,"[39] Paul reverses the cultural tradition of the wife leaving her family for the husband's, followed by the two becoming one flesh as the climax of the pericope. She is him, and he is her. She has not lost her own identity as the image-bearer of God, nor has he, but they are bonded as one, just as the church is bonded with Christ. The joining of their transformed identities in mutual submission, love, and self-sacrifice creates a new paradigm for first-century marriage, one that carries out the

---

38. *Neaer.* 5.122, LCL 351.444–47. I am using this quote, with full knowledge that it predates the Ephesian letter by three-four hundred years, to illustrate that similar attitudes continued to prevail into the first century. For more, see Satlow, *Jewish Marriage in Antiquity*; and Mendelsohn, "The Family in the Ancient Near East," 24–40.

39. "ἀντὶ τούτου καταλείψει ἄνθρωπος τὸν πατέρα καὶ τὴν μητέρα καὶ προσκολληθήσεται πρὸς τὴν γυναῖκα αὐτοῦ, καὶ ἔσονται οἱ δύο εἰς σάρκα μίαν. See fn. 26. It is noteworthy that in the preceding verse (5:30d) "for we are members of his body," some manuscripts (Western and Byzantine MSS) add at the end, "from his flesh and from his bones," apparently influenced by Genesis 2:23, albeit the shorter text is supported by the earlier and better MSS (P46, ℵ*, A, B, 33, 81, 1739*, 1881).

AN EVANGELISTIC MARRIAGE CODE

missio Dei and invites the outsider in with the hope of transforming their own marriages in like manner.

Paul goes on to say, "This mystery is great, but I am speaking about Christ and the church" (5:32). Throughout 5:22–29 he deploys analogy, using the comparative particles "as" (ὡς) and "just as" (καθώς), to show how Christ is an example for the husband's love (5:25), how the church's submission to Christ is an example for the wife to submit to her husband (5:22, 24), how a man should take care of his wife just as he takes care of himself (5:28), and how Christ's care for the church is an example of how men should care for their wives (5:29). But, in 5:30–32 Paul never deploys a comparative particle. He never says, "we are members of his body 'just as' the husband and wife are one flesh in marriage." He does not use ὡς and καθώς in 5:30–32 to compare analogy to reality. Instead, he comes right out and says, "we are (ἐσμέν) members of [Christ's] body" (5:30) and then backs this up with Genesis 2:24, "the two will become (ἔσονται) one flesh" (both words coming from εἰμί [to exist]). Two people existing as one flesh. Genesis 2:24 is about reality, not analogy.[40]

The fact that Paul refers to the one flesh notion of Genesis 2:24 both in warning against being joined to a prostitute as a transactional relationship with no real hope of intimacy or oneness (1 Cor 6:15–16), contrasted with his endorsement of marriage as the exact opposite (Eph 5:31), warrants further discussion of the Genesis 2 creation account.[41] Assuming that Adam and Eve are both created in God's image (Gen 1:27), both are told to rule over the creatures of the earth, both are told to be fruitful and multiply (1:28), and Eve is appointed as עזר כנגדו which is traditionally translated as "a suitable helper" (2:18) for Adam, should her role as "helper" be defined as one who is subordinate to Adam? Is the translation אעשה־לו עזר כנגדו as "I will make a helper suitable for him" accurate to describe their relationship? In the rest of creation are female birds, fish, animals and so forth, subordinate helpers to the males or would their relationship be better defined as "partners"? Given the influence of a patriarchal reception history of Eve upon the interpretation of the text, perhaps a more appropriate translation

---

40. Is Paul presenting marriage as a type of the relationship of Christ to the church, or the union of Christ and the church serves a model for how husbands and wives should relate? The essence of this mystery has been debated for centuries and is too large a conversation to embark on here. For more on the scope of the debate, see Arnold, *Ephesians*, 555–59. See also Lang's detailed treatment of "mystery" in the Pauline corpus in *Mystery and the Making of a Christian Historical Consciousness*.

41. See 4.1.1 for the Genesis 1 creation account.

of אעשה‑לו עזר כנגדו is "I will make a partner suitable for him."[42] God makes Adam from the ground (2:7) but makes Eve with a rib from his side (2:21) whereupon seeing her Adam says, "This is now bone of my bones and flesh of my flesh; she shall be called woman for she was taken out of man" (2:23). The words for "man" (איש) and "woman" (אשה) are customary Hebrew words to differentiate the sexes; neither is a personal name.[43] Adam does not name Eve until after the fall (3:20). His use of איש and אשה express nothing more than differentiation of man and woman. In 2:24 the narrator adds, "Therefore, a man shall leave his father and mother and be joined to his wife and the two shall become one flesh" (2:24); followed by, "The two of them were naked, the man and his wife, and were not ashamed" (2:25). The man leaves his parents and forms a partnership with his wife as one flesh. There is nothing of hierarchical relationship in the text. If anything, 2:25 indicates a mutual trust between equals in nakedness without shame because they are of the same flesh. This is the notion that Paul seeks to express by quoting 2:24 in Ephesians 5:31 in the context of "for we are members of [Christ's] body" (5:30). The mutual partnership of woman and man is restored in a marriage of body and spirit between two individuals who trust each other and function as one, having in common the flesh of each other and the flesh of Christ.[44] Paul has raised up the united Eve and Adam in the

---

42. For more see Morse, *Encountering Eve's Afterlives*, 96–100; Giles, "The Genesis of Equality," 28.4; Coleson, "Creation and Alienation (Genesis 1–3)," esp. I.B.5 "The Preparation of the Lone 'ādām (2:18–20)" in support of the translation of אעשה‑לו עזר כנגדו as "I will make for him a power/strength corresponding/equal to him." Also see Higgins, "Anastasius Sinaita and the Superiority of Woman," 255–56, where she observes that of the forty-five occurrences of the word in the LXX, forty-two refer to the help from someone stronger who does not need help. God is the helper in Exod 15:2; 18:4; Deut 33:7, 26, 29; Juds 5:23; 1 Sam 7:12; Esth 4:17; Job 22:25; and in twenty-four occurrences in Psalms. Also in Sir 51:2; Isa 8:13; 17:1; 25:4; 50:7; 2 Macc 3:39. Helper stands in parallel with the name of God in 2 Sam 22:42, denotes a helper of the weak in Job 29:12, and a helper in battle in Isa 63:5.

43. See also Ramsay, "Is Name-Giving an Act of Domination in Genesis 2:23 and Elsewhere," 24–35, where he writes, "The exclamation in Gen 2:23 is a cry of discovery, of recognition, rather than a prescription of what this creature built from his rib shall be. An essence which God had already fashioned is recognized by the man and celebrated in the naming. The essence which he perceives in this new creature determines the name, rather than vice versa. The 'ādām names the 'iššā, but it is an act of discernment rather than an act of domination" (35).

44. Marshall, "Community is a Body," 841, raises a pertinent question, and answer: "So do Christ and the church become 'one flesh' in marriage and sexual intercourse? This seems to be the conclusion drawn by the metaphorical mapping of Gen 2:24 onto the conceptual metaphor church is a wife and Christ is a husband. What does this conclusion

very first marriage as the example to emulate over the independent goddess who roamed the mountains with bow and spear.

6.7 SUMMARY

The purpose of Ephesian marital *Haustafel* is not to ensure good citizenry within Hellenistic society or the survival of the emerging church or the establishment of gender marital hierarchy for all time (see sect. 1.1 and 1.7). Rather the marital code reflects the place of husband and wife in the household of God as part of the kingdom of Christ (5:32) that is empowered by the ongoing presence of the Holy Spirit (cf. 1:13; 3:16; 5:18) to evangelize the world.[45]

Mutual submission (5:21) holds the pericope together with the notion of "we can all live sacrificially for one another" as restored image-bearers of God in reverence to Christ who lives sacrificially for the believer (5:21–22). The believing Ephesian husband and wife have lost sight of this or may never have understood this, as evidenced by their pursuit of relational independence over interdependence, which Paul seeks to correct through admonitions to mutually submit (5:21–22, 24), love and respect (5:25, 28, 33), sacrifice (5:25), nourish and cherish (5:29), and unite as one flesh (5:31). Their mistaken identity of what it means to be image-bearers for Christ is due to the adverse influence of Artemis upon their thought world, which

---

mean? Perhaps we should not push the metaphor too far. After all, Ephesians calls Gen 2:24 'a great mystery,' indicating the hiddenness, incompleteness, and tension inherent in the metaphor. But the use of the term μυστήριον may also provide a clue. In Ephesians, 'mystery' refers to the once hidden but now revealed (3:5) plan of God to unite Jews and Gentiles, circumcised and uncircumcised, into 'one new human in the place of two' (ἵνα τοὺς δύο κτίσῃ ἐν αὐτῷ εἰς ἕνα καινὸν ἄνθρωπον, 2:15). Read in light of the direct reference to Gen 2:24 in Eph 5:31, this verse echoes the narrative of creation: one human is separated into two, who then unite to become 'one flesh.' Two types of people in a divided humanity become one humanity, 'fellow heirs and members of the same body' (συγκληρονόμα καὶ σύσσωμα, 3:6). Ephesians 5:30 clarifies what body this is: 'We are members of [Christ's] body' (μέλη ἐσμὲν τοῦ σώματος αὐτοῦ). Ephesians, moreover, addresses its audience as 'heirs' (1:11, 14, 18; 3:6; 5:5) and 'children' (1:5; 4:14; 5:1, 8) and uses language that elicits the source domains of household and family (2:19, 3:15, 5:21–6:9). The purpose of a man's leaving his father and mother, marrying, and becoming 'one flesh' with his wife is for reproduction—in Gen 1:28 terms, for 'filling the earth' (πληρώσατε τὴν γῆν). The mysterious sexual union of Christ and the church, therefore, produces children and heirs who are 'one new humanity.'"

45. For additional discussion see Mutter, "Ephesians 5:21–33 as Christian Alternative Discourse," 14.

has distorted their idea of what the *imago Dei* looks like in them to be that of independence. Using inscription, allusion, and analogy, Paul selects language from their long history with Artemis to call the Ephesian couple to a fulfilling marriage of one flesh interdependence as self-sacrificing equals that will evangelize the unbeliever to new kingdom relationships that reflect the unity of all creation under God.

7

Conclusion

7.1 SUMMARY AND CONCLUSIONS

Why did Paul write his Ephesian marriage *Haustafel*? To support gender subordination as God ordained? To protect the emerging church? Or did he write it to achieve something bigger? In answering that question, I argued that one must move beyond the intertextual debate and read the marriage code alongside local epigraphy, which was visible to everyone in first-century Ephesus, including Paul who lived there for three years (ch. 1).[1] This would reveal the adverse influence of goddess Artemis, as an independent honorary male, upon the believer who tried to imagine what the *imago Dei* might look like in them, which runs counter to Paul's concept of the *imago Dei* in people. Their misunderstanding of what it meant to be God-like led the believer to live out marital independence over marital oneness, which is opposite to the types of relationships Paul wishes to foster in the new kingdom (Gal 3:28), relationships that would be attractive to the unbeliever based on a community of trust, love, and mutual respect.

The unending struggle for Paul to implement evangelistic new kingdom values in a resistant first-century world (ch. 2) is witnessed in his appointment of female ministry leaders (Rom 16; Phil 4:2–3), endorsement

---

1. See sect. 1.2 regarding Pauline authorship. The conclusions for this chapter, as well as prior chapters, are not predicated on Pauline authorship. For this book, "Paul" has been identified as the implied author of the letter, but the argument also stands where the author is quintessentially Paul along with an intimate knowledge of Ephesus.

of mutual bed chamber rights, celibacy, circumcision of the heart (1 Cor 7), and conflict with Corinthian men over female leadership (1 Cor 11), men who have made the Corinthian church an unattractive, evangelistically ineffective place. His struggle to displace Hellenistic hierarchic realities with new kingdom realities continues as he picks up his pen to instruct the Ephesian church about what it means to be part of the household of God (2:19), united as new creatures who are image-bearers for the reign of Christ (1:9–10; 2:11–22). Seeking the best means to get his message across clearly, Paul refers to what both he and his readers know well. Using language, inscription, and analogy relatable to their identity as former image-bearers for the goddess of the city, Paul informs them of their new identity which far surpasses their limited imagination from past experience with the goddess (ch. 3).

What precisely is Paul thinking of when he describes the *imago Christi* in the Ephesian believer? Pauline scriptures disclose a far more robust understanding of what God looks like in people than the paucity of references in the Hebrew Bible and extrabiblical sources (ch. 4), yet scholarship frequently relies on the Genesis 1 intertextual debate to decide which gender is most like God's image, thus giving them the right to rule the Ephesian household. But Paul's focus in explaining the *imago Dei* to his Ephesian audience has little to do with the Genesis 1 gender debate and much more to do with their former lives as image-bearers for Artemis, who has become a troublesome syncretistic influence, polluting Paul's evangelistic *Haustafel*. Which gender gets to rule the other is simply not on Paul's radar for Ephesian marriage. Paul's interests about the image of God in the Ephesian believer lie elsewhere. If which gender gets to rule is not on Paul's radar as he contemplates the *imago Dei* and Ephesian marriage, then what is on his mind? Moreover, what does he think the Ephesians are thinking about who they are as new creatures in married life? Overwhelming epigraphic evidence about Artemis makes clear that, when it comes to imagining what God looks like in people, the Ephesians and Paul could not be further apart. Paul goes to great length to instruct them that, as image-bearers for the God of the universe, they must exhibit conduct befitting new kingdom relationships of service to others—for them a fundamentally foreign notion of what it means to be God-like when compared to their experience with the Pantheon.

Just because Paul's *Haustafel* emphasized the primacy of united marriage identity as the means to attract unbelievers to new kingdom relationships, this does not mean that all believers were on board with Paul (ch.

5). To the contrary, literary evidence in the stories of Joseph and Aseneth, Paul and Thecla, and the young widows of 1 Timothy who don't want to remarry, present the reader with emerging attitudes of what it means to be female in and around the time of the Ephesian letter. Such attitudes are further observed in the rise of two traditions for the believer to manifest the *imago Dei* to the unbelieving world, marriage and celibacy, with Paul seemingly in favor of the former for Ephesus since he makes no mention of celibacy in Ephesians, while endorsing it in 1 Corinthians 7. However, too much should not be made of this as Paul appears to be addressing a specific problem in Ephesian marriage, hence discussion of celibacy may not be of importance to him at the moment. The fact that two parallel traditions are on the rise is further reinforced in the lives of the Cappadocians (in support of both traditions), the emergence of Christian celibate communities, the notion that devout women can become honorary men, and attitudes toward sex as sinful. Another reason, particular to Ephesus, for these diverging traditions is that the reception history of Eve as the disobedient wife makes her unattractive for the gentile Ephesian woman wanting to be like God, while the reception history of Artemis as an honorary man is attractive. Paul wishes to correct negative attitudes about marriage and Eve by esteeming the matron as the holy and blameless bride of Christ (5:25–30) and resurrecting Eve the wife as one of such great value that the husband would separate from his family, leaving all behind to join with her (5:31, cf. Gen 2:24), a particularly poignant statement given that tradition was for the wife to leave her family for him.

Why did Paul write his Ephesian marriage *Haustafel*? Though contextually informative to the problem with Ephesian marriages, the rise of a celibate tradition is not Paul's chief concern. Paul intends for all new creation relationships to reflect the harmony of Christ's reign in heaven and on earth, but Ephesian marriage on earth at present is far from this (ch. 6). Paul's chief concern is that an Ephesian marriage made up of two individuals acting independently of one another will have the same ineffective evangelistic outcome as the male-dominated church of 1 Corinthians 11. Paul's evangelistic mission in Ephesus and Asia Minor, as witnessed in the Acts 19 account of his assault on Artemis and continued in his Ephesian letter, has been compromised by the syncretistic influence of the goddess on believing spouses. Establishing gender hierarchy was of no interest to Paul, neither was appeasing Caesar, but offering restored relationships as a slice of what life could be for the new believer was something he would indeed die for. Paul could not allow Ephesian marriage to reflect anything other than this, hence he paints a thirteen-verse picture of mutual submission, trust, and loving self-sacrifice that would lead to relational fulfillment for the believing couple while attracting the non-believer to the hope of a similar life in a new world. His implicitly evangelistic marital *Haustafel* is part of an explicitly evangelistic letter which is part of the larger story of his three-year mission (cf. Acts 19) to win Ephesus and all of Asia to Christ.

7.2 CONTRIBUTION TO KNOWLEDGE

This book challenges long-held views regarding why Paul wrote the Ephesian marital code, and the best method for its interpretation, at four points. First, scholarship has placed significant weight (perhaps too much weight) on intertextual relationships between the Ephesian *Haustafel*, Paul's undisputed letters, and the Genesis creation and "fall" accounts to uncover what Paul thought about the *imago Dei* in people and its bearing on gender relationships in the new kingdom. The decades-long intertextual debate between complementarian and egalitarian scholars has been supplemented with in-depth socio-historical research on the status of women in antiquity and lexicological discussion over the meaning of κεφαλή in various contexts. While helpful, the application of intertextuality, lexicology, and literary evidence revealing male attitudes toward women proved insufficient to enlighten specific writer and reader context for the Ephesian letter with its exceptionally long marital code. This book engages with representative *Haustafeln* scholars, representative intertextual debates, and literary sources to point out the impasse to which the discussion has arrived and to offer a way forward that focuses on re-reading Ephesians against the *Sitz im Leben* of the Ephesian audience gleaned from epigraphical evidence about their social and religious context which Paul knew and used well.

Second, the importance of the artifactual and epigraphic evidence surrounding the Artemis cult, which has been largely overlooked by *Haustafeln* scholarship, deserves close examination. In so doing the overwhelming presence of Artemis upon Ephesian identity moves to center stage suggesting that her adverse influence had polluted Paul's intentions for how the Ephesians should think about themselves relationally, especially in marriage. Why should Artemis get to move to center stage as the example of who believing matrons want to be like? Why not prelapsarian Eve, or restored Eve, the honored matron? Hesiod's Pandora as well as Jewish and Christian reception histories of Eve had so poisoned the well against women with an irremovable mantle of sin that it was easy for the Ephesian matron to misunderstand being Christ-like to mean living as an honorary man, like Artemis. Beyond this, the weight of epigraphical and artifactual evidence makes clear that the goddess herself is the nearest, albeit incorrect, reference for the gentile believer trying to imagine what God in them looks like. This explains the length to which Paul goes to reorient their new identity (sect. 3.4; 4.2.6) as united with the Jews in Christ under the God of Israel (Eph. 2:11–22), and his thirteen-verse pericope extolling mutually submissive tender care of one's spouse in united identity as precisely what it means to be the *imago Christi*. Paul's interest is not in marital hierarchy or combatting celibacy per se, but in combatting the selfish notion that new creation spouses need not love self-sacrificially when such love is the hallmark of Paul's evangelistic message inviting the unbeliever to join a new kingdom with earthly relationships that look like heaven.

Third, re-reading this material in light of Paul's evangelistic intent reveals how the image of God is portrayed in relationships in the community of faith. Rather than a clever gimmick to recruit unbelievers, Paul's evangelistic strategy is to allow the power of transformed relationships in the new kingdom speak for themselves. Paul does not consider the unbeliever to be naïvely duped by fraudulent claims, as evidenced in Demetrius' frustration that Paul has spread a message throughout Asia that gods made with human hands are not gods at all (Acts 19:10–11), a point on which Paul and the Ephesus Jews agree. Rather, Paul's logical appeal is that relationships empowered by the Holy Spirit at multiple levels (husband/wife, children/parents, master/slave) will be evidence enough to the observer that something is fundamentally different between the way believers treat each other compared to the rest of the world. Unlike gods made by human hands or how the residents of Ephesus might perceive themselves as image-bearers for Artemis, it becomes clear that believers treat one another as if they were God-like and in so doing they become God-like. As the *imago Dei* the believer represents the God of the universe with a message of how life is lived in heaven and can be lived on earth, a life where the non-believer can join in as an equal regardless of gender or other social status.

Fourth, this re-reading of the material changes the notion of power relationships in the new kingdom as demonstrated by his image-bearers. Paul shows no interest in the *imago Dei* making one the authority over another. It plays no part in his thoughts about what it means to be God-like.

Even a complementarian notion of the husband as the benevolent ruler-leader-servant has no presence on the canvas of Paul's Ephesian painting.[2] Rather, reminiscent of Jesus' "Whoever wants to be first must be last of all and servant of all" (Mark 9:35), Paul reshapes the new creation husband as a κεφαλή who serves his wife as Christ serves the church (5:26–28) and the wife as one who submits to (5:22, 24) and respects (5:33) her husband's lead in self-sacrificing love as the manner in which she should also live, nothing more. Paul has no requirement for the matron to submit to the husband's authority according to Hellenistic values because her husband as a new creation *imago Dei* is no longer the same man. The former way of life no longer exists for either of them if they so choose. They mutually submit to one another out of reverence to Christ (5:21) as the Lord (5:22) according to his relational standards as residents of his new kingdom. Notions of who is in charge, so ever present in their former lives, now have no grounds. Paul's particular attention to the wife's "submit" and "respect" as bookends to the husband's "love" is Paul's assurance to her that this is not a return to an old way of living, but a mutual submission to sacrificial love that she need not fear.

In sum, re-reading the Ephesian marital code against the background of Artemis in combination with Paul's new creation theology and evangelistic intent has the potential to reset the conversation concerning NT *Haustafeln*. One can move away from complementarian/egalitarian debates based largely on intertextuality to new ground emphasizing the *Sitz im Leben* of reader and writer context combined with intertextuality. If the Ephesians were not thinking about the priority of gender from Genesis 1 when it came to being godlike, and if Paul, knowing his audience, was not thinking about this either in his Ephesian letter, then what might this mean for his Colossian correspondence and their *Sitz im Leben*, or 1 Timothy? Colossians might echo Paul's Ephesian desire for relational harmony between spouses as equals being an attractive alternative for the outsider. And Paul's use of Eve's deception and Adam's birth priority would not be tied to the idea of Paul laying down the nature of gender relationships for all time, but to his need to address a temporal problem about the female teachers in Timothy's letter that was out of character for believers who are the *imago Dei* (sect. 5.1.4). Sharing the geography of Asia Minor with Ephesus, one then might question what Peter's intent in his marital code is, given the situation in life for his diaspora audience. Perhaps, like Paul, which gender

---

2. For example, see Arnold's complementarian explanation, *Ephesians*, 564–72.

is most like God from Genesis 1 is also not on Peter's mind. But this is another book for another time.

As well, one must wonder if Lee-Barnewall is at least partially correct in saying, "The concept that all people are created equal and endowed with certain inalienable rights comes from the Enlightenment and would have been 'thoroughly alien' to the ancient world." She continues, "The predominant belief instead was that people were by nature created unequal, as evidenced physically (males as dominant and females as inferior), socially (parents would be superior to children, freeborn superior to slaves), and ethnically (Greeks vs. barbarians)."[3] The notion of human equality being a post-Enlightenment phenomenon and, relevant to my work, not a first-century phenomenon is a debate worthy of further discussion. It may be possible to argue that the language of relational equality is not so appropriate to the marriage *Haustafel* as the language of transformed relationship in Christ within hierarchy. But the seeds of relational equality across socio-economic boundaries are sown in texts (Gen 1:27, 2:18; Gal 3:28; Rom 16; 1 Cor 7, 11; 12:13; Col 3:11; Eph 5:21) despite predominant beliefs that people were created unequal, precisely because inequality contradicts what it means to be created in the *imago Dei*. Lee-Barnwell's comment may stem from the idea that freedom from gender hierarchy was the privilege of the select few, the female philosophers and wealthy women who could insulate themselves from the social realities of the common matron. However, true inequality might be in practice, the language of relational equality does not appear to be so "thoroughly alien" as one might expect, hence deserves more investigation. Also, another book for another time.

7.3 IMPLICATIONS FOR THE WORLD TODAY

How might this book contribute to the conversation on a practical level? Ephesians 5:21–33 is far from a fixed first century social code to be indiscreetly mapped onto marriage today. Neither is it to be viewed as outdated and ignored. Written at the first-century intersection of Greco-Roman and Christian culture, Paul's *Haustafel* represents a template for Christian response to social practice in any century. In light of the lordship of Christ (5:21) Paul instructs the readers in any age that their conduct has implications beyond the Christian community. They have a responsibility to the outsider. To reduce the text to "who gets to lead and who gets to follow"

3. See her page 85 in *Neither Complementarian* and my sect. 1.7.5, fn. 118.

mirrors Hellenistic hierarchic values, is divisive, and misses Paul's point of new beings in marital oneness and shared identity. Or, to reduce the text to the "give and take" of Roman patronage makes marriage a transactional relationship, the very thing Paul warns against in becoming one flesh with a prostitute (1 Cor 6:15–16). Neither are appealing for any century, but sacrifice based on true love for another without seeking something in return is admired in every century. Cultures change and cultures vary in different parts of the world at any given time, but notions of mutual submission, self-sacrifice, trust, and love can live within any culture while transforming all.

Bibliography

PRIMARY SOURCES

Achilles Tatius. *Leucippe and Clitophon*. Translated by Stephen Gaselee. LCL. Cambridge: Harvard University Press, 1964.
———. *Achilles Tatius*. Translated by Stephen Gaslee. LCL. London: Heinemann, 1917.
Aelian. *Historical Miscellany*. Translated by N. G. Wilson. LCL. Cambridge: Harvard University Press, 1997.
———. *On Animals*. Translated by A. F. Schofield. LCL. Cambridge: Harvard University Press, 1958.
Aeschylus. *Suppliant Maidens*. Translated by Herbert Weir Smith. 2 vols. LCL. Cambridge: Harvard University Press, 1926.
Antipater of Sidon. *Greek Anthology*. Translated by W. R. Paton. 5 vols. LCL. Cambridge: Harvard University Press, 1995–2000.
Apollonius of Tyana. *Letters*. Translated by Robert J. Penella, Leiden: Brill, 1979.
Aristeas Judaeus. *Letter of Aristeas*. Edited by R. H. Charles. Oxford: Clarendon, 1913.
Aristotle. *Politics*. Translated by H. Rackham. 23 vols. LCL. Cambridge: Harvard University Press, 1932.
Athenaeus. *The Deipnosophists*. Translated by Charles B. Gulick. 7 vols. LCL. Cambridge: Harvard University Press, 1957–63.
Augustine. *City of God*. Translated by George McCracken. LCL. Cambridge: Harvard University Press, 1930.
———. *Letters, To Simplicanus*. Translated by James Houston Baxter. LCL. Cambridge: Harvard University Press, 1930.
Basil. *Homily 10 & 11, Ascetical Works by Saint Basil*. Translated by Sister Monica Wagner. The Fathers of the Church. Washington, DC: Catholic University of America Press, 1962.
———. *Letter* 28. LCL. Cambridge: Harvard University Press, 1926.
———. *Letter* 204. LCL. Cambridge: Harvard University Press, 1930.
———. *Letter* 207. LCL. Cambridge: Harvard University Press, 1930.
Callimachus. *Hymns and Epigrams*. Translated by Alexander W. Mair. LCL. Cambridge: Harvard University Press, 1977.
Cicero. *De Natura Deorum*. Translated by Harris Rackam. 29 vols. LCL. Cambridge: Harvard University Press, 1933.

BIBLIOGRAPHY

Clement of Alexandria. *The Instructor*. Savage MN: Lighthouse Christian Publishing, 2018.

———. *Stromateis*. Edited by Thomas Helton; translated by John Ferguson. The Fathers of the Church. Washington, DC: Catholic University of America Press, 1992.

Cyprian. *On the Dress of Virgins*. Translated by Roy Deferrari. The Fathers of the Church. Washington, DC: Catholic University of America, 1958.

———. *Testimonies*. Translated by Rev. Ernest Wallis. Treatises of Cyprian 12. Edinburgh: T&T Clark, 1886.

Demosthenes. *Orations*. Translated by A. T. Murray. 7 vols. Cambridge: Harvard University Press, 1939.

Dio Chrysostom. *Discourses*. Translated by J. W. Cohoon. 5 vols. LCL. Cambridge: Harvard University Press, 1961–64.

Diogenes Laertius. *Vitae Philosophorum*. Translated by R. D. Hicks. 2 vols. LCL. Cambridge: Harvard University Press, 1979–80.

Dionysius of Halicarnassus. *Roman Antiquities*. Translated by Earnest Gray. 7 vols. LCL. Cambridge: Harvard University Press, 1937–50.

Euripides. *Iphigeneia in Tauris*. Translated by Richmond Lattimore. London: Oxford University Press, 1974.

Grenfell, Bernard P. *An Alexandrian Erotic Fragment and Other Greek Papyri Chiefly Ptolemaic*. Oxford: Clarendon, 1896.

Grenfell, Bernard P., and Arthur Hunt. *The Oxyrhynchus Papyri Part II*. London: Egypt Exploration Fund, 1899.

Guresvich, Eliyahu, *Tosefta Berakhot*. Las Vegas NV: Kindle Edition, 2010.

Herodotus. *History*. Translated by Alfred D. Godley. 4 vols. LCL. Cambridge: Harvard University Press, 1957–61.

Hesiod. *Theogony. Works and Days. Testimonia*. Translated by G. W. Most. LCL. Cambridge: Harvard University Press, 2007.

Homer. *Hymns*. Translated by M. L. West. LCL. Cambridge: Harvard University Press, 2003.

———. *Iliad*. Translated by A. T. Murray; revised by William F. Wyatt. 2 vols. LCL. Cambridge: Harvard University Press, 1924.

———. *The Odyssey*. Translated by A. T. Murray; revised by George E. Dimock. 2 vols. LCL. Cambridge: Harvard University Press, 1919.

Iamblichus. *Life of Pythagoras*. Translated by Thomas Taylor. London: J. M. Watkins, 1818.

Ignatius. *Letters*. Translated by Bart Ehrman. Cambridge: Harvard University Press, 2003.

Irenaeus of Lyons. *Against Heresies*. London: Aeterna, 2016.

Jerome. *Against Jovinianus*. Translated by W. H. Fremantle, G. Lewis, and W. G. Martley. Nicene and Post-Nicene Fathers, 2nd Series, vol. 6. 1893. Revised and edited for New Advent by Kevin Knight, 2021. https://www.newadvent.org/

Josephus. *Against Apion*. Translated by H. St. J. Thackary. LCL. Cambridge: Harvard University Press, 1926.

———. *Antiquities*. Translated by H. St. J. Thackary et al. 23 vols. LCL. Cambridge: Harvard University Press, 1930–65.

———. *The Jewish Wars*. Translated by H. St. J. Thackary. 3 vols. LCL. Cambridge: Harvard University Press, 1927–28.

Justin Martyr. *Apology* in *Ancient Christian Writers: The First and Second Apologies*. Translated by Leslie William Barnard. Mahwah NJ: Paulist, 1997.

———. *Dialogue with Trypho*. San Francisco: Fig Books, Kindle Edition, 2012.

Livy. *History of Rome*. Translated by B. O. Foster. 14 vols. LCL. Cambridge: Harvard University Press, 1919.
Minucius Felix. *Octavius*. Translated by T. R. Glover and Gerald Rendall. LCL. Cambridge: Harvard University Press, 1931.
Nazianzen, Gregory. *Select Orations of Saint Gregory Nazianzen*. Translated by Charles Gordon Brown and James Edward Swallow. London: Aeterna, 2016.
Nyssen, Gregory. *De Hominis Opificio*. On the Making of Man. Saint Gregory of Nyssa Collection. 7 vols. London: Aeterna Press, 2016.
———. *De Virginitate, Saint Gregory of Nyssa Ascetical Works*. Translated by Virginia Woods Callahan. The Fathers of the Church. Washington, DC: Catholic University of America Press, 1999.
———. *The Life of Saint Macrina*. Translated by Kevin Corrigan. Reprint, Eugene, OR: Wipf & Stock, 2005.
Origen. *Homilies on Joshua*. Translated by Barbara Bruce; edited by Cynthia White. The Fathers of the Church. Washington, DC: Catholic University of America Press, 2012.
———. *On First Principles*. Edited by G. W. Butterworth. 1936. Reprint, Eugene, OR: Wipf and Stock, 2012.
———. *The Song of Songs Commentary and Homilies*. Translated by R. P. Lawson. New York: Newman, 1956.
Orpheus. *Orphic Hymn 2*. Translated by Thomas Taylor. 1824. https://www.theoi.com/Text/OrphicHymns1.html
———. *Orphic Hymn 36*. Translated by Thomas Taylor. 1824. https://www.theoi.com/Text/OrphicHymns1.html
Pallidus. *Lausiac History*. Translated by W. K Lowther Clarke. London: Macmillan, 1918.
Pausanias. *Description of Greece*. Translated by W. H. S. Jones. 5 vols. LCL. Cambridge: Harvard University Press, 1954–61.
Petronius. *Satyricon*. Translated by Michael Heseltine, W. H. D. Rouse; revised by E. H. Warmington. LCL. Cambridge: Harvard University Press, 1913.
Philo. *The Contemplative Life*. Translated by F. H. Colson. LCL. Cambridge: Harvard University Press, 1941.
———. *Every Good Man is Free*. Translated by F. H. Colson. LCL. Cambridge: Harvard University Press, 1941.
———. *Hypothetica*. Translated by F. H. Cohen. LCL. Cambridge: Harvard University Press, 1941.
———. *On the Cherubim*. Translated by F. H. Cohen and G. H. Whitaker. LCL. Cambridge: Harvard University Press, 1929.
———. *On the Creation*. Translated by F. H. Colson and G. H. Whitaker. LCL. Cambridge: Harvard University Press, 1929.
———. *On Rewards and Punishments*. Translated by F. H. Cohen. LCL. Cambridge: Harvard University Press, 1939.
———. *On the Special Laws*. Translated by F. H. Cohen. LCL. Cambridge: Harvard University Press, 1937.
———. *Questions and Answers on Genesis*. Translated by R. Marcus. LCL. Cambridge: Harvard University Press, 1953.
Plato. *Cratylus*. Translated by Harold North Fowler. LCL. Cambridge: Harvard University Press, 1941.
———. *Lysis. Symposium. Gorgias*. Translated by W. R. M. Lamb. 12 vols. LCL. Cambridge: Harvard University Press, 1925.

BIBLIOGRAPHY

Pliny the Elder. *Natural History*. Translated by H. Rackham. 10 vols. LCL. Cambridge: Harvard University Press, 1947–63.

Pliny the Younger. *Letters and Panegyricus*. Translated by Betty Radice. 2 vols. LCL. Cambridge: Harvard University Press, 1969.

Plutarch. *Moralia*. Translated by Frank Cole Babbit et al. 15 vols. LCL. Cambridge: Harvard University Press, 1927–69.

———. *Parallel Lives*. Translated by Bernadotte Perrin. 5 vols. LCL. Cambridge: Harvard University Press, 1959–71.

———. *Whether an Old Man Should Engage in Public Affairs*. Translated by Harold North Fowler. LCL. Cambridge: Harvard University Press, 1991.

Pseudo-Zacharias Rhetor. *Joseph and Aseneth*. Translated by C. Burchard. In *Old Testament Pseudepigrapha*, volume 2, edited by J. H. Charlesworth. Garden City, NY: Doubleday, 1985.

Seneca the Younger. *Moral Essays*. Translated by John W. Basore. 3 vols. LCL. Cambridge: Harvard University Press, 1935.

Sophocles. *Electra*. Translated by Hugh Lloyd-Jones. LCL. Cambridge: Harvard University Press, 1994.

Strabo. *Geography*. Translated by Horace L. Jones. 8 vols. LCL. Cambridge: Harvard University Press, 1960–70.

Suetonius. *Claudius, Lives of the Caesars V*. Translated by J. C. Rolfe. LCL. Cambridge: Harvard University Press, 1914.

———. *Life of Augustus*. Translated by D. Wardle. Oxford: Oxford University Press, 2014.

———. *Lives of the Caesars*. Translated by J. C. Rolfe. 12 vols. LCL. Cambridge: Harvard University Press, 1914.

Suidas s.v. *Lysizonos gune* (girdle-loosening woman). Translated by Suda Online. Byzantine Greek Lexicon, 10th century CE.

Tacitus. *Agricola, Germania, Dialogue on Oratory*. Translated by M. Hutton; revised by R. M. Ogilvie, E. H. Warmington, Michael Winterbottom. 5 vols. LCL. Cambridge: Harvard University Press, 1914.

———. *Annals Book I*. Translated by Clifford Moore. LCL. Cambridge: Harvard University Press, 1931.

———. *Annals, Book IV*. Translated by John Jackson. LCL. Cambridge: Harvard University Press, 1937.

———. *Annals*. Translated by John Jackson. 5 vols. LCL. Cambridge: Harvard University Press, 1969–70.

Tertullian. *Tertullian Collection*. London: Aeterna, 2016.

Thucydides. *History of the Peloponnesian War*. Translated by C. F. Smith. 4 vols. LCL. Cambridge: Harvard University Press, 1919.

Ulpian. *Rules of Ulpian*. The Civil Law, including the Twelve Tables, the Institutes of Gaius, the Rules of Ulpian, the Opinions of Paulus, the Enactments of Justinian and the Constitutions of Leo. Translated by Samuel Parsons Scott. Cincinnati, OH: Central Trust, 1932.

Xenophon of Athens. *Anabasis*. Translated by Carleton Brownson. LCL. Cambridge: Harvard University Press, 1998.

———. *An Ephesian Tale: Anthia and Habrocomes*. Translated by Jeffrey Henderson. LCL. Cambridge: Harvard University Press, 2009.

———. *Memorabilia. Oeconomicus. Symposium. Apology.* Translated by E. C. Marchant; revised by Jeffrey Henderson. 7 vols. LCL. Cambridge: Harvard University Press, 2013.

SECONDARY RESOURCES

Aland, Kurt, and Barbara Aland, et al. *Novum Testamentum Graece.* 28th ed. Stuttgart: Deutsche Bibelgesellschaft, 2012.
Allan, John. "The 'in Christ' Formula in Ephesians." *New Testament Studies* 5 (1958–59) 54–55.
Allison, R. W. "'Let the Women Be Silent in the Churches,' (1 Cor 14:33b–36): What Did Paul Really Say, and What Did It Mean?" *Journal for the Study of the New Testament* 32 (1988) 27–60.
Anadolu-Okur, Nilgün. *From Cybele to Artemis: Motherhood and Great Mothers of Ancient Anatolia in Motherhood in Antiquity.* Edited by Dana Cooper and Claire Phelan. London: Palgrave Macmillan, 2017.
Arnold, Clinton. *Ephesians.* Zondervan Exegetical Commentary on the New Testament 10. Grand Rapids: Zondervan, 2010.
Arnold, Irene. "Festivals of Ephesus." *American Journal of Archaeology* 76 (1972) 17–22.
Aspegren, Kersten. *The Male Woman: A Feminine Ideal in the Early Church.* Uppsala Women Studies, Women in Religion 4, edited by Renee Kieffer. Uppsala: Almqvist and Wiksell, 1990.
Aune, David. *The Blackwell Companion to the New Testament.* Atlanta: Scholars, 2010.
Balch, David. "Household Codes." In *Greco-Roman Literature and the New Testament,* edited by David Aune, 25–50. Atlanta: Scholars, 1988.
———. *Let Wives be Submissive: The Domestic Code in 1 Peter.* The Society of Biblical Literature Monograph Series. Atlanta: Scholars, 1981.
———. "Paul, Families, and Households." In *Paul in the Greco-Roman World: A Handbook,* edited by J. Paul Sampley, 258–92 New York: Trinity, 2003.
Barclay, John. "Paul and Philo on Circumcision." In *Pauline Churches and Diaspora Jews,* 61–80. Grand Rapids: Eerdmans, 2011.
Barth, Karl. *Church Dogmatics.* Translated by J. W. Edwards, O. Bussey, and Harold Knight. Edinburgh: T&T Clark, 1958.
Barth, Markus. *Ephesians.* New York: Doubleday, 1974.
Batey, Richard. *New Testament Nuptial Imagery.* Leiden: Brill, 1971.
Bauer W. *A Greek-English Lexicon of the New Testament and Other Early Christian Literature.* Translated by William F. Arndt and Wilbur Gingrich; revised by F. Wilbur Gingrich and Frederick W. Danker. 2nd ed. Chicago: University of Chicago Press, 1979.
Baugh, S. M. "Cult Prostitution in New Testament Ephesus: A Reappraisal." *Journal of Evangelical Theological Society* 42 (1999) 443–60.
———. *Ephesians.* Bellingham WA: Lexham Academic, 2016.
Beard, Mary. "The Sexual Status of Vestal Virgins." *The Journal of Roman Studies* 70 (1980) 12–27.
Beattie, Gillian. *Women and Marriage in Paul and His Early Interpreters.* Journal for the Study of the New Testament Supplemental Series 296. London: T&T Clark, 2005.

Belz, Lisa Marie, "The Rhetoric of Gender in the Household of God: Ephesians 5:21–33 and Its Place in Pauline Tradition." PhD Dissertation. Chicago: Loyola University, 2013.
Best, Ernest. *A Critical and Exegetical Commentary on Ephesians*. International Critical Commentary. Edinburgh: T&T Clark, 2001.
———. *Ephesians*. London: Bloomsbury, 2004.
———. "Who Used Whom? The Relationship of Ephesians and Colossians." *New Testament Studies* 43 (1997) 72–96.
Bilezikian, Gilbert. *Beyond Sex Roles: What the Bible Says about a Woman's Place in Church and Family*. Grand Rapids: Baker, 1985
Bird, Phyllis. "Male and Female He Created Them: Gen. 1:27b in the Context of the Priestly Account of Creation." *Harvard Theological Review* 74 (1981) 125–59.
Blomberg, Craig. "Neither Hierarchicalist nor Egalitarian: Gender Roles in Paul." In *Paul and His Theology*, edited by Stanley E. Porter, 283–326. Leiden: Brill, 2006.
Boatwright, Mary Taliaferro. "Plancia Magna of Perge: Women's Roles and Status in Roman Asia Minor." In *Women's History and Ancient History*, edited by Sarah Pomeroy, 249–72. Chapel Hill, NC: University of North Carolina Press, 1991.
Boyarin, Daniel. "Paul and the Genealogy of Gender." *Representations* 41 (Winter 1993) 1–33.
Brenk, F. E. "Artemis of Ephesos: An Avant Garde Goddess." *Kernos* 11 (1998) 157–71.
Briggs, Sheila. "Slavery and Gender." In *On the Cutting Edge: The Study of the Women in Biblical Worlds, Essays in Honor of Elisabeth Schüssler Fiorenza*, edited by Jane Schaberg, Alice Bach, and Esther Fuchs, 171–92 New York: Continuum, 2004.
Brinks, C. L. "'Great Is Artemis of the Ephesians': Acts 19:23–41 in Light of Goddess Worship in Ephesus." *The Catholic Biblical Quarterly* 71.4 (2009) 776–94.
Brooke, George. *The Dead Sea Scrolls and the New Testament: Essays in Mutual Illumination*. London: SPCK, 2005.
Brower, Kent, and Mark Elliott, eds. *Eschatology in Bible and Theology*. Downers Grove, IL: InterVarsity, 1997.
Brown, Raymond. "Nature and Origin of the New Testament." In *An Introduction to the New Testament*, 1–6. New Haven, CT: Yale University Press, 2010.
———. *An Introduction to the New Testament*. New Haven, CT: Yale University Press, 1997.
Bruce, F. F. *The Epistles to Colossians, to Philemon and to the Ephesians*. Grand Rapids: Eerdmans, 1959.
———. *New Testament History*. New York: Doubleday, 1983.
———. *Paul Apostle of the Free Spirit*. Exeter, UK: Paternoster, 1977.
Burton, Henry Fairfield. "The Worship of the Roman Emperors." *The Biblical World* 40.2 (1912) 80–91.
Callahan, Brahm. "Living Off the Dead: The Relationship between Emperor Cult and the Cult of the Saints in Late Antiquity." Master's thesis, Boston College, 2008.
Cameron, Averil. "Sacred and Profane Love: Thoughts on Byzantine Gender." In *Women, Men and Eunuchs: Gender in Byzantium*, edited by Liz James, 1–23. London: Routledge, 1997.
Campbell, Douglas. *Framing Paul: An Epistolary Biography*. Grand Rapids: Eerdmans, 2013.
Campbell, Ken, M. *Marriage and Family in the Biblical World*. Downers Grove, IL: InterVarsity, 2003.

Campbell, William. "Unity and Diversity in the Church: Transformed Identities and the Peace of Christ in Ephesians." *Irish Biblical Studies* 27 (2006) 15–31.

Carney, Elizabeth Donnelly. *Arsinoë of Egypt and Macedon: A Royal Life*. Oxford: Oxford University Press, 2013.

Carson, D. A., D. J. Moo, and L. Morris. *An Introduction to the New Testament*. Grand Rapids: Zondervan, 2005.

Cervin, Richard, S. "Does *Kephale* Mean 'Source' or 'Authority' in Greek Literature? A Rebuttal." *Trinity Journal* 10 NS (1989) 85–112.

Chalupa, Aleš. "How Did Roman Emperors Become Gods? Various Concepts of Imperial Apotheosis." *Anodos. Studies of the Ancient World* 6–7 (2006–7) 201–7.

Clanton, Jann Aldridge. *In Whose Image? God and Gender*. New York: Crossroad, 1990.

Clark, Elizabeth. *Saint Augustine on Marriage and Sexuality*. Washington, DC: Catholic University of America Press, 1997.

———. "Ideology, History, and the Construction of Woman in Late Ancient History." *Journal of Early Christian Studies* 2.2 (1994) 154–84.

Clarke, Kemp Lowther. *St. Basil the Great: A Study in Monasticism*. Cambridge: Cambridge University Press, 1913.

Clines, David J. A. *What Does Eve Do to Help? and Other Readerly Questions to the Old Testament*. Journal for the Study of the Old Testament, Supplement 94. Sheffield, UK: JSOT Press, 1990.

Cohick, Lynn. *Ephesians*. New Covenant Commentary Series. Eugene, OR: Cascade, 2010.

———. *Women in the World of the Earliest Christians: Illuminating Ancient Ways of Life*. Grand Rapids: Baker Academic, 2009.

Coleson, Joseph. "Creation and Alienation (Genesis 1–3)." In *Genesis 1–11: A Commentary in the Wesleyan Tradition,* Kindle loc 2402–2560. New Beacon Bible Commentary. Kansas City: Beacon Hill, 2012.

Collins, Billie Jean, et al. *The SBL Handbook of Style*. Atlanta: SBL, 2014.

Collins, Raymond. *1 & 2 Timothy and Titus: A Commentary*. Louisville, KY: Westminster/John Knox, 2002.

Comfort, Phillip, and David Barrett. *The Text of the Earliest New Testament Greek Manuscripts*. Wheaton, IL: Tyndale, 2001.

Corley, Kathleen. *Private Women, Public Meals: Social Conflict in the Synoptic Tradition*. Peabody, MA: Hendrickson, 1993

Cotterell, Peter, and Max Turner *Linguistics and Biblical Interpretation*. Downers Grove, IL: InterVarsity, 1989.

Cranfield, C. E. B. *A Critical and Exegetical Commentary on the Epistle to the Romans*. Edinburgh: T&T Clark, 1975.

Cueva, Edmund. *The Myths of Fiction: Studies in the Canonical Greek Novels*. Ann Arbor, MI: University of Michigan Press, 2004.

D'Angelo, Mary Rose. "Women Partners in the New Testament." *Journal of Feminist Studies in Religion* 6 (1990) 65–86.

Daly, Mary. *Beyond God the Father: Toward a Philosophy of Women's Liberation*. Boston: Beacon, 1973.

Das, A. Andrew. "A Narrative of the Imperial Cult in Asia Minor." In *Paul and the Stories of Israel,* edited by A. Andrew DAS, 179–216 Minneapolis: Fortress, 2016.

Davis, Stephen. *The Cult of St. Thecla: A Tradition of Women's Piety in Late Antiquity*. New York: Oxford University Press, 2001.

BIBLIOGRAPHY

Dawes, Gregory. *The Body in Question: Metaphor and Meaning in the Interpretation of Ephesians 5:21-33.* Leiden: Brill, 1998.
de Ste Croix, G. E. M. "Some Observations on the Property Rights of Athenian Women." *Classical Review* 20 (1970) 273-78.
de Wette, W. M. L. *Introduction to the Canonical Books of the New Testament.* Translated by Frederick Frothingham. Boston: Crosby, Nichols, and Company, 1858.
DeConick, April. *The Original Gospel of Thomas in Translation.* LONDON: T&T Clark, 2006.
Deming, Will. *Paul on Marriage and Celibacy: The Hellenistic Background of 1 Corinthians 7.* Grand Rapids: Eerdmans, 2004.
deSilva, David. *Honor, Patronage, Kinship and Purity: Unlocking New Testament Culture.* Downers Grove, IL: InterVarsity, 2000.
———. "Patronage and Reciprocity: The Context of Grace in the New Testament." *Ashland Theological Journal* 31 (1999) 32-84.
Dittenberger, Wilhelm, and Karl Purgold. *Die Inschriften von Olympia.* In *Olympia: Die Ergebnisse der von dem Deutschen Reich Veranstaltung Ausgrabung,* vol. 5, edited by Ernst Curtius and Friedrich Adler, 110-11. Amsterdam: Hakkert, 1966.
Dmitriev, Sviatoslav. *City Government in Hellenistic and Roman Asia Minor.* New York: Oxford University Press, 2005.
Dover, K. J. "Classical Greek Attitudes to Sexual Behavior." *Arethusa* 6.1 (1973) 59-73.
Dundry, Ross "'Submit Yourselves to One Another': A Socio Historical Look at the Household Code of Ephesians 5:15—6:9." *Restoration Quarterly* 41 (1999) 27-44.
Dunn, James D. G. *The Epistles to the Colossians and Philemon: A Commentary on the Greek Text.* NIGTC. Carlisle, UK: Paternoster, 1996.
———. *Romans 9-16.* Word Biblical Commentary 38B. Nashville: Thomas Nelson, 1988.
———. *The Theology of Paul the Apostle.* Grand Rapids: Eerdmans, 1998.
Ehrman, Bart. *A Brief Introduction to the New Testament.* Oxford: Oxford University Press, 2004.
———. *The New Testament: A Historical Introduction to the Early Christian Writings.* Oxford: Oxford University Press, 1997.
Elliott, James Keith, *The Apocryphal New Testament: A Collection of Apocryphal Christian Literature in an English translation.* Oxford: Clarendon, 1999.
Ellis, T. A. "Is Eve the 'Woman' in Sirach 25:24?" *Catholic Biblical Quarterly* 73 (2011) 723-42.
Emerson, R. W. *Essays, Lectures and Orations.* London: William S. Orr, 1848.
Engberg-Pedersen, Troels. *Paul in His Hellenistic Context.* Minneapolis: Fortress, 1995.
Engelmann, Helmut, et al. *Die Inschriften von Ephesos.* Komission für die Archchäologische Erforschung Kleinasiens bei der Österreichischen Akademie der Wissenschaften, *Die Inschriften von Ephesos.* 10 vols. Bonn: Habelt, 1979-84.
Evanson, Edward. *A New Testament: Or the New Covenant According to Luke, Paul, and John.* London: R. Taylor, 1807.
Evridiki, Leka. "Artemis of Ephesus (Statue)." *Encyclopaedia of the Hellenic World, Asia Minor* (2002): http://www.ehw.gr/l.aspx?id=7556. Sylbvrgii, Frederici. entry 'Δαιτίς in *Etymologicum Magnum.* Lipsiae: Apvd. Io. Avg. Gottl. Weigei (1816) 228-29.
Fatum, Lone. "Image of God and Glory of Man: Women in the Pauline Congregations." In *The Image of God: Gender Models in Judaeo-Christian Tradition,* edited by Kari Elisabeth Borrenson, 71-79. Minneapolis: Fortress, 1995.

Faust, Eberhard. *Pax Christi et pax Caesaris: religionsgeschichtliche, traditionsgeschichtliche und sozialgeschichtliche Studien zum Epheserbrief.* Göttingen: Vandenhoeck & Ruphart, 1993.
Fee, Gordon. *First Epistle to the Corinthians.* Grand Rapids: Eerdmans, 1987.
Field, James, Jr. "The Purpose of the Lex Iulia et Papia Poppaea." *The Classical Journal* 40.7 (1945) 398–416.
Finegan, J. *The Archaeology of the New Testament: The Mediterranean World of the Early Christian Apostles.* Boulder, CO: Westview, 1981.
Fiorenza, Elisabeth Schüssler. *In Memory of Her: A Feminist Theological Reconstruction of Christian Origins.* New York: Crossroad, 1983.
Fishwick, Duncan. *The Imperial Cult in the Latin West: Studies in the Ruler Cult of the Roman Empire.* Etudes préliminaires aux religions orientales dans l'empire romain 2.1. Leiden: Brill, 1991.
Fitzmyer, Joseph. "Another Look at *Kephale* in 1 Corinthians 11:3." *New Testament Studies* 35 (1989) 503–11.
———. *Romans.* The Anchor Bible Commentary. New York: Doubleday, 1993.
Flanagan, N. M., and E. H. Snyder. "Did Paul Put Down Women in 1 Cor 14:34–36?" *Biblical Theology Bulletin* 11 (1981) 10–12.
Fleischer, Robert. *Artemis von Ephesos und verwandte Kultstatuen aus Anatolien und Syrien, Etudes préliminaires aux religions orientales dans l'empire romain* 35. Leiden: Brill, 1973.
Foster, Christopher, G. *The Corinthian Correspondence in Light of Early Jewish Mysticism in the Dead Sea Scrolls.* Wissenschaftliche Untersuchungen zum Neuen Testament 2. Reihe 575. Tübingen: Mohr Siebeck, 2022.
Fowl, Stephen. *Ephesians: A Commentary.* Louisville, KY: Westminster John Knox, 2012.
Frame, John. "Men and Women in the Image of God." In *Recovering Biblical Manhood & Womanhood: A Response to Evangelical Feminism*, edited by John Piper and Wayne Grudem, 225–32. Wheaton, IL: Crossway, 2006.
Frank, Richard "Augustus' Legislation on Marriage and Children." *California Studies in Classical Antiquity* 8 (1975) 41–52.
Frayer-Griggs, Daniel. "The Beasts at Ephesus and the Cult of Artemis." *Harvard Theological Review* 106 (2013) 459–77.
Friesen, Steven. "The Cult of the Roman Emperors in Ephesus: Temple Wardens, City Titles, and the Interpretation of the Revelation of John." In *Ephesos: Metropolis of Asia*, edited by Helmut Koester, 229–50. Cambridge: Harvard University Press, 2004.
———. *Twice Neokoros: Ephesus, Asia and the Cult of the Flavian Imperial Family.* Leiden: Brill, 1993.
Garroway, Joshua. *The Beginning of the Gospel: Paul, Philippi, and the Origins of Christianity.* London: Pelgrave MacMillan, 2018.
Gaudemet, Jean. "Le statut de la femme dans l'Empire romain." In *Rec. de la Société Jean Bodin XI, La femme,* 225–60. Bruxelles: Editions de la Librairie Encyclopedique, 1959.
Gempf, Conrad. "Pseudonymity and the New Testament." *Themelios*, Jan-Feb 1992, 8–10.
Gese, Michael *Das Vermachtnis des Apostels: Die Rezeption der paulinischen Theologie im Epheserbrief.* Wissenschaftliche Untersuchungen zum Neuen Testament 99. Tübingen: Mohr Siebeck, 1997.
Giles, Kevin. "The Genesis of Equality." *Priscilla Papers* 28.4 (2014) https://www.cbeinternational.org/resource/genesis-equality-part-1/.

Gill, Christopher "The School in the Roman Imperial Period." *The Cambridge Companion to the Stoics*, edited by Brad Inwood, 33–58. New York: Cambridge University Press, 2003.

Gladd, Benjamin, and Matthew Harmon. *Making All Things New: Inaugurated Eschatology for the Life of the Church*. Grand Rapids: Baker Academic, 2016.

Glahn, Sandra. *Nobody's Mother: Artemis of the Ephesians in Antiquity and the New Testament*. Downers Grove, IL: InterVarsity, 2023.

Glancy, J. A. "Obstacles to Slaves Participation in the Corinthian Church." *Journal of Biblical Literature* 117 (1998) 481–501.

Gnilka, Joachim. *Der Epheserbrief*. 1977. Reprint, Freiburg: Herder, 2002.

Gombis, Timothy G. "A Radically New Humanity: The Function of the Haustafel in Ephesians." *Journal of the Evangelical Theological Society* 48 (2005) 317–30.

Goodspeed, E. J. *The Meaning of Ephesians*. 1933. Reprint, Eugene, OR: Wipf & Stock, 2012.

Gottstein, Alon Goshen. "The Body as an Image of God in Rabbinic Literature." *The Harvard Theological Review* 87.2 (1994) 171–95.

Grenfell, Bernard P. *An Alexandrian Erotic Fragment and Other Greek Papyri Chiefly Ptolemaic*. Oxford: Clarendon, 1896.

Grenfell, Bernard P., and Arthur Hunt. *The Oxyrhynchus Papyri Part II*. London: Egypt Exploration Fund, 1899.

Grenz, Stanley. "Jesus as the Imago Dei: Image-of-God Christology and the Non-Linearity of Theology." *Journal of the Evangelical Theological Society* 47.4 (2004) 617–28.

Gritz, Sharon Hogden. *Paul, Women Teachers, and the Mother Goddess at Ephesus: A Study of 1 Timothy 2:9–15 in Light of the Religious and Cultural Milieu of the First Century*. Lanham, MD: University Press of America, 1991.

Grossman, Maxine. "Postmodern Questions and Sexuality Studies." In *T&T Clark Companion to the Dead Sea Scrolls*, edited by George Brooke and Charlotte Hempel, 246–58. London: Bloomsbury, 2018.

Grudem, Wayne. *1 Peter*. Tyndale New Testament Commentaries. Grand Rapids: Eerdmans, 2007.

———. "Does Kephale Mean 'Source' or 'Authority Over' in Greek Literature? A Survey of 2,336 Examples." *Trinity Journal* 6NS (1985) 38–59.

———. *Evangelical Feminism and Biblical Truth*. Wheaton, IL: Crossway, 2004.

———. "The Meaning of *Kefalh* ('head'): A Response to Recent Studies." *Trinity Journal* 11 (1990) 3–72.

Gundry-Volf, Judith. "Beyond Difference? Paul's Vision of a New Humanity in Galatians 3:28." In *Gospel and Gender: Trinitarian Engagement with Being Male and Female in Christ*, edited by D. A. Campbell, 8–36. London: T&T Clark, 2003.

Guthrie, Donald. *New Testament Introduction*. Downers Grove, IL: InterVarsity, 1990.

———. *The Pastoral Epistles*. Leicester, UK: InterVarsity, 1990.

Hadas-Lebel, Mireille. *Philo of Alexandria: A Thinker in the Jewish Diaspora*. Leiden: Brill, 2012.

Hanson, R. P. C. "A Note on Origen's Self-Mutilation." *Vigiliae Christianae* 20 (1966) 81–82.

Harrill, James Albert. *Slaves in the New Testament: Literary, Social and Moral Dimensions*. Minneapolis: Fortress, 2006.

Harrill, James Albert. *Slaves in the New Testament: Literary, Social and Moral Dimensions*. Minneapolis: Fortress, 2006.

Harris, Stephen. *The New Testament: A Student's Introduction*. New York: McGraw-Hill, 2002.
Harrison, Verna. "Allegory and Eroticism in Gregory of Nyssa." *Semeia* 57 (1992) 113–30.
Hartog, Paul. "Polycarp, Ephesians, and Scripture," *Westminster Theological Journal* 70 (2008) 255–75.
Hays, Richard. *Echoes of Scripture in the Letters of Paul*. New Haven, CT: Yale University Press, 1989.
Head, Barclay V. *On The Chronological Sequence of the Coins of Ephesus*. London: Rollin & Feuardent, 1880.
Heine, Ronald, and F. Piere. *The Commentaries of Origen and Jerome on St. Paul's Epistle to the Ephesians*. New York: Oxford University Press, 2002.
———. "Recovering Origen's Commentary on Ephesians from Jerome." *Journal of Theological Studies* 51.2 (2000) 478–514.
Hekster, Olivier. *Emperors and Ancestors: Roman Rulers and the Constraints of Tradition*. Oxford Studies in Ancient Culture and Representation. Oxford: Oxford University Press, 2015.
Henderson, Suzanne Watts. "Taking Liberties with the Text: The Colossian Household Code as Hermeneutical Paradigm." *Interpretation* 60 (2006) 420–32.
Hengel, Martin. "The Pre-Christian Paul." In *The Jews among Pagans and Christians*, edited by Judith Lieu, John North, and Tessa Rajak, 29–52. London: Routledge, 1992.
Hering, James. *The Colossian and Ephesian Haustafeln in Theological Context: An Analysis of Their Origins, Relationship, and Message*. American University Studies 7.260. New York: Lang, 2007.
Hess, Richard. "Equality, with and without Innocence: Gen 1–3." In *Discovering Biblical Equality*, edited by Ronald Pierce and Rebecca Groothuis, 79–95. Downers Grove, IL: InterVarsity, 2005.
Higgins, Jean. "Anastasius Sinaita and the Superiority of Woman." *Journal of Biblical Literature* 97 (1978) 255–56.
Hoehner, Harold W. *Ephesians: An Exegetical Commentary*. Grand Rapids: Baker Academic, 2002.
Hoekema, Anthony. *Created in God's Image*. Grand Rapids: Eerdmans, 1986.
Hogden Gritz, Sharon. *Paul, Women Teachers, and the Mother Goddess at Ephesus: A Study of 1 Timothy 2:9–15 in Light of the Religious and Cultural Milieu of the First Century*. Lanham, MD: University Press of America, 1991.
Horowitz, Maryanne Cline. "The Image of God in Man: Is Woman Included?" *The Harvard Theological Review* 72 (1979) 175–206.
Horrell, David. *Becoming Christian: Essays on 1 Peter and the Making of Christian Identity*. The Library of New Testament Studies 394. London: T&T Clark, 2013
———. "Ethnicization, Marriage, and Early Christian Identity: Critical Reflections on 1 Corinthians 7, 1 Peter 3, and Modern New Testament Scholarship." *New Testament Studies* 62.3 (2016) 439–60.
Horsley, G. H. R. "The Inscriptions of Ephesos and the New Testament." *Novum Testamentum* 34.2 (1992) 105–65.
Howard-Johnston, James, and Paul Hayward. *The Cult of Saints in Late Antiquity and the Middle Ages*. Oxford: Oxford University Press, 1999.
Hübner, Hans. *An Philemon. An die Epheser*. Handbuch zum Neuen Testament 12. Tübingen: Mohr Siebeck, 1997.

Hull, Gretchen Gaebelein. *Equal to Serve: Men and Women Working Together Revealing the Gospel*. Grand Rapids: Baker, 1987.
Hunter, David. *Marriage and Sexuality in Early Christianity*. Minneapolis: Fortress, 2018.
Hurley, James B. *Man and Woman in Biblical Perspective*. Leicester, UK: InterVarsity, 1981.
Immendörfer, Michael. *Ephesians and Artemis: The Cult of the Great Goddess of Ephesus as the Epistle's Context*. Tübingen: Mohr Siebeck, 2017.
Isbell, Charles David. *How Jews and Christians Interpret Their Sacred Texts: A Study in Transvaluation*. Eugene OR: Resource, 2014.
Jobes, Karen. *1 Peter*. Baker Exegetical Commentary on the New Testament. Grand Rapids: Baker Academic, 2005.
Johnson, Edna. *A Semantic and Structural Analysis of Ephesians*. Dallas: SIL International, 2008.
Johnston, George. *Ephesians*. The Interpreter's Dictionary of the Bible, vol. 2. Nashville: Abingdon, 1999.
Karaman, Elif Hillel. *Ephesian Women in Greco-Roman and Early Christian Perspective*. Tübingen: Mohr Siebeck, 2018.
Karwiese, Stefan. "Ephesos: C Numismatischer Teil." In *Paulys Realencyclopädie der classischen Altertumswissenschaft*, 297–364 Supplement 12. Realencyklopädie für protestantische Theologie und Kirche. Stuttgart: Druckenmüller, 1970.
———. *Groß is die Artemis von Ephesos. Die Geschichte einer der großen Städte Antike*. Vienna: Phoibos, 1995.
———. *Die Münzprägung von Ephesos*. Vienna: Böhlau, 1995.
Kearsley, R. A. "Women in Public Life in the Roman East: Iunia Theodora, Claudia Metrodora and Phoebe, Benefactress of Paul." *Tyndale Bulletin* 50.2 (1999) 189–211.
Keener, Craig S. "Marriage." In *The Dictionary of New Testament Background*, edited by Craig A. Evans and Stanley E. Porter, 680–93. Downers Grove, IL: InterVarsity, 2000.
———. *Paul Women & Wives: Marriage and Women's Ministry in the Letters of Paul*. Grand Rapids: Baker Academic, 1992.
Keil, Josef. "Die erste Kaiserneokorie von Ephesos." *Numismatische Zeitschrift* 52 (1919) 115–20.
Kennedy, George. *New Testament Interpretation through Rhetorical Criticism*. Chapel Hill, NC: University of North Carolina Press, 1984.
Khobnya, Svetlana. "Preparing Women for Ministry in 1 Cor 14:34–35 and 1 Tim 2:8–15." *Didache* 19.1 (2020) 1–9.
———. "So That They May Be Won Over without a Word: Reading 1 Peter through a Missional Lens." *European Journal of Theology* 29.1 (2019) 7–16.
Kilner, John. "Humanity in God's Image: Is the Image Really Damaged." *Journal of Evangelical Theological Society* 53.3 (2010) 601–17.
Kirbihler, François. "Les prêtresses d'Artémis à Éphèse (Ier siècle av. J.-C.–IIIe siècle apr. J.-C.) ou comment faire du neuf en prétendant restaurer un état ancien?" In *Dialogues d'histoire ancienne*, Supplement 18, 21–79. Besançon: Franche-Comté University Press, 2018.
King, Helen. "Bound to Bleed: Artemis and Greek Women." In *Sexuality and Gender in the Classical World: Readings and Sources*, edited by Laura K. McClure, 109–27. Oxford: Blackwell, 2002.
Kitchen, Martin. *Ephesians*. London: Routledge, 1994.
Kim, Seyoon. *The Origin of Paul's Gospel*. Tübingen: Mohr Siebeck, 1981.

Kraemer, Ross. *Her Share of the Blessings: Women's Religions among Pagans, Jews, and Christians in the Greco-Roman World*. Oxford: Oxford University Press, 1992.
Kreider, Alan. *Worship and Evangelism in Pre-Christendom*. Cambridge: Grove, 1995.
Kreitzer, Larry. "A Numismatic Clue to Acts 19.23–41: The Ephesian Cistophori of Claudius and Agrippina." *Journal for the Study of the New Testament* 30 (1987) 59–70.
Lampe, Peter. "Acts 19 im Spiegel der ephesischen Inschriften." *Biblische Zeitschrift* 36 (1992) 59–76.
Lang, T. J. *Mystery and the Making of a Christian Historical Consciousness: From Paul to the Second Century*. BZNW. Berlin: de Gruyter, 2015.
———. "Sealed for Redemption: The Economics of Atonement in Ephesians." In *Atonement: Jewish and Christian Origins*, edited by M. Botner et al., 155–70. Grand Rapids: Eerdmans, 2020.
Larkin, William J. *Ephesians: A Handbook on the Greek Text*. Waco, TX: Baylor University Press, 2009.
Lee-Barnewall, Michelle. *Neither Complementarian nor Egalitarian: A Kingdom Corrective to the Evangelical Gender Debate*. Grand Rapids: Baker Academic, 2016.
Levinskaya, Irina. *The Book of Acts in Its First-Century Setting. Volume 5, Diaspora Setting*. Grand Rapids: Eerdmans, 1996.
Levison, J. R. "Is Eve to Blame? A Contextual Analysis of Sirach 25:24." *Catholic Biblical Quarterly* 47 (1985) 617–23.
———. "The Exoneration of Eve in the Apocalypse of Moses 15–20." *Journal for the Study of Judaism in the Persian, Hellenistic, and Roman Period* 20 (1989) 135–50.
Lichtenecker, Elisabeth. "Die Kultbilder der Artemis von Ephesos." Inaugural dissertation zur Erlangung des Doktorgrades einer hohen philosophischen Fakultät der Universität zu Tübingen, 1952.
Liddell, H. G., and R. Scott. *A Greek-English Lexicon*. Revised by Henry Stuart Jones and Roderick McKenzie. Supplemental Edition. E. A. Barber, et al. Oxford: Clarendon, 1968.
LiDonnici, L. R. "The Images of Artemis Ephesia and Greco-Roman Worship: A Reconsideration." *Harvard Theological Review* 85 (1992) 391–415.
Lincoln, Andrew T. *Ephesians*. Word Biblical Commentary. Nashville: Thomas Nelson, 1990.
Long, Frederick. "Paul's Theology in Greco-Roman Political Context." In *Christian Origins and Greco-Roman Culture*, edited by Stanley Porter and Andrew Pitts, 255–309. Leiden: Brill, 2013.
Macdonald, Dennis Ronald. *The Legend and the Apostle: The Battle for Paul in Story and Canon*. Philadelphia: Westminster, 1983.
———. *There is No Male and Female: The Fate of a Dominical Saying in Paul and Gnosticism*. Harvard Dissertations in Religion 20. Philadelphia: Fortress, 1987.
MacDonald, Margaret. "Beyond Identification of the Topos of Household Management: Reading the Household Codes in Light of Recent Methodologies and Theoretical Perspectives in the Study of the New Testament." *New Testament Studies* 57 (2011) 65–90.
———. *Colossians and Ephesians*. Sacra Pagina Series 17. Collegeville, MN: Liturgical, 2008.
———. *Early Christian Women and Pagan Opinion: The Power of the Hysterical Woman*. Cambridge: Cambridge University Press, 1996.

———. *Pauline Churches: A Socio-Historical Study of Institutionalization in the Pauline and Deutero-Pauline Writings*. Society for New Testament Studies Monograph Series 60. Cambridge: Cambridge University Press, 1988.

———. "Reading Real Women through the Undisputed Letters of Paul." In *Women and Christian Origins*, edited by Ross Shepard Kraemer and Mary Rose D'Angelo, 199–220. New York: Oxford University Press, 1999.

———. "Was Celcus Right: The Role of Women in The Expansion of Early Christianity." In *Early Christian Families in Context: An Interdisciplinary Dialogue*, edited by David Balch and Carolyn Osiek, 157–84. Grand Rapids: Eerdmans, 2003.

MacGregor, Kirk. "1 Corinthians 14:33b–38 as a Pauline Quotation-Refutation Device." *Priscilla Papers* 32.1 (Winter 2018) https://www.cbeinternational.org/resource/1-corinthians-1433b-38-pauline-quotation-refutation-device/

Macurdy, Grace Harriet. "Queen Eurydice and the Evidence for Woman Power in Early Macedonia." *The American Journal of Philology* 48.3 (1927) 201–14.

Mansfeld, Jaap. "Theology." In *The Cambridge History of Hellenistic Philosophy*, edited by Algra Keimpe et al., 452–78. New York: Cambridge University Press, 1999.

Manus, C. U. "The Subordination of Women in the Church: 1 Cor 14:33b–36 Reconsidered." *Review of African Theology* 8 (1984) 183–95.

Marshall, Jill. "Community Is a Body: Sex, Marriage, and Metaphor in 1 Corinthians 6:12—7:7 and Ephesians 5:21–33." *Journal of Biblical Literature* 134.4 (2015) 833–47.

Matthews, Shelly. "Fleshly Resurrection, Wifely Submission, and the Myth of the Primal Androgyne: The Link between Luke 24:39 and Ephesians 5:30." In *Delightful Acts: New Essays on Canonical and Non-canonical Acts*, edited by Harold W. Attridge et al., 101–8 Tübingen: Mohr Siebeck, 2017.

Mattingly, Harold. *Roman Coins*. London: Methuen, 1928.

Maurer, Christian. "Der Hymnus von Epheser 1 als Schüssel zum ganzen Briefe." *Evangelische Theologie* 11 (1951–52) 151–72.

Mayer, Annemarie. *Sprache der Einheit im Epheserbrief und in der Ökumene*. Tübingen: Mohr Siebeck, 2002.

Mealand, D. L. "The Extent of the Pauline Corpus: A Multivariate Approach." *Journal for the Study of the New Testament* 18.59 (1996) 61–92.

Meeks, Wayne A. *The First Urban Christians: The Social World of the Apostle Paul*. 2nd ed. New Haven, CT: Yale University Press, 2003.

Mellor, Ronald. ΘΕΑ ΡΩΜΗ: *The Worship of the Goddess Roma in the Ancient World*. Hypomnemata 42. Göttingen: Vandenhoeck & Ruprecht, 1975.

Ménage, Gilles. *The History of Women Philosophers*. Translated by Beatrice Hope Zedler. Lanham, MD: University Press of America, 1984.

Mendelsohn, Isaac. "The Family in the Ancient Near East." *The Biblical Archaeologist* 11.2 (1948) 24–40.

Meriç R., Merkelbach R., et al. *Inschriften griechischer Städte aus Kleinasien: Die Inschriften von Ephesos, 17.1, 7.1, 3003*. Habelt: Bonn, 1981.

Metzger, Bruce. *A Textual Commentary on the Greek New Testament*, Peabody, MA: Hendrickson, 2002.

Meyer, Wilhelm. *Vita Adea et Evae* (1878). The Life of Adam and Eve Collection. Leeds, UK: Digital Ink, 2020.

Mickelsen, B., and A. Mickelsen. "What Does *Kephale* Mean in the New Testament?" In *Women, Authority and the Bible*, 101–4. Downers Grove, IL: InterVarsity, 1986.

Middleton, Richard. *The Liberating Image: The Imago Dei in the Symbolic World of Genesis 1.* Grand Rapids: Brazos, 2005.
Miletic, Stephen Francis. *One Flesh: Eph. 5:22-24, 5:31 Marriage and the New Creation.* Rome: Editrice Pontificio Instituto Biblico, 1988.
Miller, Colin. "The Imperial Cult in the Pauline Cities of Asia Minor and Greece." *Catholic Biblical Quarterly* 72 (2010) 314-32.
Milne, Pamela. "The Patriarchal Stamp of Scripture: The Implication of Structural Analysis for Feminist Hermeneutics." In *A Feminist Companion to Genesis*, edited by Athalya Brenner, 146-72. Sheffield, UK: Sheffield Academic Press, 1993.
Mitton, C. L. *The Epistle to the Ephesians.* Oxford: Oxford University Press, 1951.
Moffatt, J. *An Introduction to the Literature of the New Testament.* Edinburgh: T&T Clark, 1918.
Moltmann, Jürgen. *The Coming of God, Christian Eschatology.* Minneapolis: Augsburg Fortress, 1996.
Moo, Douglas. *The Epistle to the Romans.* Grand Rapids: Eerdmans, 1996.
Morse, Holly. *Encountering Eve's Afterlives: A New Reception Critical Approach to Genesis 2-4.* Oxford: Oxford University Press, 2020.
Muddiman, John. *A Commentary on the Epistle to the Ephesians.* London: Continuum, 2001.
Murphy-O'Connor. Jerome *Paul the Letter-Writer: His World, His Options, His Skills.* Collegeville, MN: Liturgical, 1995.
Mussies, G. "Pagans, Jews, and Christians at Ephesos." In *Studies on the Hellenistic Background of the New Testament*, edited by P. W. van der Horst and G. Mussies, 182-85. Utrecht: Faculteit der Godgeleerdheid Rijksuniversiteit Utrecht, 1990.
Mutter, Kelvin. "Ephesians 5:21-33 as Christian Alternative Discourse." *Trinity Journal* 39NS (2018) 3-20.
Niskanen, Paul. "The Poetics of Adam: The Creation of אדם in the Image of אלהים." *Journal of Biblical Literature* 128.3 (2009) 417-36.
Norris, F. W. "Deification: Consensual and Cogent." *Scottish Journal of Theology* 43.4 (1995) 411-28.
O'Brien, Peter T. *The Letter to the Ephesians.* Pillar New Testament Commentary. Grand Rapids: Eerdmans, 1999.
Oakes, Peter. *Empire Economics and the New Testament.* Grand Rapids: Eerdmans, 2020.
Ortland, Raymond. "Male-Female Equality and Male Headship (Genesis 1-3)." In *Recovering Biblical Manhood and Womanhood*, edited by John Piper and Wayne Grudem, 95-112 Wheaton, IL: Crossway, 1991.
Osiek, Carolyn, et al. *A Woman's Place: House Churches in Earliest Christianity.* Minneapolis, MN: Fortress, 2006.
Osiek, Carolyn. "The Bride of Christ (Ephesians 5:22-33): A Problematic Wedding." *Biblical Theology Bulletin* 32.1 (2002) 29-39.
Osiek, Carolyn, and David Balch. *Families in the New Testament World: Households and House Churches.* Louisville, KY: Westminster John Knox, 1997.
Oster, Richard. *A Bibliography of Ancient Ephesus.* New York: Scarecrow, 1987.
———. "Ephesus Was a Religious Center under the Principate, I. Paganism before Constantine." In *Aufstieg und Niedergang der römischen Welt: Geschichte und Kultur Roms im Spiegel der neueren Forschung 2.18.3, Principat*, edited by Hildegard Temporini and Wolfgang Haase, 1725-26. Berlin: de Gruyter, 1990.
———. "Holy Days in Honor of Artemis." In *New Documents Illustrating Early Christianity: A Review of the Greek Inscriptions and Papyri Published in 1979*, edited by G. Horsley,

74–82. Sydney: The Ancient History Documentary Research Centre, Macquarie University, 1987.

Padgett, Alan. *As Christ Submits to the Church: A Biblical Understanding of Leadership and Mutual Submission*. Grand Rapids: Baker Academic, 2011.

Payne, Philip. "Fuldensis, Sigla for Variants in Vaticanus, and 1 Cor. 14:34–35." *New Testament Studies* 41 (1995) 240–62.

———. "Galatians 3:28's Application of Paul's New Creation Teaching to the Status of Women in Christ." *Male Authority in Context: A Special Edition Journal of Christians for Biblical Equality* (2012) 11–16.

———. *Man and Woman, One in Christ*. Grand Rapids: Zondervan, 2009.

———. "Ms. 88 as Evidence for a Text without 1 Cor. 14.34–35." *New Testament Studies* 44 (1998) 152–58.

———. "Response." In *Women Authority and the Bible*, edited by Alvera Mickelsen, 101–4. Downers Grove, IL: InterVarsity, 1986.

Peppiatt, Lucy. *Women and Worship at Corinth: Paul's Rhetorical Arguments in 1 Corinthians*. Eugene OR: Cascade, 2015.

Perkins, Pheme. *Ephesians*. ANTC. Nashville: Abingdon, 1997.

Petroelje, Benjamin. *The Pauline Book and the Dilemma of Ephesians*. London: T&T Clark, 2021.

Perriman, Andrew. "The Head of a Woman: The Meaning of Κεφαλή in 1 Cor. 11:3." *Journal of Theological Studies* 45 (1994) 602–22.

———. *Speaking of Women: Interpreting Paul*. Leicester, UK: Apollos, 1998

Perrin, Norman. *A Modern Pilgrimage in New Testament Christology*. Philadelphia: Fortress, 1974.

Pervo, Richard. *The Making of Paul: Constructions of the Apostle in Earliest Christianity*. Minneapolis: Fortress, 2010.

Pierce, Ronald, and Rebecca Merrill Groothuis. *Discovering Biblical Equality: Complementarity without Hierarchy*. Downers Grove, IL: InterVarsity, 2004.

Piper, John, and Wayne Grudem, eds. *Recovering Biblical Manhood and Womanhood: A Response to Evangelical Feminism*. Wheaton, IL: Crossway, 1991.

Pomeroy, Sarah. *Goddesses, Whores, Wives, and Slaves: Women in Classical Antiquity*. New York: Schocken, 1995.

———. *Spartan Women*. Oxford: Oxford University Press, 2002.

———. "Spartan Women among the Romans: Adapting Models, Forging Identities." In *Memoirs of the American Academy in Rome, Supplementary Volumes*, Vol. 7, 221–34. Ann Arbor, MI: University of Michigan Press, 2008.

Price, Simon. "From Noble Funerals to Divine Cult: The Consecration of Roman Emperors." In *Riches of Royalty: Power and Ceremonial in Traditional Societies*, edited by David Cannadine and Simon Price, 56–105. Cambridge: Cambridge University Press, 1987.

———. *Rituals and Power: The Roman Imperial Cult in Asia Minor*. Cambridge: Cambridge University Press, 1984.

Price, Theodora Hadzisteliou. *Kourotrophos: Cults and Representations of the Greek Nursing Deities*. Leiden: Brill Archive, 1978.

Porter, Stanley. "When and How Was the Pauline Canon Compiled?" An Assessment of Theories." In *The Pauline Canon*, 95–127. Atlanta: Society of Biblical Literature, 2004.

Ramsay, George. "Is Name-Giving an Act of Domination in Genesis 2:23 and Elsewhere." *The Catholic Biblical Quarterly* 50.1 (1988) 24–35.

Ramsay, William Mitchell. "Early History of Province Galatia." In *Anatolian Studies Presented to William Hepburn Buckler*, edited by W. M. Calder and Josef Keil, 209–26. Publications of the University of Manchester 265 Manchester: Manchester University Press, 1939.

Redding, Ann Holmes. "Not Again: Another Look at the Household Codes." In *Eve & Adam*, edited by Kristen E. Kvam et al. 455–62 Bloomington, IN: Indiana University Press, 1999.

Richards, Randolph. *Paul and First-Century Letter Writing: Secretaries, Composition, and Collection*. Downers Grove, IL: InterVarsity, 2004.

Richter, Donald. "The Position of Women in Classical Athens." *Classical Journal* 67 (1971) 1–8.

Ridderbos, Herman. *Paul: An Outline of His Theology*. Translated by John Richard de Witt. Grand Rapids: Eerdmans, 1975.

Robbins, Vernon. "Socio-Rhetorical Interpretation." In *The Blackwell Companion to the New Testament*, edited by David E. Aune, 192–219. Chichester, UK: John Wiley and Sons, 2010.

———. *The Tapestry of Early Christian Discourse: Rhetoric, Society, and Ideology*. London: Routledge, 1996.

Robert, L. "Inscriptions de Chios du Ier siècle de notre ère." In *Études épigraphiques et philologiques*, 128–33 Paris: Champion, 1938.

Roberts, Alexander, et al. *The Ante-Nicene Fathers: The Writings of the Fathers Down to AD 325*. Vol. 1. New York: Cosmo Classics, 2007.

Roberts, Alexander, and James Donaldson. *The Ante-Nicene Fathers: Translations of the Writings of the Fathers Down to AD 325*. Vol. 2. Edinburgh: T&T Clark, 1867.

Robinson, E. S. G. "The Coins from the Ephesian Artemision Reconsidered." *The Journal of Hellenic Studies* 71 (1951) 156–67.

Rogers, Guy. "Constructions of Women at Ephesos." *Zeitschrift für Papyrologie und Epigraphik* 90 (1992) 215–23.

———. *The Mysteries of Artemis of Ephesos: Cult, Polis, and Change in the Greco-Roman World*. New Haven, CT: Yale University Press, 2012.

———. *The Sacred Identity of Ephesos: Foundation Myths of a Roman City*. London: Routledge, 1991.

Rogers, Justin. "Origen in the Likeness of Philo: Eusebius of Caesarea's Portrait of the Model Scholar." *Studies in Christian–Jewish Relations* 12.1 (2017) 1–13.

Romano, I. B. "Early Greek Cult Images and Cult Practices." In *Early Greek Cult Practice. Proceedings of the fifth International Symposium at the Swedish Institute at Athens, 26–29 June 1986*, edited by R. Hagg, N. Marinatos, G. Nordquist, 127–34. Stockholm: Swedish Institute at Athens, 1988

Rousseau, Phillip. *Basil of Caesarea*, Berkeley, CA: University of California Press, 1994.

Ruether, Rosemary Radford. "*Imago Dei*, Christian Tradition and Feminist Hermeneutics." In *The Image of God: Gender Models in Judaeo-Christian Tradition*, edited by Kari Elisabeth Borrenson, 267–91. Minneapolis: Fortress, 1995.

Russell, Norman. *The Doctrine of Deification in the Greek Patristic Tradition*. Oxford: Oxford University Press, 2004.

Sampley, J. Paul. *And the Two Shall Become One Flesh: A Study of Traditions in Ephesians 5:21–33*. Society for New Testament Studies Monograph Series 16. Cambridge: Cambridge University Press, 1971.

BIBLIOGRAPHY

Sanders, J. N. "The Case for Pauline Authorship." In *Studies in Ephesians*, edited by F. L. Cross, 9–20. Oxford: Mowbray, 1956.

Satlow, Michael. *Jewish Marriage in Antiquity*. Princeton, NJ: Princeton University Press, 2001.

Schaff, Philip, ed. *Ante-Nicene Fathers*, Vol. 4. Grand Rapids: Eerdmans, 2000.

———. *History of the Christian Church: Nicene and Post-Nicene Christianity from Constantine the Great to Gregory the Great*. Vols.1–2. Edinburgh: T&T Clark, 1981.

———. *History of the Christian Church: Nicene and Post-Nicene Christianity from Constantine the Great to Gregory the Great*. Vol. 3. New York: Scribner's Sons, 1889.

Schaff, Philip, and Henry Wace. *Nicene and Post Nicene Fathers*, Series 2. Vol. 5. New York: Scribner's Sons, 1917.

Scherrer, Peter. "The City of Ephesus from the Roman Period to Late Antiquity." In *Ephesos*, edited by Helmut Koester, 1–25 Harvard Theological Studies 41. Valley Forge, PA: Trinity, 1995.

Schleiermacher, F. D. E. *Einleitung in das Neue Testament, Sämmtliche Werke*. Berlin: Reimer, 1845.

Schnackenburg, Rudolf. *The Epistle to the Ephesians*. Edinburgh: T&T Clark, 2001.

Schüssler Fiorenza, Elizabeth. *In Memory of Her: A Feminist Theological Reconstruction of Christian Origins*. New York: Crossroad, 1983.

Smith, Shively. *Strangers to Family: Diaspora and 1 Peter's Invention of God's Household*. Waco, TX: Baker University Press, 2016.

Snodgrass, Klyne. *Ephesians*. NIV Application Commentary. Grand Rapids: Zondervan, 1996.

Stallard, Mike. "Gender Neutral Translations: The Controversy over the TNIV." *Journal of Ministry and Theology* 7.1 (2003) 5–26.

Strelan, Rick. *Paul, Artemis, and the Jews in Ephesus*. Berlin: de Gruyter, 1996.

Sunberg, Carla. *The Cappadocian Mothers: Deification Exemplified in the Writings of Basil, Gregory, and Gregory*. Eugene OR: Pickwick, 2017.

Sutherland, C. H. V. *The Roman Imperial Coinage*. Vol. 1. London: Spink, 1984.

Swindler, Leonard. *Women in Judaism: The Status of Women in Formative Judaism*. Metuchen, NJ: Scarecrow, 1976.

Syme, Ronald. *The Roman Revolution*. Oxford: Clarendon, 1939.

Tagliabue, Aldo. *Xenophon's Ephesiaca: A Paraliterary Love-Story from the Ancient World*. Elde, Netherlands: Barkhuis, 2017.

Tanzer, Sarah. "Ephesians." In *Searching the Scriptures: A Feminist Commentary*, edited by Elizabeth Schüssler Fiorenza, 325–48 New York: Crossroad, 1994.

Tarn, W. W., and G. T. Griffith. *Hellenistic Civilization*. Cleveland, OH: Meridian, 1952.

Tarus, David. "Imago Dei in Christian Theology: The Various Approaches." *Online International Journal of Arts and Humanities* 5 (2016) 18–25.

Taylor, Joan E. *Jewish Women Philosophers of First-Century Alexandria: Philo's 'Therapeutae' Reconsidered*. New York: Oxford University Press, 2003

Thacker, Alan. "Loca Sanctorum: The Significance of Place in the Study of the Saints." In *Local Saints and Local Churches in the Early Medieval West*, edited by Alan Thacker and Richard Sharpe, 1–44 Oxford: Oxford University Press, 2002.

Thesleff, Holger. *The Pythagorean Texts of the Hellenistic Period*. Abo, Finland: Abo Academi, 1965.

Thielman, Frank. *Ephesians*. Baker Exegetical Commentary on the New Testament. Grand Rapids: Baker Academic, 2010.

Thompson, Dorothy Burr. "A Portrait of Arsinoe Philadelphos." *American Journal of Archaeology* 59.3 (1955) 199-206.
Todd, Robert "The Stoics and Their Cosmology in the First and Second Centuries AD." In *Aufstieg und Niedergang der römischen Welt: Geschichte und Kultur Roms im Spiegel der neueren Forschung* 36.3. Principat, 1365-78 Berlin: De Gruyter, 1989.
Tolbert, Mary. "Philo and Paul: The Circumcision Debates in Early Judaism." In *Dem Tod nicht flauben: Sozialgeschichte der Bibel; Festscrriff für Luise Schottroff zum 70. Geburtstag*, edited by Frank Crüsemann et al. 394-407. Gütersloh: Güutersloher Verlagshaus, 2004.
Towner, Philip. *The Letters to Timothy and Titus*. Grand Rapids: Eerdmans, 2006.
Towner, W. S. "Clones of God: Genesis 1:26-28 and the Image of God in the Hebrew Bible." *Interpretation* 59 (2005) 341-56.
Trebilco, Paul. "Asia." In *The Book of Acts in Its Greco-Roman Setting*, edited by David W. J. Grill and Conrad Gempf, 291-362 Grand Rapids: Eerdmans, 1994.
———. *The Early Christians in Ephesus, from Paul to Ignatius*. Grand Rapids: Eerdmans, 2007.
———. *Jewish Communities in Asia Minor*. Society for New Testament Studies Monograph Series 69. Cambridge: Cambridge University Press, 1991.
Treggiari, Susan. *Roman Marriage: Lusti Coniuges from the Time of Cicero to the Time of the Ulpian*. Oxford: Oxford University Press, 1991.
Trell, B. L. "The Temple of Artemis at Ephesos." In *The Seven Wonders of the Ancient World*, edited by P. A. Clayton and M. J. Price, 87-88. London: Routledge, 1988.
Trible, Phyllis. *God and the Rhetoric of Sexuality*. Philadelphia: Fortress, 1984.
Trobisch, David. *Paul's Letter Collection*. Bolivar, MO: Quiet Waters, 2001.
Valentine, Katy Elaine. *For You Were Bought with a Price: Sex, Slavery, and Self-Control in a Pauline Community*. GlossaHouse Dissertation Series 4. Wilmore, KY: GlossaHouse, 2017.
van Bremen, Riet. *The Limits of Participation: Women and Civic Life in the Greek East in the Hellenistic and Roman Periods*. Amsterdam: Gieben, 1996.
———. "Women and Wealth." In *Images of Women in Antiquity*, edited by Averil Cameron and Amélie Khurt, 223-42 Detroit: Wayne State University Press, 1983.
Vermaseren, Maarten J. *Cybele and Attis: The Myth and the Cult*. Translated by A. M. H. Lemmers. London: Thames and Hudson, 1977.
Vogt, Kari. "'Becoming Male:' A Gnostic and Early Christian Metaphor." In *The Image of God: Gender Models in Judaeo-Christian Tradition*, edited by Kari Elisabeth Borrenson, 217-42 Minneapolis, MN: Fortress, 1995.
Wace, Henry, and Philip Schaff, eds. *Nicene and Post Nicene Fathers*, Series 2. Vol. 7. New York. The Christian Literature Company, 1894.
Ware, Bruce. "Male and Female Complementarity and the Image of God." In *Biblical Foundations for Manhood and Womanhood*, edited by Wayne Grudem, 14-23. Wheaton, IL: Crossway, 2002.
Watson, Alan. *The Spirit of Roman Law*. Athens, GA: University of Georgia Press, 1995.
Watson, Duane. "Why We Need Socio-Rhetorical Commentary and What It Might Look Like." In *Rhetorical Criticism and the Bible*, edited by Stanley Porter and Dennis Stamps, 129-57 London: Sheffield Academic Press, 2002.
Webb, William. *Slaves, Women, and Homosexuals: Exploring the Hermeneutics of Cultural Analysis*. Downers Grove, IL: InterVarsity, 2001.

BIBLIOGRAPHY

Wenham, David. *Paul: Follower of Jesus or Founder of Christianity?* Grand Rapids: Eerdmans, 1995.
West, M. L. *Hesiod Theogony and Works and Days.* Oxford: Oxford University Press, 1988.
Westermann, Claus. *Genesis 1–11: A Commentary.* Minneapolis: Fortress, 1984.
Westfall, Cynthia Long. *Paul and Gender: Reclaiming the Apostle's Visions for Men and Women in Christ.* Grand Rapids: Baker Academic, 2016.
White, Rachel Evelyn. "Women in Ptolemaic Egypt." *Journal of Hellenic Studies* 18 (1898) 264–65.
Whiston, William. *The Complete Works of Flavius Josephus.* Green Forest AR: New Leaf, 2008.
Wider, Kathleen. "Women Philosophers in the Ancient Greek World: Donning the Mantle." *Hypatia* 1.1 (1986) 21–62.
Wilhelm, Friedrich. "Die Oeconomica der Neupythagoreer Bryson, Kallikratidas, Perktione, Phintys." In *Rheinisches Museum für Philologie,* vol. 70, 161–223. Bad Orb, Germany: Sauerländers, 1915.
Wilkin, Robert Louis. *Spirit of Early Christian Thought: Seeing the Face of God.* New Haven, CT: Yale University Press, 2003.
Winter, Bruce. *After Paul Left Corinth.* Grand Rapids: Eerdmans, 2001.
———. *Roman Wives, Roman Widows: The Appearance of New Women and the Pauline Communities.* Grand Rapids: Eerdmans 2003.
Wire, Antoinette Clark. *The Corinthian Women Prophets: A Reconstruction through Paul's Rhetoric.* Minneapolis: Fortress, 1990.
Witherington, Ben. *The Letters to Philemon, the Colossians, and the Ephesians: A Socio-Rhetorical Commentary on the Captivity Epistles.* Grand Rapids: Eerdmans, 2007.
———. *Women in the Earliest Churches.* Cambridge: Cambridge University Press, 1988.
———. *Women and the Genesis of Christianity.* Cambridge: Cambridge University Press, 1990.
Wizenburg, Justin. *Ephesians and Empire: An Evaluation of the Epistle's Subversion of Roman Imperial Ideology.* WUNT 2. Tübingen: Mohr Siebeck, 2022.
Wood, A. S. *Ephesians.* Grand Rapids: Zondervan, 1978.
Wright, Martin. *The Dividing Wall: Ephesians and the Integrity of the Corpus Paulinium.* The Library of New Testament Studies 646. London: T&T Clark, 2021.
Wright, N. T. *Jesus and the Victory of God.* London: SPCK, 1996.
Yoder Neufeld, Thomas R. *Ephesians.* Believers Church Bible Commentary. Scottsdale, PA: Waterloo, 2002.

General Index

Achaia, 12
Achilles Tatius, 73–74, 120–21
Acts 19 riot, 101–4, 108, 149
Acts of Paul and Thecla, 122, 124–26, 136
Adam, 7, 23, 33, 44, 82–83, 82n10, 110–11, 112, 123, 133–34, 151–53
Aelian, 146
Against Neaera (Demosthenes), 150
Agrippina, 14–15, 95
Alexander, 16–17, 125
analogy, 151
Andronicus, 38, 38n9
Anthia and Habrocomes (Xenophon), 119
Antiochus III, 15–16, 15n49
Antony, Marc, 56, 64, 93
Apocalypse of Moses, 111, 134
Apocryphal writings, 79
Apollo, 64, 89, 91n47, 92, 117, 124
Apollo (city), 94
Apollonis (city), 73
Apollonius of Tyana, 99
Aquila, 38, 38n8
Arete, 57
Argeia, 57
Ariadne, 70
Arignote, 57
Aristotle, 4n13, 29, 55n6, 57, 58–59, 58n25, 134n125
Arsinoë II (Queen), 55–56
Artemis/Artemis cult, 6–8, 11, 13–17, 19–20, 22, 26, 54, 62–63
  and authority, 124
  and Caesar, 93–96
  contribution to knowledge, 158–61
  of Ephesus, 91–93
  Eve and Artemis reception histories compared, 121
  Greek Artemis, 89–90
  as hometown goddess, 100–104
  image-bearers for, 97–100
  image of, 72–73
  influence of, 32, 104–7
  in inscription and analogy, 63–72
  mistaken identity in a sacred community, 142, 142–43n14, 145
  reception history of, 117–21
  rise of two traditions, 121–31
  turning away many from, 139
  wealthy women and prominent priestesses, 73–75
Artemisia, 57, 119
Artemision temple, 13, 36n2
  Acts 19 riot, 102–3
  background, 63–72
  closed to matrons, 90, 90n43
  Ephesian believing matron, 148
  images of Artemis, 72–73
  imperial images, 95–96
  inscriptional evidence, 64–72, 97–100
  many-breasted Artemis, 92–93
  reception histories of Artemis, 120–21
  wealthy women and prominent priestesses, 74–75
Aseneth, 122–23, 137
Aspasia, 57
Athens, Greece, 55
Augustine, 134, 134n125

183

GENERAL INDEX

Aurelia, 71, 118
authorship, Pauline, 8–10, 8n25, 10n32,
    11n32, 36–37, 51–52, 66, 155n1;
    authenticity of, 8–10

Basileia, 74
Basil the Great, 126–28
believing women, 3, 40, 110, 137
Ben Sirah, 111, 134
Bird, Phyllis, 83–85
breasts, 91–92, 91n47
bride of Christ, 31n106, 129–30, 146–47,
    157
building terminology, 66–67, 66n69,
    67n73, 67n74

Caesar, Augustus, 59–60, 93–96, 131–32
Caesar, Julius, 10, 56, 93, 108, 110,
    131–32, 137
Callimachus, 74, 117–18
Cappadocians, 110, 126, 130–31, 137
Caracalla (Emperor), 93n51
Carthage, 133
celibacy, 38–39, 109–10, 131–36, 137, 147
Chios, 74
Christ, 2–8, 41–47
    analogy with reverence for Artemis,
        69
    and the church, 28, 31, 65, 71n103,
        72n109, 131, 149, 150, 151n40,
        152–53n44
    Ephesians and Colossians, 51–52
    expansion of Christ's kingdom,
        138–39
    new humanity, 79–80
    new identity in, 104–7
    riches, 68
    subordination to, 18
    theology of reversal, 32–33
    See also new kingdom
Christian God, 103–4
Christology, 51
church fathers, 13, 47, 49, 109n1, 110
Cicero, 73
circular letter, 11–14, 140
circumcision, 39–40, 106
citizenship, 70, 99n85

city-state, 4n, 4n13, 62
Classical period, 57
Claudia Metrodora, 74
Claudius, 14–15, 60, 72, 95
Clement of Alexandria, 49, 115, 129, 134
Cleopatra VII, 56
Clines, David, 84–85, 87
Clitophon, 74
cohesion among believers, 25–26
coinage, 14–15, 72, 95, 100
Colossae, 12, 148n29
Colossian *Haustafeln*, 51
Colossians, relevance of to Ephesians,
    51–52
Commercial Agora, 67
Commodus, 103
complementarians, 2–3, 3n7, 23, 33,
    144–45
composition date for the letter, 10–11,
    10–11n32
The Contemplative Life (Philo), 132
Corinth, 12, 38–51, 142
Cos, 94
cosmos, 51
Council of Constantinople, 136
Council of Ephesus, 136
Cyprian, 133

Daitis festival, 119
Damo, 57
daughters, 139
Deborah, 16
deification, 96
Demetrius, 14–15, 102, 159
Demosthenes, 55n2, 150
Der Kleine Katechismus (Small
    Catechism) (Luther), 2n4
deutero-Pauline authorship, 8n25
De Vita Macrinae (Nyssen), 129
de Wette, W. M. L., 8n24
Dialogue with Trypho (Justin Martyr),
    114
Diana, 90
Diaspora Jews, 9–10, 15–17, 22
Die Inschriften von Ephesos, 63
Diodorus Cronus, 57
Diotima of Mantinea, 57

GENERAL INDEX

divorce, 38–39
Dolabella, 16
dominion, 83–84
Domitian, 94–95

early Christians writings, 27, 27n92, 109
early rabbinic era, 9
earthly hierarchical structures, 2, 144
egalitarian anthropology, 84, 84n22
egalitarianism, 48–49
egalitarians, 2–3, 3n7, 23, 33, 144–45
Egyptian women, 56
emerging church, 2–4, 24–25, 35, 133, 153
Emmelia, 126–31
emperor cult, 95–96
ephebes, 100, 100n88
Ephesian Artemis, 100–104
Ephesian believers, 26, 137, 139–41, 145
Ephesian believing husband, 148–50, 153–54
Ephesian believing matron, 146–48
Ephesian believing wife, 153–54
Ephesian Christians, 67, 86n30
Ephesian correspondence, 47, 52, 103, 104
Ephesian letter, 8–17, 28, 36–37, 48, 50, 59, 61, 122, 140
    Acts 19 riot, 103–4
    backdrop of the, 65
    objective of the, 121
    shared identity with Artemis, 97
Ephesian marital *Haustafel*, 23–35, 77
    authorial context, 42
    defined, 2n4
    Ephesian believing husband, 148–50
    evangelistic relationships in a sacred community, 142
    expand Christ's kingdom and change the world, 138–39
    Hellenistic social structures, 141
    inscriptional evidence, 63–72
    introductory questions, 10–17
    Karaman's good citizen marital code, 26–28
    and Lee-Barnewall, 33–34
    marital interdependence, 47
    marriage hierarchy, 1–8
    methodology, 19–20
    Osiek's compliance and defiance marital code, 25–26
    relevance of Colossians, 51
    scholarly landscape of, 81
    scholarship concerning, 2n5
    scope and limitation, 21–22
    Westfall's reciprocity marital code, 30–32
    where to begin, 18–19
Ephesians
    Artemis in inscription and analogy, 64–72
    and celibacy, 131–36
    concept of the image of God *(imago Dei)*, 88–107
    evangelism in the face of persecution, 139–41
    interdependence, message of, 141–42
    introductory questions, 8–17
    and Lee-Barnewall, 33
    relevance of Colossians to, 51–52
    undisputed letters, 36
Ephesian Tale (Xenophon), 119–20, 121
Ephesian women, 73–75, 111, 117, 121, 124, 137, 148, 157
Ephesian Women in Greco-Roman and Early Christian Perspective (Karaman), 26–28
Ephesos, 99
Ephesus, 77, 93, 109–10
    Acts 19 riot, 101–4
    citizenship in, 70
    destination of the letter, 11–17
    Ephesian Artemis, 91–93
    Ephesian believing husband, 148–50
    Ephesian believing matron, 147–48
    image-bearers for Artemis, 97–100
    imperial cult, 94–96
    influence of Artemis, 63–72
    Karaman's good citizen marital code, 27
    role of women in ancient philosophy, 56–59
    socio-historical analysis, 19–20
    wives in Ephesus are not in God's image, 42
Epicurus, 57

GENERAL INDEX

equality, 3, 5–6, 25, 27–28, 30–31, 32–34, 36, 49, 52, 55, 58–59, 81n9, 82, 82n11, 85, 87, 161
Essenes, 132–33, 135
eunuch priests, 135
Euodia, 37
Euripides, 102
Eusebius of Caesarea, 136
Eutuches, 118
evangelism
    evangelistic mission/intent of Paul, 6–7, 7n23, 10–11, 17, 28, 110
    evangelistic relationships in a sacred community, 141–42
    in the face of persecution, 139–41, 139n3
    Paul's objective, 39
    relevance of Colossians to Ephesians, 52
    Smith's survival marital code, 28–29
    theology of reversal, 34
Evanson, Edward, 8n24
Eve, 6, 23, 33, 109, 110–11
    one flesh notion of Genesis 2:24, 150–53
    original sin, 133–34
    reception history of, 111–17
exiles of the Dispersion, 140
extrabiblical contexts, 23–24

false teachings, 124, 124n79
Fatum, Lone, 42–45
female autonomy, 61, 110, 122
female slaves, 40
female subordination, 43–48
fertility, 83–84, 92
festivals, 103, 119–20
flaming arrows, 70
forgiveness, 106

Gaius Iulius Atticus, 118
Galatia, 48, 140
Galli, 135
gender
    creation language applied to, 4–5
    frame of reference, 19
    gender equality, 3, 5, 27–28, 30, 82, 87

gender hierarchy, 2, 5, 29, 157, 161
hierarchy, Aristotle's, 29
image of God *(imago Dei)*, 80–86
    in new kingdom relationships, 145–46
    and Westfall, 30–32
Genesis 2 creation, 47–48, 47n43, 151–53
gentile believers, 22, 26, 37, 66, 86–87, 104, 111, 116–17, 159
gerucia of Ephesus, 103
G. Norbanus Flaccus, 16
Goodspeed, E. J., 8n25
Gorgonia, 129–30
The Gospel of Thomas, 115
Gospels, 21–22, 71–72n107, 100n93
Great Theatre, 67
Greek Artemis, 89–90, 91n45, 92
Greeks, 9–10, 17, 92, 146
    and barbarians, 34n118, 64n63, 97n74, 161
    Greek cultural and philosophical influence, 37n5, 54–59
Gregory of Nazianzus, 126, 129–30
Gregory of Nyssa, 116n42, 126–27, 126n88

hairstyles, 41–46
harmony in the household, 4, 4n13
"head" (κεφαλή), 2–4, 19, 23–25, 47, 144–45, 158–60
head coverings, 19, 41–47, 42n23, 53
Hellenism
    emphasis on marriage and family, 131–32
    gender subordination, 2
    Hellenistic patriarchy, 33, 36, 47
    Hellenistic social structures, 6–7, 141, 143–46
    new kingdom discourse, 4
    "sexual immorality" (πορνεία), 40
    and women, 123–25
Hellenistic period, 57
Hera, 70
Heraklea, 74
Hesiod, 116–17
hierarchy
    earthly hierarchical structures, 2, 144
    gender, 5, 29, 157, 161

GENERAL INDEX

hierarchical Hellenism, 52, 108, 156, 162
hierarchical oneness marital code, 32–34
hierarchical order, 43
hierarchical relationships, 2, 23
marital hierarchy, 48, 51
patronage, 31
Hillel, 113
Hipparchia of Maroneia, 57
holiness, 109
Holy Spirit, 4, 80, 88, 104, 105, 143–44, 153, 159
Homer, 70
Homeric Hymn 27, 117
Homilies on Genesis (Origen), 115–16
Homily on the Song of Songs (Origen), 116
Horowitz, Maryanne Cline, 82
household codes/management, 4, 4n13, 7, 24, 27, 28–29, 30, 52, 123
household metaphor, 141
household of God, 140, 142, 143–44, 156
Hymn 3 to Artemis, 117
hymns, 117–18

identity
Acts 19 riot, 101–4
Ephesian believing husband, 148
Ephesian believing matron, 147
fundamental shift in, 28
image-bearers for Artemis, 97–100
mistaken identities in a sacred community, 142–46
mistaken identity in a sacred community, 142–43n14
in new creation, 6, 17
new identity in Christ, 7–8, 104–7
one flesh notion of Genesis 2:24, 150–51
presence of Artemis upon Ephesian identity, 158–59
social identity, 74–75
Westfall's reciprocity marital code, 30–31
Ignatius, 133
Iliad (Homer), 70
image-bearers, 17, 107–8

Acts 19 riot, 101–4
for Artemis, 88–89, 97–100
for Christ, 7, 96
Ephesian believing matron, 148
for the God of the universe, 104–7
image of Artemis, 71, 72–73
image of God *(imago Dei)*, 3–8, 17, 77, 78–86, 107–8
celibacy, trajectory of, 131–36
Ephesian believing husband, 150
Ephesian believing matron, 148
Ephesian Christians, 67
Ephesians' concept of, 88–107
frame of reference, 19–20
and gender, 80–86
mistaken identities in a sacred community, 142–46
model for a female restored in the, 126, 130
objective of the Ephesian letter, 121
restored, 3, 6, 11, 73, 105, 109n1, 131
rise of two traditions, 110–31
transforming in the life of the Ephesian believer, 105–7
two traditions of, 109
and women, 42–44
imago Artemis, 108
imago Christi, 79, 106, 108, 109, 117
imperial cult, 62, 93–96
imperial temple, 94–96, 98
inaugural eschatology, 3–4, 41, 130
indigenous household codes, 5n17
inheritance, 4–5, 68, 68n80, 75, 105
inscriptional evidence, 14, 63–72, 75, 97–100, 101–3, 107, 147
interdependence, 6, 21, 47–48, 109–10, 137, 141–42, 143, 148, 153–54
intertextuality, 19, 80
intimacy, 96
Iphigenia Among the Taurians (Euripides), 102
Irenaeus, 136
Irenaeus of Lyons, 114
Israel, 104

Jerome, 134–35
Jerusalem, 10, 10n29, 28, 105n109

187

GENERAL INDEX

Jerusalem temple, 36n2, 66, 66n71
Jewish literature, 111, 113–14
Jewish seven sons of Sceva, 17
Jewish War, 10
Jews, 9–10, 15–17, 22, 62, 75, 87, 102n101, 105n109, 117, 153n44, 159
Joseph, 122–23, 137
Josephus, 16, 112, 114
Joshua, Rabbi, 113
Julia, 38
Julian Marriage Laws, 131–32
Junia, 38
Justin, 133
Justin Martyr, 114, 135

Karaman, Elif, 24, 26–28, 34–35
Kitchen, Martin, 8n25, 9
Koressos Gate, 100

Lady/Lord, 69
Lang, T. J., 4–5
Lee-Barnewall, Michelle, 25, 32–34, 35, 82, 82n15, 161
Leontion, 57
Leto, 92
Leucippe and Clitophon (Achilles Tatius), 73–74, 120–21
lexicology/lexical exegesis, 3–4, 19, 23–24, 158
Lex Julia laws, 10, 131–32
Lex Papia laws, 132
LiDonnici, Lynn, 91
Lincoln, Andrew, 51
Livia, 60, 60n37, 94
living letters, 4–5
L. Lentulus Crus, 16
Long, Fredrick, 61–62
loving sacrificially, 143–46
Luke, 17, 103, 139
Luther, Martin, 2n4
Lysimachus, 72

MacDonald, Margaret, 139n3
Macedonian women, 55
MacGregor, Kirk, 49–50
Macrina the Elder, 126–31
Macrina the Younger, 126–31

male teachers, 46, 53
Marcion, 11, 11–12n33
Marcus Aurelius Hortensius, 118
Marian, 38
marital hierarchy, 48, 51
marital interdependence, 47, 109
martyrdom, 29
Mary, 136
Megabyzi, 135
Melissa, 57
Melite, 74
Menexene, 57
Messalina, 60
metaphors, 141–42
Middleton, Richard, 84–86
Miletus, 16, 94
ministry leaders, 19, 36, 37–38, 45
Minuscius Felix, 91, 133
Mishnah, 113
mistaken identities, 142–43n14, 142–46, 153–54
modern world, 87
Morse, Holly, 110, 112, 116
mutual interdependence, 47
mutual submission, 3, 6, 18–19, 23, 30, 33–34, 59, 143–46, 150–54, 158, 160, 162
mutual subordination, 18, 51
Myia, 57
Mysteries of Artemis, 119
"mystery" rituals, 71–72

national religious cults, 60
Natural History (Pliny the Elder), 132
Neither Complementarian nor Egalitarian (Lee-Barnewall), 32–34
Nereus, 38
Nero, 72–73
new creation, 4–5, 17, 19, 24, 33, 41, 52, 80, 80n7, 105–6, 107, 139
new humanity, 79–80, 81, 104–6, 142
new kingdom, 4–5, 8, 41, 43, 47, 49, 62, 146–48, 149, 150, 155–60
 attract unbelievers to new kingdom relationships, 139, 154, 156
 egalitarians, 144–45
 Ephesian believing husband, 148–49

GENERAL INDEX

Ephesian believing matron, 147–48
identity, 28
interpreting the household codes, 24
theology of reversal, 32–34
women in Corinth, 38–39
new self, 28, 52, 73, 75, 80, 106, 108
new world order, 37, 39–40, 48, 141
Nicaea, 93
Niskanen, Paul, 85–86
Nonna, 129–30
nurturing relationships, 91–93, 91n47
Nyssen, Gregory, 126–31, 126n87

Octavius (Minucius Felix), 91
Odyssey (Homer), 70
old self, 75, 80, 106
old-world order, 37, 110, 144
one flesh notion of Genesis 2:24, 150–53
On the Creation of the World (Philo), 112
On the Human Condition (Basil the Great), 127
Oration 8 (Nazianzen), 129
Oration on Holy Baptism (Gregory of Nasianzus), 129
Origen, 13, 110n1, 115–16, 115n37, 126–31, 126n87, 128n96, 136, 136n134, 136n137
original sin, 133–34
Orphic Hymn 2 to Prothyraia, 117–18
Osiek, Carolyn, 24, 25–26, 34
Oster, Richard, 91–92

Pamphile, 57
Pandora, 116–17
Pantacleia, 57
Pastoral Epistles, 49
patriarchal reading of Genesis 1, 33, 47, 87, 107, 151–52
patronage hierarchy, 31
Paul, 1–8, 36–37, 77, 138–39
Acts 19 riot, 101–4
Acts of Paul and Thecla, 122, 124–26, 136
and Artemis, 100–104
Artemis in inscription and analogy, 63–72
and celibacy, 131–36

circumcision, 39–40
concept of the image of God (*imago Dei*), 78–88
destination of the letter, 11–17
Ephesian Artemis, 91–92
Ephesian believing husband, 148–50
Ephesian believing matron, 146–48
Ephesians and Colossians, 51–52
Ephesians' message of interdependence, 141–42
evangelism in the face of persecution, 139–41
evangelistic mission/intent of, 6–7, 7n23, 10–11, 17, 28, 110
evangelistic relationships in a sacred community, 141–42
frame of reference, 19–20
fundamental shift in identity, 28
gender and image of God (*imago Dei*), 81–86
gender dominance, 43, 47–48
gentile believers in Ephesus, 87–88
Gospels, 21–22
hairstyles and head coverings, 41–47
image-bearers, 88–89
image-bearers for Artemis, 97–99
image-bearers for the God of the universe, 104–7
and intimacy, 96
introductory questions, 8–17
male and female, 48–49
metaphors, 141–42
ministry leaders, 37–38
mistaken identities in a sacred community, 142–46
notion of "head" (κεφαλή), 24
one flesh notion of Genesis 2:24, 150–53
role of women in ancient philosophy, 56, 59
Roman political influence, 61–62
"sexual immorality" (πορνεία), 38–41
social and political influences, 62–63
textual interpolation of silencing women, 49–50
theology of reversal, 33–34

189

GENERAL INDEX

Paul (continued)
    undisputed letters, 8n25, 11n32, 21, 36–37, 52–53, 105
    Westfall's reciprocity marital code, 30–32
    and women, 123–24
Paul and Gender (Westfall), 30–32
Paullus Fabius Persicus, 67
Paul's gospel, 12, 14, 45, 93
Pax Romana, 25
Payne, Philip, 49
Peppiatt, Lucy, 42–48, 50
Perictione, 57, 58
Persa, 38
persecution, 139–41
Persia, 9
personal holiness, 108, 108n119, 126, 133, 137
Peter, 22, 28–29, 37, 138, 139–41, 160–61
Petronius, 61
Philo of Alexandria, 16, 72, 111–12, 114, 132
Phintys, 57
Phoebe, 37
Pisidian Antioch, 16
Plato, 58–59, 89
Pliny the Elder, 132
Pliny the Younger, 140n8
Politics (Aristotle), 4n13
Pompillius Carus Pedo, 98
post-canonical Christian writers, 114, 116–17, 137
priests of Cybele, 135
Priscilla, 38
processions, 71, 92n50, 100, 101, 106, 106n114, 119–20, 146
Pro Flacco (Cicero), 73
prophets, 48, 49, 50, 53
Protoevangelium of James, 136
Proverbs, 112–13
pseudonymous authorship, 8–9, 36–37
Ptolemy II, 55
purification of Artemis statues at processions, 71, 146
purity, 70–71, 125, 141
Pythagorean School, 56–57
Pythagorean women, 57

reception history of Artemis, 109, 117–21, 122, 137, 157
reception history of Eve, 6, 21, 109, 111–17, 122, 137, 151–52, 157
Republican period, 60
riches, 26, 52, 57, 68, 138, 148
rights, 33, 52–53, 55, 156
Roman coinage, 95
Roman patronage system, 31, 35, 162
Roman political influence, 59–62
Roman Senate, 64, 94, 96n69, 98–99
Roman way of life, 25–26
Rome's elite, 131–32
Ruether, Rosemary Radford, 83–84

Sabbath, 16
sacrificial living, 20, 34, 141, 142–44
Salutaris Foundation, 99–100
Salutaris Inscription, 65–66, 71, 92, 103, 146, 146n20
Second Enoch, 79
Second Temple Jewish writings, 109, 116–17
Second Temple Judaism, 4, 5n17, 61
Seleucia, 125–26
self-control, 38–41, 41n18, 45, 135–36
self-sacrifice/self-sacrificial love, 7–8, 19, 30–31, 158, 159–60
    Ephesian Artemis, 93
    Ephesian believing husband, 150
    expand Christ's kingdom and change the world, 138
    "head" (κεφαλή), 145
    and intimacy, 96
    theology of reversal, 32–34
Servilius Isauricus, 16
sex as sinful, 20, 110, 131, 133–35, 137, 157
"sexual immorality" (πορνεία), 38–41
sexual interdependence, 142
shared identity, 7–8, 97, 147, 162
silencing women, 49–51
Simon ben Jochai, Rabbi, 113–14
Sitz im Leben, 5, 36, 56, 59, 130, 158–60
slaves, 4n13, 19, 40–41, 51, 52, 120, 140–42, 144, 161
Smith, Shively, 24–25, 28–29, 35

Smyrna, 94, 133
social and political influences, 62–63
social equality, 36
social reforms, 140n8
social status, 1–2, 5, 33–34, 88, 132, 159
socio-historical analysis, 19–20
Socrates, 57, 89
Spartan women, 55
stags, 92
State Agora, 64
Strabo, 13n38, 68, 71
Strangers to Family (Smith), 28–29
strategic survival, 5, 25, 28–29, 31, 35
Strelan, Rick, 146
Stromata VI (Clement of Alexandria), 115
submission passages in 1 Peter, 28–29
"submitting yourselves" (ὑποτασσόμενοι), 18, 25, 143–44
Sunberg, Carla, 126–30
Syntyche, 37

Talmud, 113–14
Taurian Artemis, 102
Temple of Croesus, 66
temples, 60, 66–68, 93–96, 93n51, 148n29. *See also* Artemision temple
Tertullian, 11, 11–12n33, 49, 114, 114n29
Thargelion, 64
Thaumaturgus, Gregory, 110n1, 126–27, 126n87, 126n88
Theano, 57
Thecla, 124–26, 136, 137
Theognis, 57
Theogony (Hesiod), 116–17
theological reversal, 32–34
theosis, 105, 105n110, 126–31
Therapeutae, 132, 135
Tiberius, 94
Titus, 66
Tolbert, Mary, 39
To the Church of Neocaesarea (Basil the Great), 127
Tryphaena, 125
Tryphena, 38
Tryphosa, 38

Tyrannus, 12, 17

undisputed letters of Paul, 8n25, 11n32, 21, 36–37, 52–53, 105

Valentine, Katy, 40
virginity
  of Artemis, 89–90, 89n39, 92–93, 117–18
  of Mary, 136n138
  in Nyssen, 129–30
  virgin birth, 134n125
virgins, 39n11, 60n42, 120–21, 124–26, 132–36

wealthy women and prominent priestesses, 73–75
Westfall, Cynthia, 25, 30–32, 35, 42, 44–45, 82
widows of Ephesus, 123
wifely submission, 18, 35, 51
A Woman's Place (Osiek), 25–26
women, 5–6, 5n17, 110
  and egalitarians, 3, 3n7
  evangelism in the face of persecution, 139–40
  gender and image of God *(imago Dei)*, 80–86
  Greek cultural and philosophical influence, 54–59
  hairstyles and head coverings, 41–47
  in leadership, 37–38
  reception histories of Eve and Artemis, 111–21
  Roman political influence, 59–61
  "sexual immorality" (πορνεία), 38–41
  sexual transgressions, 112–13
  silencing, 49–51
  social and political influences, 62
  social roles available for, 150
  stories of independence, 121–31
  wealthy women and prominent priestesses, 73–75
  Westfall's reciprocity marital code, 30–32

Xenophon of Athens, 68, 119–20, 121

Scripture Index

OLD TESTAMENT

Genesis

1	83–84, 87–88, 156, 161
1:22	83
1:26	43, 77, 78n2, 83, 87, 115n37
1:26–27	23, 46, 78, 79, 80–81, 81n10, 82
1:26–28	78n2, 79, 81, 82n11, 84, 85
1:26–27a	43
1:27	19, 48n46, 77, 78n2, 78n3, 82, 83, 84, 85–86, 86n30, 151, 161
1:27a	83, 84, 85
1:27b	83, 84, 85
1:27c	83, 84, 85
1:27b–28	43
1:27–28	87
1:28	83, 84, 85, 151, 153n44
2:7	115, 152
2:16–17	23
2:17	110
2:18	23, 42n22, 47n43, 151, 161
2:20	23
2:21	152
2:21–22	46, 82
2:23	23, 150n39, 152, 152n43
2:23–24	19n63, 44
2:24	xix, 19, 33, 71n103, 84, 86n30, 123, 137, 141–42n10, 147n27, 149n37, 150–53, 152–53n44, 157
2:25	152
3	134
3:1	111–12
3:1–5	110–11
3:6	111
3:7	111
3:6–8	110
3:12	33
3:12–13	110
3:15	134n125
3:15–16	110
3:16b	111n2
3:20	152
5:1	78
5:1–2	78n2, 81n10, 82, 86
5:1–3	85
5:3	81–82n10
6:19	84
7:9	84
9:6	78
41:45	122

Exodus

15:2	152n42
18:4	152n42
34:29–35	79n6

SCRIPTURE INDEX

Leviticus
15:16	135
15:19	135

Numbers
11:2	31n106

Deuteronomy
32:18	81
33:7	152n42
33:26	152n42
33:29	152n42

Judges
5:23	152n42

1 Samuel
7:12	152n42

2 Samuel
22:42	152n42

Isaiah
7:14	134n125
8:13	152n42
17:1	152n42
25:4	152n42
42:14	81
49:15	81
49:15–16	31n106
50:7	152n42
63:5	152n42
65:17	80n7
66:13	81
66:22	80n7

Ezekiel
16:8–14	71, 71n100

Psalms
	152n42
8:4–6	78–79
51:1	134
51:5	133
123:2–3	81
131:2	81

Proverbs
	112
2:16–19	112n16, 113n21
5:2–11	112n16, 113n21
5:15–18	112n16, 113n21
6:24–35	112n16, 113n21
7:5–27	112n16, 113n21
11:16	112n16, 113n21
11:22	112n16, 113n21
12:3	112n16, 113n21
19:13	112n16, 113n21
21:9	112n16, 113n21
21:19	112n16, 113n21
22:14	112n16, 113n21
23:27–28	112n16, 113n21
25:24	112n16, 113n21
27:15–16	112n16, 113n21
30:20	112n16, 113n21
31:3	112n16, 113n21

Job
22:25	152n42
29:12	152n42

Esther
4:17	152n42

NEW TESTAMENT

Matthew
1:25	136n138
13:11	71–72n107
18:4	32
19:11	135
20:16	32
22:30	133
22:31	135
23:12	32

SCRIPTURE INDEX

Mark

4:11	71–72n107
9:35	32, 160
10:31	32
12:25	133, 135
15:40	136n138f

Luke

2:7	136n138
7:25	147
8:10	71–72n107
13:17	147
13:30	32
14:11	32
18:14	32
20:34–35	115
22:26	32

John

19:25–29	136n138

Acts

1:21–26	38n9
2:22–29	99n85
2:37	38n9
2:42	38n9
6:2	38n9
6:6	38n9
7:54–60	28–29
8:1	28
13:1–3	38n9
13:46	17n59
14:1	17n59
14:14	38n9
15	103n104
16:3	37n6
17:1	17n59
17:10	17n59
17:17	17n59
17:23	61
18:2	38n8
18:6	17n59
18:19	17n59
18:24–28	63n50
18:26	38n8
19	86n31, 101–2, 139, 149, 157–58
19:8–10	16, 17
19:9–10	12
19:9–20	12
19:10	102
19:10–11	104, 159
19:13–16	16, 17
19:13–17	17
19:20	102
19:21–41	101
19:23–27	12
19:23–40	95n66
19:26	14, 102
19:26–27	102, 139
19:27	15, 102
19:28	17, 69n83, 98, 102
19:28–41	102
19:32–34	16
19:33	17
19:34	17, 98
19:35	15, 64, 97n71, 101, 102, 149
19:37	102–3
20:31	12, 63n50
20:32	71n99, 146n19
22–26	11n32
22:3	37n5
23:6	37n5
24:27	11n32
26:4	37n5
26:18	71n99, 146n19

Romans

1:1	33
2:4	68
2:24–25	103n104
4:13	68n82
4:14	68n82
5:12	134
5:12–21	134
5:15a	134
6:12	38
6:14–15	37
6:15	38
7:1–6	37

SCRIPTURE INDEX

Romans (continued)

8:1–17	106n112
8:17	68n82
8:29	79, 105
9:23	68
11:1	37n5
11:12a/b	68
11:33	68
12:8	38n7
12:10	33
13:14	37
14	103n104
14:17	4
16	19, 45, 155–56, 161
16:1–2	37
16:3	38n8
16:6	38
16:7	38
16:12	38
16:34	38

1 Corinthians

	48n45
1:2	71n99, 146n19
1:6–7	48
1:10	53
1:10–17	49n47
1:12	45n37
1:18	32
1:23–24	32–33
2:3	48
2:7	72n107
2:9	38
2:11–12	48
2:14	48
2:20	106
3	67n74
3:1–2	31n106
3:1–4	141
3:1–21	49n47
3:3	53
3:4	45n37
3:5–9	141
3:9–10	52
3:9–15	141
3:9–17	67n73
3:16	66–67, 67n74
3:16–17	141
3:17	67n74, 141
3:18–21	49n47
4:1	72n107
4:1–2	141
4:8–13	49n47
4:10	48, 147
4:14–21	141
5:1	53
5:1–12	49n47
5:6	49n47
5:23	48
5:31	48
6:1–11	49n47
6:6	53
6:9	68n82
6:9–10	5
6:11	71n99, 71n102, 146n19
6:12–13	45n37
6:12–17	141
6:12–20	49n47
6:15	142
6:15–16	141, 142n10, 151, 162
6:16	149n37
6:17	142
6:18	141
6:19	67n74, 141
6:19–20	4, 141
7	19, 21, 39n11, 40, 45, 48, 50, 131, 131n108, 156, 157, 161
7:1	38, 45n37
7:1a	39n11
7:1b	39n11
7:2–9	19, 38
7:3–4	39
7:3–5	142
7:6–7	142n11
7:7	38
7:8	39, 49, 50
7:10–11	39
7:12–14	39, 52
7:13	49, 50
7:17–20	19, 39, 40, 45
7:19	39n12, 40

7:21	41	14:2	72n107
7:21–24	19, 40	14:33b–36	50n49
7:32–35	38	14:34–35	19, 49, 50–51, 50n48
8	103n104	14:34–36	50n49
8:1	45n37	14:35	49, 50
8:4	45n37	15:5	22n66
8:6	51n50	15:6	38n9
8:8	45n37	15:7	38n9
9:20–22	10	15:8	38n9
9:21	37	15:9	37n5
10:15	68n82	15:28	51n50
10:23	45n37, 53	15:39–40	149n37
11	45, 48, 156, 157, 161	15:45	79
11:2–3	46, 47	15:49	79, 88, 105
11:2–16	19, 42	15:50	5, 68n82
11:3	41, 43	15:51	72n107
11:3–9	43	16:19	38n8
11:4	41		
11:5	19, 41, 48, 49, 50	**2 Corinthians**	
11:5–6	44		12
11:6	46	1:1	12
11:7	41, 43, 44, 79	2:17–18	80, 105–6
11:7–9	43	2:20	80
11:7–10	47–48	3:2–3	4
11:7–19	47–48	3:18	79, 88
11:8	42	4:4	79
11:9	42	4:4–6	79
11:10	42, 42n23	4:5	33
11:11	48	4:6	79
11:11–12	47, 48	4:10–11	149n37
11:14	41	5:16–20	80n7
11:14–15	44	5:16–21	80, 88
11:15	41, 44	6:16	67n74
11:17	45, 53	11:2	147n26
11:17–22	49n47	11:3	134
11:33	49	11:22	37n5
11:34–35	49		
12	48	**Galatians**	
12:4–11	48		12, 48n45
12:13	48, 161	1:2	12
12:21–24	48	1:10	33
12:25	34, 48	1:13–14	37, 37n5
12:25–26	48	1:13–17	37n5
12:27–31	48	1:15–16	37
12:28	48	2	103n104
13:1–7	49n47	2:3	37
13:2	72n107		

SCRIPTURE INDEX

Galatians (continued)

2:12–14	37
2:14	37
3–4	5
3:28	23, 34n118, 37, 39, 48–49, 81, 83, 88, 128, 155, 161
3:28c	43
4:19	31n106
5:11–12	103n104
5:21	5
5:22–23	40, 45
6:12–16	80, 80n7, 88, 103n104, 106

Ephesians

1:1	8n25, 11, 69, 99n86, 107n116, 140
1:3	69, 143
1:4	69, 99n86, 107n116
1:5	153n44
1:6	11, 140
1:7	68, 99n86, 107n116, 148
1:8	11, 140
1:9	72n107, 72n108, 99n86, 107n116
1:9–10	72, 72n109, 156
1:10	1, 51n50, 99n86, 105, 107n116, 143
1:11	99n86, 107n116, 153n44
1:12	99n86, 107n116
1:13	11, 69, 99n86, 105, 107n116, 140, 153
1:14	68, 68n81, 153n44
1:15	8n25, 11, 63n50, 69, 140
1:15–23	104n106
1:17	69, 104, 104n106
1:17–18	105
1:18	4, 11, 68, 68n81, 69, 140, 148, 153n44
1:18–20	1
1:19	67n77, 67–68
1:20	99n86, 107n116
1:20–22	105
1:20–23	143
1:23	51n50
2	67n74
2:1–3	17, 87, 135
2:2	25
2:4	11, 17, 68, 140
2:4–10	87
2:5	11, 17, 105, 140
2:5–6	75, 94n56, 108
2:5–10	104
2:6	2
2:7	68, 99n86, 105, 107n116, 148
2:8	11, 140
2:10	99n86, 105, 107n116, 140
2:11	104
2:11–12	104
2:11–16	75
2:11–18	87, 104
2:11–22	59n34, 75, 108, 156, 159
2:12	70, 70n98, 99n84, 99n85
2:13	17, 99n86, 107n116
2:13–18	104
2:14–15	17, 66n71
2:15	99n86, 107n116, 153n44
2:16	17, 106
2:18	11, 140
2:18–20	106
2:19	69, 70, 70n98, 99n84, 99n85, 104–5, 140, 142, 153n44, 156
2:19–22	104
2:20	106
2:20–22	66, 67n73, 148
2:21	36n2, 67n74, 69, 99n86, 104–5, 107n116
2:21–22	141
2:22	67, 104–5, 148
3:1	10n43
3:1–13	8n25, 59n34
3:2	8n25, 140
3:3	72, 72n107, 72n108

SCRIPTURE INDEX

3:3–10	72n109	5:1	2, 105, 153n44
3:4	72n107, 72n108	5:1–2	xix, 65
3:5	69, 72, 153n44	5:2	11, 140
3:6	68, 68n81, 99n86, 105, 107n116, 153n44	5:3	11, 69, 140
		5:5	68, 68n81, 153n44
3:8	68, 69, 148	5:8	2, 105, 153n44
3:8–10	26	5:9	105
3:9	51n50, 72n107, 72n108	5:14	106, 106n115
		5:15	144
3:9–10	138	5:18	18, 105, 144, 153
3:11	69, 99n86, 107n116	5:19	144
3:12	11, 99n86, 107n116, 140	5:19–20	4, 18
		5:20	69, 144
3:13	141	5:21	7, 17, 18–19, 18n61, 23, 25, 30, 33, 34, 59, 142, 143, 144, 145, 153, 160, 161
3:14–21	104n106		
3:15	104, 104n106, 153n44		
3:16	68, 105, 148, 153		
3:17	105	5:21–22	20, 144, 153
3:18	11, 69, 140	5:21–33	xviii, xix, 2, 6, 11, 20, 25, 42, 51, 59, 65, 140, 142, 143, 145, 161
3:20	105		
3:21	99n86, 107n116		
3:22–23	2	5:21—6:1	139
4–5	70–71	5:21—6:9	139–40, 153n44
4:5	71n102	5:22	7, 11n32, 18, 18n62, 19, 31, 33, 34, 142, 144, 145, 160
4:10	51n50		
4:12	69		
4:13	76, 105, 115	5:22b	143n16
4:14	153n44	5:22–23	51
4:17	28, 31	5:22–33	15n48, 23
4:17–24	25	5:22–27	30
4:17–32	105n111	5:22–29	151
4:17—5:20	25	5:23	3, 30, 69, 69n86, 144, 145
4:21	8n25, 99n86, 107n116		
4:22	52, 75, 80, 105n111, 106	5:24	7, 11n32, 34, 142, 144, 145, 151, 153, 160
4:22–24	79, 88, 105		
4:23	52, 80, 105, 105n111	5:24b	143n16
4:24	xix, 28, 31, 52, 73, 75, 80, 88, 105, 105n111, 106, 108	5:25	11, 11n32, 19, 20, 31, 140, 143, 144, 145–46, 151, 153
4:25	105n111	5:25b	143n16
4:25–32	80, 88	5:25–26	19
4:28	105n111	5:25–27	7
4:29	105n111	5:25–28	1
4:30	69, 105	5:25–29	20, 30–31, 145
4:31	105n111	5:25–30	92, 147, 157
4:32	99n86, 105n111, 107n116	5:25–31	34, 51
		5:25–33	7, 65

199

SCRIPTURE INDEX

Ephesians (continued)

5:26	19, 69, 70–71, 71n100, 146, 146n19
5:26–27	31n106, 131, 146
5:26–28	160
5:27	65, 69, 147, 147n26, 148n28
5:28	11n32, 19, 143n16, 144, 147, 151, 153
5:28a	149n37
5:28–29	149
5:28–30	7
5:29	65, 65n66, 147, 149, 151, 153
5:29a	149n37
5:30	7–8, 20, 145, 147, 151, 152, 153n44
5:30d	150n39
5:30–32	151
5:31	xix, 8, 19, 19n63, 33, 123, 137, 142n10, 147n27, 149n37, 150, 151, 152, 153, 153n44, 157
5:32	71n103, 72n107, 72n108, 72n109, 131, 151, 153
5:33	7, 31, 142, 144, 153, 160
6:1–4	140
6.4	149
6:5	144
6:5–8	51
6:5–10	140–41
6:9	51, 144
6:10	141
6:10–20	25, 25n81
6:11	25
6:11–17	141
6:12	25
6:15	25
6:16	25, 70, 70n93
6:18	11, 140
6:19	72, 72n107, 72n108, 72n109, 106
6:19–20	106, 138
6:20	106, 141
6:24	11, 69, 140

Philippians

2:1–11	33
2:6–8	32
2:6–11	51
3:4–6	37, 37n5
3:8	37
3:8–11	37
3:21	51n50, 79
4:2–3	19, 37, 45, 155–56

Colossians

	51, 68n82, 148n29
1:2	69n88
1:4	69n88
1:11	67n77
1:12	69n88
1:15	79
1:15–20	79
1:16–17	51n50
1:18	69n86, 79
1:19	51n50
1:20	51n50
1:22	69n88, 147n26
1:23—2:10	104n106
1:26	69n88, 72n107
1:27	72n107
2:2	72n107
2:7	67n73
2:9	50n51
3:1	79, 88
3:2	79, 88
3:5	52, 79, 88
3:8–9	52, 80, 88
3:10	37, 52, 79
3:10–11	80, 88
3:11	51n50, 161
3:12	69n88
3:12–17	80, 88
3:18–19	11, 14, 42, 51
3:18—4:1	139
3:22–25	51
3:24	5, 68n81
4:3	52, 72n107, 138, 141n9

4:5	52, 138	10:10	71n99, 146n19
4:16	12n34, 14	10:14	71n99, 146n19
		13:12	77n99, 146n19

1 Thessalonians

2:6–7	31n106
2:7	149n35
5:23	71n99, 146n19

2 Thessalonians

2:4	67n74
2:7	72n107

1 Timothy

	51, 122, 123, 123n77, 124n79, 124n80, 125, 133, 137, 157, 160
1:3–7	124
1:18–20	124
2:8–15	50n48
2:11	123
2:11–12	50
2:11–15	139
2:13	123
2:14	123
2:15	133
3:9	72n107
3:16	72n107
4:1–15	124
5	131, 131n108
5:3–10	139
5:3–16	124n81
5:9–16	125
5:11–15	133
5:13	123
5:14	123, 124, 133

2 Timothy

4:19	38n8

Titus

2:3–5	139

Hebrews

2:11	71n99, 146n19

James

	12
1:1	12

1 Peter

	12, 25, 28, 52
1:1	12, 140
2:11	29, 138
2:12	29, 140
2:15	138
2:17a	29
2:17d	29
2:18	29
2:21	29
3:1	29
3:1–2	29, 138
3:1–6	139
3:1–7	11, 14, 28
3:4	29
3:7	29
3:7a	29
3:7b	29
3:15	29
3:16	140
4:14	140
5:9	140

2 Peter

	12
1:1	12

Jude

	12
1:1	12

Revelation

1	12
1:4	12
1:11	12

SCRIPTURE INDEX

DEUTEROCANONICAL BOOKS

2 Esdras
3:21–27	134n123
8:44	79n3

Maccabees
18:6–8	30n105

2 Maccabees
3:39	152n42

Wisdom of Sirach (Ecclesiasticus)
17:1–12	79
25:24	111, 134
26:10–16	30n105
42:9–12	30n105
51:2	152n42

Wisdom of Solomon
1:13–14	79
2:23–24	79

OLD TESTAMENT PSEUDEPIGRAPHA

Life of Adam and Eve
18:1–2	111, 134

Apocalypse of Moses (Greek version of Life of Adam and Eve)
32:1–3	111, 134

Second Enoch
44:1–3	79
65:2	79

MISCELLANEOUS

Joseph and Aseneth
4:9–11	122
6:3	122
8:1–7	122
10:11	122
11—13	122
14—16	122
15:6	122
16:16	123
22:13	123

Testament of Reuben
5:1–2	113
5:1–3	62n49

Jerome's Vulgate
19–20	111n2

Septuagint (LXX)
22	111n2

T. Jud.
17:1	62n49